IN THE AIR FOR HIM

To Brian and Pam —
God bless you!
Ruth Schettema

IN THE AIR FOR HIM

THE STORY OF HANK SCHELTEMA AND ABWE AIR

RUTH SCHELTEMA

Association of Baptists for World Evangelism
P.O. Box 8585
Harrisburg, PA 17105-8585
(717) 774-7000
abwe@abwe.org

ABWE Canada
980 Adelaide St. South, Suite 34
London, Ontario N6E 1R3
(519) 690-1009
office@abwecanada.org

 PUBLISHING®

IN THE AIR FOR HIM
The Story of Hank Scheltema and ABWE Air
Copyright © 2006 by ABWE Publishing
Harrisburg, Pennsylvania 17105

First printing, May 2006
Second printing, January 2008

Library of Congress Cataloging-in-Publications Data
(application pending)

In the Air for Him
    Autobiographical, Non-fiction, Missionary
    ISBN-10: 1-888796-36-7
    ISBN-13: 978-1-888796-36-0

Printed in the United States of America

ACKNOWLEDGMENTS

Writing *In the Air For Him: The Story of Hank Scheltema and ABWE Air* has been a task I never dreamed of doing until ABWE asked me to. I intended to help my husband write about his years as a missionary pilot, but God took him to Heaven before we even began. Written information and past prayer letters from ABWE pilots had been filed over many years, and from these I gleaned details to guide me. All of the pilots, past and present, as well as the wives of the pilots who are now in Heaven with Hank, assisted me by checking for accuracy and providing me with their personal stories. To them all I express my sincere appreciation and hope that I have been accurate in the many details.

Of necessity, in the process of editing, many pages from the original manuscript have been cut. This explains why you will find no reference in the book or on the timeline to several ABWE missionary pilot-appointees who either did not make it to the field or did not become involved in aviation on the field.

I am immensely grateful to my editor, Mrs. Shirley Brinkerhoff, who patiently walked with me through the process of correcting and improving my manuscript. Her expertise, talent, and creativity as a published author were invaluable to me. Through her persistent questions, she also impressed upon me how important it is to accommodate the reader by clarifying aviation terms common to pilots and me. I hope we accomplished this.

I also thank God for my children, whose inestimable assistance and encouragement so greatly motivated me.

I agreed to work on this book partly because The Association of Baptists for World Evangelism, Inc., with whom Hank and I have served since 1958, facilitated its publication. I am most appreciative of their assistance, especially that of the Media Department.

In retrospect, I realize how many faithful friends have been praying for me as I researched, evaluated, and wrote these chapters. This book is the product of those prayers, and for this "I thank my God upon every remembrance of you" (Phil 1:3).

By God's grace and for His glory,

Ruth E. Scheltema

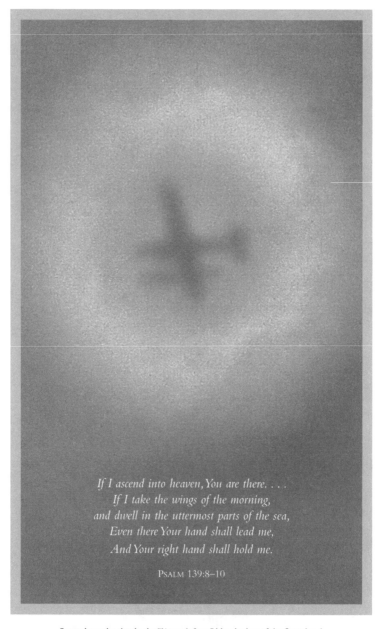

If I ascend into heaven, You are there. . . .
If I take the wings of the morning,
and dwell in the uttermost parts of the sea,
Even there Your hand shall lead me,
And Your right hand shall hold me.

PSALM 139:8–10

From above the clouds, the "Airman's Cross" (the shadow of the floatplane)
is reflected in the halo of a rainbow, reminding the pilot of God's presence.

ONE

EMERGENCY IN THE AMAZON

Pedro, a Brazilian rubber worker, signaled frantically from the shore to my husband, Hank Scheltema, who was taxiing his float-plane up the Ituí River, one of the many tributaries of the mighty Amazon River in Brazil.

"Help, Senhor Henrique! Hurry!"

Until that moment, this flight had been one of Hank's routine, bi-monthly trips to hold preaching services at the rubber collector's hut on the Ituí. But now, he faced an unexpected emergency.

Hank snapped off the floatplane's master switch and adjusted the rudders so he could steer across the swirling current to the muddy bank, where dugout canoes cluttered the shoreline. The whirling prop stilled as he opened the cabin door and stepped out onto the float, where he steadied himself against the wing strut, bracing for the lurch of the float thudding against the riverbank.

Again, Pedro shouted. "Hurry, Senhor Henrique—a *cascavel* bit Francisco!"

Hank grabbed an oar and a rope from the cabin, jumped off the float and plunged the oar into the soft clay, then quickly knotted the rope around it to secure the plane. He snatched his medical kit from the cargo pod, knowing that the bite of the *cascavel,* or rattlesnake, could prove fatal in minutes.

I'm sure I have anti-venom in my kit, Hank thought, hastening behind Pedro as he led the way through the tangled brush, but he worried that the victim might be too far gone.

"How long since he was bitten?" he asked. "Has anything been done to help him?"

Pedro answered, "We cut open the puncture and sucked out

the venom, but his leg is swelling already."

Ahead in the tall grass, almost concealed by a group of onlookers, Francisco writhed in pain. Hank dropped to his knees beside him and injected the anti-venom serum, then drafted two onlookers to help carry the injured man to the riverfront. "We've got to get Francisco to the plane so I can fly him to the hospital. I'll come back next week to hold the Bible study."

When they reached the river, Hank took Francisco from the two helpers and began to carry him cautiously down the steep embankment. Just as he turned to yell, "Someone please untie the rope and bring the oar," Hank slipped and lost his balance, but managed to land solidly on the ground, with Francisco in his lap, and not in the river. With great care, he finally got the injured man safely aboard the plane and took off in the direction of Benjamin Constant and the nearest hospital.

As they flew, Hank's thoughts drifted back to the flights he'd made a few years earlier with missionary Allen Franz in Alaska. It was there he had first seen lives rescued through missionary aviation and had learned the amazing ways airplanes could save missionaries time and physical hardship in their travel to remote, isolated places. Peering out his side window at the winding Ituí below, Hank reflected on how different it was to fly over the frozen tundra of Alaska as compared to this steaming jungle to which God had brought him. He had never realized, back then, how useful his training as a medical technician in the US Army would be when he became a missionary pilot. Now, though, he thanked God for it. He hoped that this forty-minute trip by plane, in place of a three-day river trip by canoe, would save Francisco's life.

Save him, Lord, Hank pleaded silently.

When they neared Benjamin Constant, Hank banked the plane and began descending to the small tributary that flowed in front of our house and hangar. Official permission to operate a radio between the plane and our home base had been stalled in bureaucratic red tape, so Hank had no way to advise me of Francisco's emergency. But I had heard the roar of the engine surging up onto the ramp of the floating hangar and was already running toward it, slipping and sliding down the crude steps carved into the muddy riverbank.

While Hank and the hangar guard lowered Francisco, weak and nauseated from air sickness, from the plane's cabin, I brought the speedboat alongside so they could get him aboard. After all he'd been through, Francisco still faced a fifteen-minute boat ride downriver to the hospital.

By God's grace, Francisco survived that snakebite, even though he continued to suffer side effects years later. Not long after that emergency flight, Francisco and Francisca, his wife, received Christ as Savior. Because Francisco was physically unable to return to the Ituí headwaters to collect rubber, they settled in Benjamin Constant, where they joined the First Regular Baptist Church. They adopted a Ticuna Indian baby, Raimundo, who later professed Christ, attended the church school, and furthered his education in Manaus, where he joined a Baptist church and remains faithful to the Lord today.

THE BEGINNING OF ABWE AVIATION CHURCH PLANTING

This was just one of many lifesaving flights Hank made as ABWE's first missionary pilot to the Amazon. He knew from experience that the plane would help him save lives in emergencies. With it, he could also spare other missionaries hours of bone-wearying travel and could distribute their mail and food supplies. Although aviation had the potential to make missions safer and more efficient, Hank believed that missionary aviation had to be more than a taxi service, and certainly more than eight-hour days doing mechanical work on aircraft engines and airframes.

Hank longed to use his airplane to reach isolated people groups along the Amazon River tributaries, waterways so remote that the only efficient way to get to them would be via float-plane, and he wanted to be not only the pilot, but the preacher as well. His heart's desire was to lead people to Christ, to teach those people to live by God's Word taught in a local setting of believers, and to see them pass on their faith to future generations.

Since he both piloted and maintained the floatplane, Hank trusted God to provide all things needed to keep the plane "up in the air for Him," which became Hank's motto. By God's grace and for His glory, Hank partnered with Americans, Brazilians, and Indians to plant or help in many church ministries. Through his aerial surveys of the Amazon River and its tributaries, which spread from the borders of Peru, Colombia, and Brazil, the ministry of ABWE expanded to several new preaching points and stations. Eventually, the missionary aviation work Hank began became ABWE Air, and spread into seven different countries.

FROM MICHIGAN TO THE AMAZON

What events prepared Herwin Henry (Hank) Scheltema for this lifelong work?

He grew up on a farm outside of Grand Rapids, Michigan. He and his brothers helped work the farm, supervised by their father, who also worked in town as a meter reader. One fall day, when the cornstalks had been gathered and loaded on a wagon, Hank and a neighbor boy worked together to fill the silo, pitching and leveling the chopped husks until late afternoon. Sweaty and thirsty, the boys decided to climb down for water. They pushed their forks into the silage and started down the metal rungs of the silo ladder. Before Hank's friend reached the bottom, they heard a noise above them and looked up to see a pitchfork plummeting toward them. Still on the ladder, Hank pressed tightly against the silo, warned his friend with a yell, and protected his head with one arm while the pitchfork whizzed past him. His friend, now on the ground, was not as fortunate. Before he could step back, the pitchfork slammed into his skull and knocked him to his knees. Hank yanked the fork from his friend's head and arranged for him to be taken immediately to the hospital. Miraculously, Hank's friend survived. But it was through this experience that Hank realized he was not prepared to die. Later that night, shaking and trembling, he climbed to the hayloft in the barn and asked the Lord to forgive his sins and save him.

As a teen, Hank's mother, Betty, had longed to be a missionary, but her father needed her help on the farm. Years later, Betty watched Hank, her second child, listen intently to a missionary nurse from Africa tell her stories at the Scheltema dinner table. Betty prayed silently, *Will Hank be the one I've prayed would go in my place, Lord?* And so it was. God used the stories of medical missionaries, whom Hank's parents often invited for Sunday dinner, to give him a desire to be a missionary doctor.

Four years into his premedical studies at Calvin College, in Grand Rapids, Hank was drafted into the US Army, where he served as a medical technician with the Alaskan ski troops, an experience that changed his direction.

"I'm not sure that God wants me to be a missionary doctor after all," he wrote. His mother frowned as she read this line in Hank's letter, then smiled as she read on. "The more I fly here and see how important an airplane is to work in remote Eskimo villages, the more I want to be a missionary pilot. I just read *Jungle Pilot,* by Nate Saint, and that clinched it! When I get my discharge, I'll finish my degree at Calvin, then go on to get my flight ratings. My medical background should come in handy no matter where I go as a missionary pilot."

I (Ruth) attended Hank's home church, Wealthy Street Baptist, in Grand Rapids, and after his discharge from the Army in 1953, we were married. In 1954, Hank enrolled at the Chicago Aeronautical University and earned his A & P (Airframe and Powerplant) license. We returned to Grand Rapids in 1956, where I completed my mission courses at the Grand Rapids

Baptist Bible Institute, now Cornerstone University. Hank also took seminary courses there.

One day, while we were students, Hank came bounding into the trailer where we lived, alongside the Thornapple River south of Grand Rapids, shouting, "Ruth, guess what? I just got a job managing the Hastings Airport. Not only will it give us more money for food, but I can work on aircraft in exchange for flight time. This way, I can log enough hours to complete my private license *and* earn my commercial rating—and do both for less money than I thought!"

Hank had already purchased a wrecked single-engine airplane, repaired it, and installed floats for landing on water. The Thornapple River served as the runway where he taught himself to handle the floatplane. When he went to be checked out for his floatplane rating, the instructor told him, "You don't need lessons. You already handle it like a pro."

By 1958, with two children in tow and a third on the way, both Hank and I had completed our training for missionary service. We applied to the Association of Baptists for World Evangelism (ABWE) and attended fall candidate classes. At that time, ABWE still held staunchly to its policy that missionaries should be church planters only, and we had to convince the mission board that aviation could be a viable way to help plant churches, especially in remote, hard-to-reach places where transportation was a problem.

Hank began by explaining it to them this way: "Visualize the distance between the office here in Philadelphia and the house in Germantown where we stay during candidate classes. Which would you rather be? A bird flying swiftly over the many obstacles along the way or an ant crawling around, over, and under them to reach the same destination? An airplane could speed up transportation in difficult-to-reach areas by almost ten times. The pilot himself could be involved in evangelism, but he could also partner with church-planting missionaries by transporting them to and from isolated stations and serving as their supply line. In life and death emergencies, the airplane could be a lifesaver for missionaries and nationals alike." Hank's testimony and vision for the use of aviation in missions convinced the ABWE Board to change its policy. The next two years were a whirlwind of activity for us. ABWE voted to approve and appoint us to pioneer missionary aviation in the Central Amazon, and Wealthy Street Baptist Church ordained Hank in June 1959. Then Hank completed his specialized training with Missionary Aviation Fellowship in California and we finished raising our support. By January 1960, our family of five arrived for language school in Fortaleza, Brazil, in preparation for our first term of service.

USA

Philadelphia

Miami

Caicos
Great Turk
Dominican Republic
Puerto Rico

Martinique

Trinidad

Georgetown, British Guiana
Paranaribo, British Guiana
Cayene, French Guiana

Marajó

Manaus

Belem

Fortaleza

Benjamin Constant

BRAZIL

Brasília

São Paulo

● The air route Hank Scheltema and John Schlener
took to Brazil in the Aeronca Sedan floatplane

★ The 2,500-mile flight that Hank and five-year-old-son
Daniel made from Fortaleza to Benjamin Constant
in January, 1961

TWO

EARLY YEARS IN THE AMAZON

During the following months of adaptation and language learning, Hank applied and waited for the import permit to bring his Aeronca Sedan, with which he had replaced the float-plane, from Michigan to Brazil. Unexpectedly, he secured both the import license for the plane and his Brazilian pilot's license at the same time; so, in October, Hank temporarily stopped language study to travel back to the States to get the plane. Meanwhile, I was expecting the birth of our fourth child in December, so I stayed behind with our three children. Working out the details to fly the Aeronca from the US to Brazil kept Hank away from us for two months—much longer than we expected—but he finally took off from Miami on Friday, December 2. It was to be a long and difficult journey.

John Schlener, a former US Air Force navigator and now an ABWE missionary, was returning to Brazil after furlough, and he accompanied Hank on this flight. John penned the details of their trip for the May 1961 issue of the *Message,* ABWE's quarterly magazine, and the following is an excerpt about their experiences in the Caribbean:

It was a rough go, as we smashed from one swell to another until we finally cleared the last one with enough speed to be airborne. It must have been here that the pontoon braces were broken in two places on one side; this we discovered the next day. . . . Over Caicos, Hank found a hole in the turbulence and there below us lay the tiny speck of an island called Grand Turk. . . . Before we even landed we were pressed into an air-sea search for a Navy base worker who had drowned in the surf just a little before our arrival. Apparently he was eaten by sharks, since even further search the next day was fruitless.

For two days, Hank and John faced turbulence, tropical showers, poor visibility, and choppy seas as they passed over the Dominican Republic, Puerto Rico, and then took nearly five hours to refuel, clear customs, and leave Antigua on the way to Martinique. There, the police had promised to watch the plane, but the next morning, the missionaries found it partially submerged. It took them two hours of pumping out the floats by hand to get the tail out of the water. After that, they had good weather until they reached Trinidad, where high temperatures and no wind forced them to dump part of their precious gas load to get enough momentum to go airborne.

Delays in customs and refueling in Georgetown, British Guiana, caused Hank and John to arrive later than planned in Cayenne, French Guiana. Hank, though famished, stayed in the plane all night to guard it while John went to town to arrange for gas and food. The next day, head winds slowed them down and ate up their gas supply. Soon they realized they needed to make a forced landing. As they flew over the island of Marajó at the mouth of the Amazon, they spied a creek that emptied into the ocean. This would serve as a landing spot, allowing them to avoid landing in the rough surf. Before the weary travelers could sleep that night, Hank walked several miles to get gas and to close their flight plan at a nearby airport (which turned out not to be operating). John tried to sleep in a hammock tied to a tree and Hank slept in the plane. Later that night, when the tide went out, a heavy log broke loose and smashed a hole in the back of one float, but Hank managed a quick repair. John's article in the

Message continues the story:

> . . . Saturday, December 9, we took off early with just enough gas to get us to Lake Arari in the middle of Marajó. . . . When we got to the lake . . . two men waded two miles into the village and brought us ten gallons of gas, which got us to our destination, Belém (Brazil). . . . I have never seen a man handle an airplane better than Hank Scheltema, and I can truthfully say that as navigator I was never lost, but I'm grateful to say that our heavenly Father certainly watches over us. Praise the Lord!

In Belém, John met the ship that was carrying his baggage up the Amazon. Hank continued on to Fortaleza alone, where three days later, bewhiskered and gaunt from loss of weight, Hank returned safely to me and the children. He had many repairs to make on the Aeronca after this difficult flight.

FROM LANGUAGE SCHOOL TO BENJAMIN CONSTANT

While Hank was traveling back to us, the children and I packed our family's belongings into barrels for shipment from Fortaleza, where we had spent the previous year in language school, to Benjamin Constant, our ministry location on the Amazon. A month after the birth of Linda Joy, our fourth child, Hank and I began our separate trips to the Amazon. On a Tuesday morning in early February, I took one-month-old Linda, two-year-old Kim, and three-and-one-half-year-old Kisti by commercial airliner to Belém, on to Manaus, and then by Catalina seaplane to Benjamin Constant.

After mapping out the same three-leg journey for the Aeronca, Hank took our son, Danny, then almost five years old, and began the 2,500-mile cross-country flight. The ABWE Aeronca Sedan was the first single-engine seaplane to cross the largest jungle in the world. With ingenuity, Hank had rigged an extra fuel tank in one float so that he could travel 750 miles to Belém, a nonstop seven-hour flight, and then 800 miles to Manaus, the capital of Amazonas. There he would refuel for the last 800 miles to Benjamin Constant—flying almost twenty-one hours total.

Friday morning, after a night's rest in Belém, Hank pushed to get an early start; he wanted to have ample time to arrive at his next stop before nightfall, when he would no longer have enough light to fly. However, it took more time than anticipated to load extra gas for the longer flight, and this delayed his takeoff. He had a hard time breaking the water (a pilot's term for breaking free of the water's surface drag) but calculated he could still make Manaus before dark.

FORCED LANDING

As dusk neared, Hank could just make out the lights of Manaus flickering on in the distance. Suddenly, the plane's engine noise ceased. All went quiet—except for the hiss of the windmilling propeller. Knowing he had only minutes until the plane hit the water, Hank went through his checklist: nose down . . . fasten Danny's life jacket . . . secure seat belts. Thankful for the floats under them, he swooped over 200 feet of the jungle's reaching green tentacles and glided the plane down to the river, now a glimmering mirror that reflected the sunset and nearly blinded him in the fading daylight. The shadows cast by the jungle along the shoreline helped guide him to a safe landing.

Still several miles below Manaus, Hank tossed his shoes and socks on the floor, grabbed an oar from the cabin, and crawled out onto the float, leaving Danny, who had been sick from sunburn, sound asleep in his seat. Hank ignored the danger lurking in the river and sat down to paddle, his feet dangling from the front of one float. He fought the Amazon current for hours, straining every muscle, paddling the three-quarter-ton seaplane upstream until he finally reached an on-shore refinery outside of Manaus, where he notified the airport and closed his flight plan by phone. Then, exhausted, he crawled into the plane to sleep alongside Danny.

The next morning, Hank discovered the cause of the engine problem—water in the gas. Friendly Brazilians at the refinery quizzed Hank about his adventure, and though it had been a grueling experience, this conversation opened up valuable contacts at the refinery that he would need for purchasing and shipping fuel in the future. Three days later, reunited with me and the girls in Benjamin Constant, plane and pilot were prepared to go to work.

ASSISTING OTHER MISSIONARIES

Requests from missionaries to bring mail, food, and other supplies soon filled Hank's schedule, along with scheduled evangelistic meetings and shuttling missionary families to and from field council meetings.

He also began standing in for other missionaries in their absences from the field, a practice that would become an ongoing part of our lives as aviation missionaries. The first time was in the case of Dale and Martha Payne. The Paynes were expecting a baby, and with no adequate health care available locally, they needed to leave their post in Santo Antonio do Iça to travel to the US for the birth of their baby, Sharon. They wanted someone to visit and encourage both the Brazilian and Ticuna Indian congregations during their three-month absence. Hank volunteered, and flew every other week to Santo Antonio do Iça, a trip of about one-and-one-half hours by air as compared to the twenty-four-hour trip by boat.

He helped missionary families in other ways, as well, and unusual circumstances sometimes forced him to make quick decisions. During Christmas 1961, flights on commercial airlines between Manaus, Brazil, and Iquitos, Peru, had been stalled because of unresolved international problems. Six missionary kids stranded in Iquitos had no way to get home from boarding school. Hank responded, "I'm on my way. Just pray that I'll get permission to make an international flight."

It "just happened" that when Hank applied for permission to fly to Iquitos, he met the Peruvian Consul and his wife, who were stranded at the airport and were trying to get back to Iquitos for Christmas. Hank obtained aviation clearance when he promised to fly them there in the mission plane.

"Boy, were the MKs happy to see me," he told me afterward. "I squeezed all six into the cabin, strapped in two to a seat, and stacked their Christmas gifts and bags on their laps. We did it, but only because they were all lightweights."

WEIGHT & BALANCE LIMITS

To make sure he did not exceed the *Weight & Balance* limits, Hank always weighed passengers and their baggage before loading. Sometimes he required one seat to fly empty or he refused some baggage after he weighed in a couple of heavy passengers. The *Weight & Balance* limit also showed how pilots must monitor and control their own weight. Hank carefully watched his diet and jogged routinely to keep his weight down. He felt this was a necessary discipline to allow room for more baggage and the passengers whom he served.

Regarding flying the MKs home two-to-a-seat, Hank explained, "The planeload capacity is not dependent on the seats available. The F.A.A. requires a *Weight & Balance Data* sheet—a guide from the factory for loading any airplane—to be carried in the plane at all times. The useful load is stated in pounds, from which is subtracted the weight of gasoline, oil, and non-permanent equipment carried. Seats for passengers listed one adult to a seat, two children up to twelve years to a seat, or one lap child (usually two years and under) to each adult. Each passenger (lap children excluded) must be secured by a seat belt; but seat belts can be shared."

The value of air over boat travel soon became evident to the missionaries, and they came to depend on it. Flying not only saved time, but eliminated exposure in an open boat to sun and rain or to the fatigue of slamming hour after hour across turbulent waves in a small boat. Sometimes Hank sensed an element of fear in his passengers. To help, he often joked with a characteristic twinkle in his eye, "Lean back and relax. No plane has ever collided with the sky." or "Flying is not dangerous. Crashing is, but I expect a safe landing."

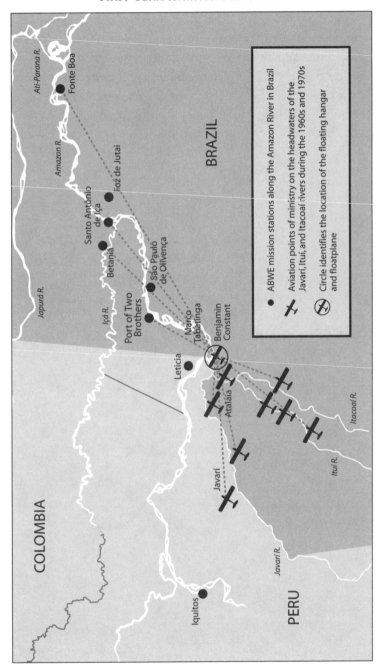

THREE ✈

INGENUITY REQUIRED

Aircraft maintenance required much of Hank's time. He often said, "For every hour of actual flying, I put in three or four hours of maintenance." The fuselage on the Aeronca Sedan, which was covered with fabric rather than metal, was delicate and required constant upkeep to repair tears and holes, and replacement parts were not available on the field. If Hank could not build a part he needed or get it in the jungle, it had to be ordered. Hank depended on his brother, Bill, a test pilot with Continental Motors, to locate, buy, and mail the part needed. Sometimes Hank had to ground the plane until that part arrived, which could be two to three weeks after Bill mailed it.

Hank stocked an emergency kit in the plane. It was filled with a variety of tools, canned sardines or cheese, fishing gear, hooks, and line. My mother, who worked at a hospital back in Grand Rapids, accumulated discarded odds and ends, such as assorted sizes of rubber tubing and surgical instruments, for Hank. They both claimed that one never knew when something discarded would come in handy. When the engine developed a problem one day, Hank proved their claim.

As we flew to a preaching point to proclaim the gospel and disciple growing believers on the Javarí River, Hank detected a slight change in engine noise. He checked it out after the service and found a wide crack in the rubber oil hose, which could cause oil starvation and seize up the bearings in the crankshaft—real trouble if it happened in the air. Hank didn't have an aviation hose, but he did have a piece of rubber tubing among the hospital discards in his toolbox. Hank, always adept at jerry-rigging, figured he could fix the problem temporarily. He fitted the tubing in the place of the cracked hose and got us safely home. In emergencies, rubber tubing came in handy more than once.

ON WINGS TO THE JUNGLE

For years, fellow missionary Jack Looney had traveled from Benjamin Constant up and down the Javarí River by riverboat, winning souls and helping the Brazilians who eked out their living by tapping rubber, harvesting lumber, gardening, hunting, and fishing. Though he had no formal medical training, he treated the people for parasites, saved snakebite victims, tended to those who were malnourished, and saved numerous lives. During Jack's furlough in 1962, Hank continued holding services on the Javarí in three of the locations Jack had established, but several other sizeable tributaries—the Ituí, the Itacoaí, and Japurá—also beckoned to Hank. He determined to visit some of the more populated sections on these tributaries that he could see from the air, in order to set up preaching points.

Following the Apostle Paul's example, Hank selected young men from the First Regular Baptist Church of Benjamin Constant or its Christian school, and took them along to train them in evangelism. In the future, five of these men went on to get formal Bible training, and all still serve the Lord in Baptist churches in Manaus.

When Hank and one of his helpers held services at preaching points, I usually accompanied them, along with one or two of our children, to play the accordion for the song service. The people told me that I was the first white missionary lady to visit these headwaters, and my presence seemed to embolden children and women—who were often too shy to approach a man—to voice their questions and doubts about salvation. After I saw their response, I went along as often as possible.

On a typical day, we held three meetings at points ranging from fifty to seventy-five miles apart. We left home around 7 a.m., carrying packed lunches and boiled drinking water for the day, and arrived back at the base by 5 p.m., an hour before sundown, when our only "landing light" turned off. One evangelistic trip involved three services and approximately ten hours of evangelism, but actual flying time took only one hour. Because folks upriver lived in isolation, they appreciated these meetings, which we prearranged so they could arrive in time for the first chorus. Canoe-loads of people traveled hours, sometimes all day, to attend. They listened eagerly, and many came to Christ.

HAZARDOUS FLYING

The airplane made it possible for us to reach these remote areas, but, in order to minister to the people there, Hank and his crew often flew in hazardous situations. Normally, having pontoons and keeping a waterway within gliding distance ensured a safe landing in an emergency, but pontoons also made the takeoff tricky, especially on the headwaters, which were narrower and shallower. The rivers we used as airstrips wound, snake-like, in narrow passages, banked by a canopy of towering trees; the wingtips of the plane barely cleared the verdant underbrush. Sometimes, to ensure a safe takeoff, Hank cut down brush to give a wider margin on either side of the tributary. At other times, when the plane had insufficient turnaround space, the local men tied a rope from their canoe to the floatplane and towed it into a better takeoff position. Hank taught other ABWE pilots his special maneuvers to fly the headwaters—though not all floatplane pilots felt comfortable doing them.

ABWE pilot Butch Jarvis described Hank's technique for taking off from a narrow waterway this way:

> Hank thrust the throttle forward to gain enough momentum to get "up on the step" (achieving the speed needed to skim across the waves) just before reaching the curve in the river. He broke the drag of the river's surface by swishing

around the curve with one float lifted out of the water, then plopped down on that float in order to pop up on the opposite float to make a turn in a curve to the opposite direction. Eventually, after a few pop-ups and snap-downs to the river, Hank would have enough speed to be able to rotate. Hank couldn't just fly straight out; he had to keep making turns until at last a long stretch of river gave room to surge with a powerful thrust upward to clear the lofty heights of the encroaching jungle.

This technique challenged the most experienced floatplane pilot, and it required courage of the passenger, as well, especially when the force of forward momentum plastered the passenger hard against the seat. He found himself resisting, straining, and leaning contrary to the pull of gravity in the curves, first to one side of the cabin, then to the other. He would hold his breath, close his eyes, and duck his head to miss the trees that seemed to speed toward him in the powerful liftoff to the sky beyond. A normal day's schedule gave just enough time to recover from one takeoff before beginning the next; yet, during the years ABWE pilots flew the headwaters, God continually protected the planes, pilots, and passengers from harm.

From time to time, ABWE Board members asked why Hank preferred to use a floatplane. Why not fly a plane with wheels? A quote from one of his reports explains his reasoning:

> After thousands of hours flying in both types of planes, over jungle, ocean, and countryside, I feel the inherent safety of a floatplane outweighs its initial extra cost, loss in speed (10–15 mph), and provides cheap insurance for the safety it gives. It provides much greater safety since a floatplane can land on water or land, or grass, in an emergency, and if crash-landed. In any other type of terrain the floats absorb the major part of the crash shock, which is not true with a

wheel plane. I realize floatplanes can't be used everywhere, but where they can, I feel they should be appropriated. With a floatplane, 99 percent of the time, we are over an excellent emergency landing site.

EXPANDING BORDERS

Along with his survey of the tributaries, which allowed Hank to extend his ministry of evangelism, he took new missionaries with him to see towns located beyond ABWE stations. At several river towns, such as São Paulo de Olivença, Porto Alfonso, and Amaturá, where he landed to talk with folks, Hank repeatedly heard, "Please send us a missionary." The mayor of Caruarí even wrote a letter to ABWE begging for a missionary. Hank ached to stop at every river town, but he knew his own limitations, and believed it unwise to begin a work where no one could regularly follow up new believers. He did squeeze in evangelism at Tonantins and Vila Nova on his monthly supply flight downriver, believing that in the future, should he be unable to continue going there, a missionary from nearby Santo Antonio do Içá might travel by boat to follow up with the people there.

"Let's expand our borders," Hank challenged his coworkers, and the missionaries responded. Soon, Ed and Dorothy Blakslee and their family moved hundreds of miles downriver to begin a church in Fonte Boa, and later, John and Sylvia Kallin and their children moved to the Foz de Jutaí. These missionaries of pioneer spirit, unusual in a used-to-conveniences world, lived great distances from their supply sources, post offices, and medical facilities. They willingly suffered physical hardship for the sake of the gospel, but relied on the pilot and plane for help.

NEEDED: A BIGGER PLANE

In the summer of 1963, we began preparing for furlough. During our first term, Hank's father had helped us construct a mission house in Benjamin Constant at the juncture of three rivers: the Javarí, the Solimões, and Javarizinho. There, Hank built the floating hangar for the Aeronca. Over the span of three years, Hank had flown 1,000 hours, started seven new preaching points in previously unreached villages and homes on distant tributaries, and saved valuable time, even lives, with his three-seat Aeronca Sedan. But he knew that the little plane could no longer meet the needs of the missionary families he served. Their children were growing up, as were ours, taking more space and increasing in weight. No longer could they all fit in the plane at one time. This became evident early one morning before a trip. I climbed into the plane and Hank belted in our four youngsters on the lightweight wooden bench he had installed in place of the original—and heavier—padded seats. At the controls, he tried time and again to break the surface of the water, but the Aeronca couldn't take off. Despite the coolness of dawn and the choppy waves out on the main river, which would normally make take-off easier, he tried repeatedly to lift off but could not. He finally admitted he would have to try something else.

Back at the floating hangar, I quickly sorted through the canvas duffel bag filled with clothing (suitcases would have been too heavy), selected about two pounds of unessential items, and handed them to the hangar guard to take back to the house. Hank siphoned off a couple gallons of gas. As he taxied out to the main river this time, he could feel the difference. The plane bounced up on the step, skimmed across the waves, and lifted off. To avoid delays and wear and tear on the engine, especially after repeated incidents like this one, something had to be resolved before next term. Hank asked the Lord for an answer.

By the time we left for furlough, he believed the Lord had given us a plan to follow.

FOUR

THE NEW PLANE—A GROUP PROJECT

The old Aeronca Sedan that we first took to the Amazon had saved time and lives; it had multiplied our outreach to remote areas where many now professed Christ.* But now a second, larger airplane was needed, one that would provide not only room for more passengers, but also, due to an extended fuel capacity, a longer range of flight. Hank had carefully researched the make and model that would best serve our needs and knew the plane would cost at least $20,000—a huge amount in 1964. But God had given us a unique plan to challenge churches to help put the Great Commission on wings. Hank called the plan "Amazon Airlift."

During our 1964 furlough, churches, Sunday school classes, and individuals, including boys and girls, caught our enthusiasm for "Amazon Airlift." We enlisted their help by breaking down the cost of the plane into 100 projects of varying cost, so that a church or individual could buy a wing or spark plugs, the windshield or the door handles. Knowing that many housewives at the time collected S & H Green Stamps, Hank and I were also glad to redeem the stamps for dollars to purchase a part on the plane.

"For example," Hank explained to his listeners, "twelve books of stamps will buy the airplane battery. Fifteen dollars will buy the compass. And anyone who gives $5,000 is offered a free trip with me to visit the Amazon."

I wrote thank-you notes and sent attractive certificates to each sponsor, and Hank regularly publicized our progress, crossing off

*The 16 mm. film, *Flight Plan Amazonas,* tells more of this story, and is available from ABWE Publications.

each part of the plane as a sponsor financed it. By April 1964, gracious gifts supplied the total need, and ABWE purchased a brand new Cessna 185 on floats.

At the dedication of the new plane, held in Grand Rapids, near the Ann Street Bridge, hundreds of faithful sponsors gathered to see what they had helped buy. Over the noise of their excitement, one could hear statements like these:

"My son gave all his savings for a bicycle to the airplane project."

"Look at that propeller! That's what our Junior Department saved to buy."

Years later, ABWE missionary to São Paulo, Brazil, Richard Sterkenburg observed, "Few will forget Hank's landing on the Grand River in Grand Rapids. At that dedication service, a young lady in the crowd decided to become a missionary, and ended up years later in Papua New Guinea. And how many youngsters became interested in missions because Hank 'divided up' the airplane into parts small enough to let children join in its purchase? I am sure that many felt a tie to that ministry because of their investment."

Christ's words, "Where your treasure is, there your heart will be also," encouraged us to believe that the majority of donors would be faithful in praying for the airplane ministry in the Amazon. And God blessed the use of this aircraft. Thirty-five years later, Allen Yoder, our son-in-law and also an ABWE pilot, would fly that same floatplane back to the States, where Hank and volunteer mechanics overhauled and updated it "for another 35 years of service," as Hank said. He added, "What an investment those sponsors made!" That Cessna is still in operation in the Amazon today.

THE NEW CESSNA ARRIVES IN THE AMAZON

In 1965, Hank took the children and me back to Benjamin Constant on a commercial flight, then returned to the States to fly the Cessna 185 to our mission station. Orville Floden, veteran ABWE missionary to Leticia, Colombia, accompanied Hank on the long trip. They flew from Grand Rapids to St. Louis and, although it was snowing heavily, installed a cargo pod which would double the usefulness of the plane. Three days later they landed in Miami, installed a radio, and adapted a float compartment to serve as an auxiliary gas tank, which would allow them to make nonstop seven-to-eight-hour flights. Hank, skilled in altering and rebuilding aircraft, connected a flexible hose from the auxiliary tank to the wing tank and installed a switch to pump fuel as needed. It worked so well that when he flew other aircraft to South America in future years, he installed a similar device.

The next leg of the journey took Hank and Orville from Miami over the Caribbean to Belize. After spending the night in Belize, they woke to find one float sinking. Waves had washed water into the cable openings of the float, contaminating the sixty extra gallons of fuel they had counted on for the next leg of the journey. Two hours of salty, gas-covered, soaked-to-the-gills work got it floating again, and this near disaster taught Hank an invaluable lesson for the rest of his career as a floatplane operator. He told Orv, "If I have anything to say about it, whenever the plane must be in the water for a long time, I'll see that the floats are dragged on to shore with the rudders up and cable openings out of the water."

Thirteen days after leaving Michigan, Hank landed on the Amazon River, dropped Orv off at the mission station in Leticia where he and Helen worked, and twenty minutes later buzzed low over our house in Benjamin Constant to announce his arrival.

To officially import the Cessna, Hank once again faced mountains of bureaucratic paper, just as he had when he imported the Aeronca during our first term. Thanks to the suggestion of ABWE missionary Richard Sterkenburg, the Brazilian mission agency, Missão Batista Regular Evangelizadora, agreed to import the Cessna and lease it for the work in Benjamin Constant, just as it had with the Aeronca.

"The task was not easy," Richard explained after working diligently for over a year to help Hank with this issue. "On more than one occasion Hank would appear unexpectedly in São Paulo 'dropping names,' that is, using names of military and government officials with whom he had cultivated goodwill, to cut through the bureaucratic red tape and move the petition forward." Until then, Hank had to fly the aircraft on a renewable, ninety-day permit. On January 17, 1965, God answered prayer and permission was granted. Hank painted the assigned Brazilian letters on the Cessna: PT-CJG, which stood for "Preaching, Teaching, Christ Jesus' Gospel."

Emergency flights involving Brazilians, Indians, and missionaries alike, had been on hold, awaiting the arrival of this newer, larger aircraft. Now they could resume. Two days after Christmas, Hank picked up missionary Jean Harrell and her daughter from Santo Antonio do Içá, where Jean and her husband, Lindsey, worked, and flew them to Benjamin Constant to be treated for malarial complications. After an emergency in Fonte Boa, Hank flew a desperately ill man to the hospital in Benjamin Constant, which then transferred him the ten miles across the river to the hospital in Leticia for an operation. On one of Hank's mail and supply flights downriver, Ed and Dorothy (Dot) Blakslee, missionaries in Fonte Boa, sent along a man with a hernia, and the Paynes, missionaries in Santo Antonio do Içá, sent a nine-year-old girl with an injured leg. Hank delivered both patients to the hospital for treatment. Then we received a telegram telling us that Ed Blakslee himself was very sick. Thanks to the Cessna, Hank was able to fly the entire family to Benjamin Constant— an 800-mile round trip—in only six hours of flying time. In the first four months back on the field, Hank flew the Cessna over 18,000 miles.

Hank and I also carried on mission work at the Benjamin Constant station where we lived. This included Sunday school, church responsibilities and baptisms, Bible classes in local schools, extensive medical work, the education of our children, and many hours of plane maintenance. Days and weeks away from our family on official ABWE business also added to Hank's responsibilities. God had given Hank gifts of physical health, ability, and diligence, for which he often gave thanks, but he soon realized he needed help.

NEW WORKERS JOIN THE AVIATION TEAM

During our 1963–64 furlough, Hank and I had met with Terry and Wilma Bowers, new ABWE appointees who would partner with us in the Amazon. Terry and Wilma hailed from Muskegon, Michigan, and had attended Grand Rapids Baptist College (now Cornerstone University), and Terry had also graduated from Moody Aviation.

When we met them at a missions banquet, we were in the midst of raising the donations for "Amazon Airlift." Terry's eyes sparkled at the thought that funds were accumulating for the Cessna, which meant that each pilot would have a plane to fly. By December 1963, the Bowerses left the States for language school in Fortaleza, Brazil. The following year, they arrived in Benjamin Constant and moved into the mission house where we had been living. Terry began flying the Aeronca and kept up the ministry at the preaching points on the Javarí River that Hank had previously reached. Their presence freed Hank to move our family and the Cessna three hours downriver to fill in at Fonte Boa for Ed and Dot Blakslee, who were going on furlough in 1965.

Wilma Bowers found, as did all the pilots' wives, how important her role as hostess was to the ministry. Many times the emergency patients that Terry or Hank transported ended up in the Bowerses' home until they were stable enough to travel home by riverboat. Wilma lovingly ministered to their needs and told them of Christ's love. Benjamin Constant was a connecting point for missionaries who came from their distant stations to get dental or medical care, buy supplies, pick up mail, or leave and re-enter Brazil, and they also found hospitality with the Bowerses.

RESCUING THE HANGAR

Wilma enjoyed all the benefits of her hard-working husband's mechanical skills in flying and maintaining the floatplane, but claimed no aviation skill for herself. However, when it came time to rescue the plane or hangar from disaster, she could do it.

She proved this on one occasion when Terry went on a supply trip downriver and had to stay overnight. Missionary pilots' wives track the weather before and during their husbands' flights, and that afternoon Wilma observed the clouds overhead billowing higher and higher. The sky darkened, the wind whipped furiously, and the palm leaves clattered noisily as a torrential rain pelted them. Branches crashed to the ground. When Wilma went to lower the window shutters against the driving rain, she saw the wind rip the floating hangar loose from its moorings on the Javarizinho River. Several huge logs, tied to the hangar for later use, also broke loose and floated downriver one by one.

With a prayer for God's help, Wilma flew into action. No doubt the neighbors laughed to see her running along the slick riverbank, kicking up mud, yelling and gesturing for someone to help rescue the hangar and wayward logs. The hangar swung away from the bank and out into the swift river current, but thanks to a second tie-down rope secured to a nearby tree, it didn't go far. However, Wilma's rescue squad of Brazilian men chased the logs far beyond the port of Benjamin Constant. When Wilma finally trudged back home, bedraggled and wet to the skin, the family's pet dog met her at the riverfront, looking bewildered.

He's probably wondering where the walk-on plank to the hangar is, she thought. *I can't put the hangar back in place, but thank the Lord, at least it's not floating off downriver.* No matter how carefully the pilots secured cables or ropes to anchor the floating hangar, each family that occupied the Javarizinho house at the Benjamin Constant station experienced a similar episode.

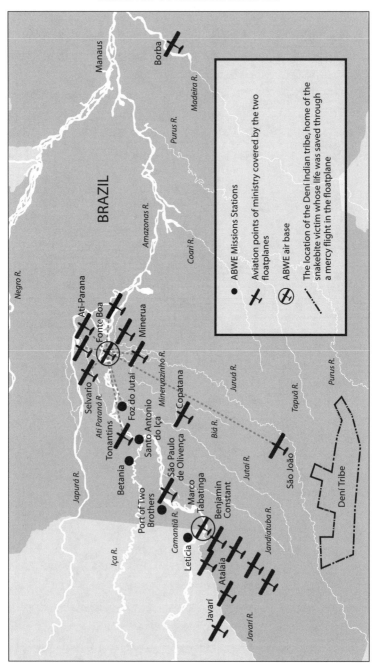

Manaus

Borba

Madeira R.

Purus R.

BRAZIL

Amazonas R.

Negro R.

Coari R.

• ABWE Missions Stations

✈ Aviation points of ministry covered by the two floatplanes

⊗ ABWE air base

—··— The location of the Deni Indian tribe, home of the snakebite victim whose life was saved through a mercy flight in the floatplane

Ati-Parana

Fonte Boa

Minerua

Mineruazinho R.

Selvario

Ati Paraná R.

Foz do Jutaí

Copatana

Juruá R.

Tonantins

Santo Antonio do Içá

Biá R.

Tapuá R.

Betania

São Paulo de Olivença

Purus R.

Port of Two Brothers

Marco Tabatinga

Jutaí R.

Deni Tribe

Camantiá R.

Benjamin Constant

São João

Leticia

Jandiatuba R.

Içá R.

Japurá R.

Javarí

Atalaia

Javari R.

FIVE

COMPASSION EVANGELISM

While Wilma and Terry Bowers were beginning their work in Benjamin Constant, Hank and I and the children were settling in at Fonte Boa to direct the growing congregation there during the Blakslee's furlough.

Weeks before we made this move, Ed and Hank visited the Ati-Paraná, a region of many rivers about an hour north of Fonte Boa. Ed regularly traveled to this region by riverboat to hold services, and Hank promised to continue the services in Ed's absence. At the same time, while checking his aeronautical map, Hank pinpointed several other tributaries in the area as possible places to evangelize beyond the distance feasible for Ed's boat ministry. Hank explored the Mineruá, the Japurá, the Jutaí, the Jandiatuba, the Juruá, the Biá, and the Negro rivers, as well as the headwaters that intertwined over the Ati-Paraná River territory. With the Cessna, we established eleven new preaching points, none more than a twenty-minute flight from Fonte Boa. Most had never before had a gospel witness.

At one preaching point on the Mineruá River Hank noticed a lady who always stood in the shadows behind the other listeners, her face well hidden behind a scarf. Curious, Hank wondered why she left each service immediately after his message. Normally, Brazilians who lived along the river were very sociable and congenial; this woman remained aloof.

Once, when Hank visited the host and hostess to reschedule a gospel service, he glimpsed the lady swinging in a hammock, not wearing her usual kerchief. Her face—what was left of it— seemed tightly pulled back, the nose sunken, and her body was covered with sores. Hank recognized the telltale marks of leprosy. When the lady realized Hank was looking at her, she quickly pulled up the drape of the hammock to hide herself. Though there was no cure, Hank provided her with medication that impeded further progress of the disease. This act of compassion opened doors to many homes, and even to other preaching points.

THE DENÍ STORY

While we were at Fonte Boa, another act of compassion opened the way for the gospel to reach an entire village. In July of that year, New Tribes missionaries Paul and Dorothy (Dot) Moran asked Hank to survey the Tapauá River and the Juruá and its tributaries south of Fonte Boa in order to locate a Dení Indian village they had heard about from riverboat traders and hoped to reach with the gospel. Hank located the village and reported back to the Morans, who then traveled there by riverboat from Manaus. However, finding the tribe from the airplane was one thing, but finding it while trekking through the jungle was another. They spent several weeks looking for the Dení without success.

The Morans had arranged for Hank to pick them up at a rendezvous point on the Purus River on December 10. Hank, never having landed on that river prior to this, skimmed the towering trees along the shoreline, searching for the white flag the Morans had promised to display. After spotting it, Hank made a go-around, checking the width of the river, the distance between bends, and the direction of the wind. The takeoff from a limited stretch is trickier than the landing, and he wanted to make sure he could get the plane up off this uninhabited, isolated stretch of river. Once he was satisfied that he could do so, he banked and slipped the plane to splash down, then cut power. The moving rudders swished against the current of the river as Hank pushed the foot pedals, steering the floatplane toward the muddy bank where the Morans and their baggage waited.

Once Dot was settled in the back passenger seat and Paul was in front beside Hank, they began taxiing for takeoff. Then Hank spotted a dugout with three Indians approaching from downriver, signaling for the plane to stop. He cut the engine, opened the cabin door, and stepped out onto the pontoon.

The two Indians paddling the dugout gestured toward their passenger, who was cradling his arm, which was wrapped in a dirty cloth. All three talked at one time in a dialect Hank didn't understand, but their pantomime revealed why they had overcome their fear to ask for help from strangers. The injured passenger, who turned out to be a teenaged boy, unwrapped his makeshift bandage. Horrified, Hank smelled and saw putrefied flesh sloughing off the boy's forearm and hand. A venomous snake had bitten him on the arm and cut off circulation to his hand.

Gangrene! Hank thought. *It's a miracle he's still alive. Lord, help us save him.*

Paul, who by now was outside the plane and standing on the other pontoon, said, "The poor kid. Can you take him with us to get help, Hank?"

"The only way to save him is to get him to the hospital in Manaus. I don't have enough fuel to take him the entire way myself, but once we reach Fonte Boa, I'll try to get him passage on your flight to Manaus, if you'll look after him and get him to a hospital."

"Of course," Paul agreed, as he helped Hank lift the Indian into the back seat next to Dot, who squinched up her nose and couldn't help saying, "Whew! What a stench!"

Hank and Paul agreed with her as the airplane bounced in the up- and downdrafts of hot turbulence. *We've got to do something about this smell. It's overwhelming,* Hank thought, growing more and more nauseated.

He turned to Dot and asked, "Do you have any perfume in your bag?"

Scrabbling through her bag, she offered Hank her roll-on deodorant. "Thanks, that'll do it," Hank said, laughing as he rubbed the deodorant under his nose. "Ahhhh. That helps." He handed the roll-on to Paul, who sheepishly did the same.

After they ramped (making a powerful surge up a sloping ramp to get the floats out of the water) the plane on the floating hangar anchored at Fonte Boa, Hank carried the injured boy, now dubbed "Chico," to the small clinic adjacent to where we were living. While Chico, frightened and bewildered, huddled on a clinic chair, Hank hurried to buy him a ticket on Panair, the Catalina seaplane that stopped on the waterfront once a week.

"You want passage for that Indian you brought with you in the floatplane today, right?" asked the agent, demonstrating the incredible speed of the *radio de cipó* (literally, "vine radio"). "No one else will travel with someone who smells like he does." He shrugged and turned away, refusing to sell Hank a ticket. "Sorry, but I can't afford to lose my other passengers."

Possible solutions to this dilemma ran through Hank's mind. *Maybe if the foul smell were removed . . . but there's no doctor here to do it. I've butchered cattle and chickens back on Dad's farm. Severing the joint between the hand and wrist shouldn't be too hard.* He realized he didn't have the proper instrument to do it, but thought that a razor blade would serve. He had plenty of dental anesthetic at the clinic to dull the pain. Reaching home, he decided that, with God's help, he would try to save Chico by cutting off his hand. Maybe then the Panair agent would sell him a ticket.

After the painful amputation, a bath, proper food, and doses of antibiotics, Chico survived to fly with the Morans to a hospital in Manaus, where a surgeon removed the rest of his arm. Concerned Christians in the US purchased an artificial arm for Chico, but by the time it reached him back at his village, he had grown used to hunting, fishing, and spearing with his one good arm.

Months later, when the Morans returned by riverboat with

Chico to his home area, they were amazed when the young Indian led them to his village and introduced them to his father, chief of the Dení tribe they had originally set out to find. Chico, later called Chief One-arm, became the instrument God used to reach the Denís for Christ and assisted the Morans in translating God's Word into his tribal language.

DETERMINING FLIGHT POLICY

We never knew when or where an emergency would occur.

One morning in Fonte Boa, as Hank sat eating breakfast and listening to a Manaus radio broadcast that customarily sent messages to interior towns, an announcer read a telegram received at the station: "Missionary Bill Barkley in Manaus calls Hank, the pilot up in Fonte Boa, to come as quickly as possible to rescue Mrs. Gerald Woods in Borba on the Madeira River. She is critically ill and has no other transportation." Although this meant nearly ten hours of flying time over solid jungle, helping missionaries such as Mrs. Woods from other mission agencies was not uncommon, and God used Hank once again to save a missionary's life.

Hank began developing ABWE aviation policy during these early years of flying in the Amazon, partly through his experience of such mercy flights. Because of the high cost of buying and transporting aviation fuel 1,000 miles from Manaus, the difficulty of obtaining repair parts from the US, exorbitant insurance costs, and the shortage of a pilot's finances, foresight had to be exercised. The Cessna floatplane burned fifteen gallons of fuel per hour; how best to cover that expense was an issue that needed to be settled. Emergency flights could consume all of Hank's available fuel, leaving little or none for evangelism and service to our missionaries who lived in isolated places—ministries that were priorities in Hank's book. He relied on the Lord's provision and wisdom to make decisions on how to use and regulate his aviation resources.

From the beginning, he determined not to use the plane as a commercial enterprise or mere taxi service open to anyone who wished to charter it. Since the plane did not have a commercial license in Brazil, he had no problem denying flights to politicians or businessmen. Though he was always available in life-and-death situations, Hank required government, military, or town officials to present a written request as proof that a flight was an emergency. Such flights were paid for in aviation fuel because receiving cash might open the way for accusation or misunderstanding, and this method covered necessary expenses.

Service flights for missionaries were another story. Hank and Terry raised extra finances from churches and supporters to cover their regular service flights for ABWE. This enabled them to make one or, often, two monthly supply trips without charge to the missionaries, as part of their ministry to the four mission stations between Leticia and Fonte Boa. When missionaries chartered the plane for medical or other personal reasons, they paid only the cost of fuel. However, to charter private flights, there had to be surplus gasoline on hand after the fuel for scheduled evangelism flights had been calculated. To celebrate a family birthday or make a memory for the children, the two pilots might include a camping or fishing trip on a sandbar or lake during travel to or from a scheduled service. In order to use the plane, money, and time wisely, Hank and Terry always tried to combine a supply trip with an evangelistic service at one or two preaching points.

THE DISAPPEARING PLANE

On one occasion, Terry scheduled a regular supply flight from Benjamin Constant to Fonte Boa. Wilma wanted to get better acquainted with the vast area downriver, so she and their two young sons, Philip and Jimmy, flew along. On the return trip, Terry planned to stop at São Paulo de Olivença. We missionaries had a standing invitation from the townspeople to stop and hold services, but a lack of personnel kept us from starting a permanent base there. Occasionally, a missionary who was passing by either boat or plane would stop to hold a service in the home of an interested Brazilian.

After tying the plane securely to the port dock at São Paulo de Olivença, Terry grabbed his satchel containing Bibles and gospel literature and started up the fifty-foot embankment. Wilma and the boys followed more leisurely, the boys pausing now and then to grab a lizard along the steep path. When Wilma stopped to catch her breath, she glanced back down at the dock and shouted, "Where's the plane? It's gone!" She spotted it floating offshore on the current moving downriver.

Frantic to stop Terry, who was disappearing over the top of the steep bank, Wilma yelled at him to come back. She told the boys to stay put, then she hurried back down the path to the dock. There she found an onlooker with a canoe who was willing to help Terry retrieve the floatplane, and eventually the gospel service went on as scheduled.

Afterward, Terry took time to investigate the incident. How had the plane come untied? Someone had cut the rope, but if anyone on the dock had seen it, they didn't offer to tell. God, however, had protected the aircraft, and Terry learned an important lesson: Always leave a hired man or responsible person in place to guard the plane.

SIX

THE NEED FOR RADIO COMMUNICATION

The presence of two ABWE pilots, miles apart on the Amazon River, pointed up a growing problem—lack of communication. This lack was not just between home base and airplane, but between missionary stations as well. A pilot's wife had no way to make contact with her husband from the time he left until he returned, even in an emergency.

In 1966, Terry planned a survey flight to river settlements a short distance downriver from Benjamin Constant and arranged with Jacó, a leader in the Santo Antonio congregation, to accompany him. Jacó and two other men often helped Terry in evangelistic meetings at preaching points, and they all hoped that someone would invite them to hold a service in a home in one of the settlements. The Lord blessed, and by afternoon, they had witnessed to some and had scheduled future meetings. With one eye on the weather, because tropical storms usually develop in the afternoon heat, Terry urged his helpers to get to the plane in order to leave before a storm hit.

As soon as they boarded, rain and wind blasted them. "Well, at least we tried," Terry said. He spotted a familiar lake below and went in for a quick landing, hoping to wait out the storm, but it was not to be. "This'll be an all-nighter," he predicted, noting the early darkness and dripping sky. The three men settled down as best they could to spend the night inside the cabin of the Aeronca Sedan.

Aware of the storm but unable to communicate with Terry, Wilma figured that he would return early the next morning. A pilot's wife must depend on a sovereign God to keep calm at such

39

times. However, when there was still no sign of the Aeronca Sedan by noon the next day, she called the hangar guard to get the speedboat ready. She planned to cross the river and report the plane missing at the military base in Tabatinga. Just then, the floatplane buzzed above the hangar, and Wilma gave a sigh of relief. But when Terry explained what had delayed his return, she couldn't believe her ears.

"You did *what*?" she demanded.

Sheepishly, Terry confessed that the men couldn't resist dropping a fishing line in the lake before their return flight. "And before we knew it, it was almost noon," he confessed.

After cooling down, Wilma had to admit that fresh fish would taste good, and she did rejoice to hear the results of the survey flight. This incident further highlighted the need for radio contact.

About this time, Panair, the national seaplane that had flown a weekly circuit between Manaus and Benjamin Constant, went bankrupt, leaving some of the missionaries downriver with no communication with the outside world. The seriousness of the situation became evident when Dorothy Blakslee sent an urgent note to Hank via the pilot on Panair's final stop at Fonte Boa. The note asked him to fly down as soon as possible to get her husband, Ed, who once again was gravely ill. Without the plane, the Blakslees would have had to make a tortuous 450-mile trip in an undependable speedboat, slamming against turbulent waves, constantly watching for submerged logs and sandbars during violent rainstorms, in order to reach a hospital. To complicate this situation, the military required that Hank report all flights departing and arriving, but he had no government license to operate a radio in the plane and so could not contact them. Before leaving to help the Blakslees, he had to check in and out at the military post upriver, thirty-five minutes away by speedboat. When Hank finally arrived in Fonte Boa, friends carried Ed by stretcher to the plane, and Hank flew him to Benjamin

Constant, where he was diagnosed with malaria and a urinary tract infection. A lot of time and effort could have been saved had radio contact been possible.

In Brazil during the 1960s, sending a message to a town that had telegraph capability might work in an emergency, but it was not reliable. Telephones—nonexistent within a town or between towns in this area of Brazil—cost hundreds of dollars, when available. But communication had become an absolute necessity and Hank needed to find a way to put it in place. Once again, Hank looked to his friend and coworker Richard Sterkenburg, who was thousands of miles away in São Paulo, to help buy single side-band radios and procure licenses to operate them from Benjamin Constant, Santa Rita Port of Two Brothers (named for ABWE missionaries and brothers, Paul and John Schlener, who ministered together there for nearly forty years,* Betania, Santo Antonio do Içá, Fonte Boa, and, later on, Foz de Jutaí.

Before we left on furlough in February 1963, the Amazon Field Council members had voted unanimously that Hank could begin the negotiations to buy the radios. The ABWE Board approved their plan and agreed to advance the funds until each missionary could repay their part of the cost. Months of follow-up dragged into years. Hank and I asked churches to pray that this project be completed. Four years later, Hank grew hopeful when he received word that the radio technician assigned to bring and install the radios would need transportation from Manaus to our area. But the technician never arrived. Communication flew back and forth between Hank and Richard Sterkenburg, who worked to discover why the technician had never shown up with the radios. The radio company promised that the technician would arrive within thirty days, but they never set a date. Hank didn't care to make another ten-hour

---

*Port of Two Brothers; The Amazing Story of Two Missionary Brothers and Their Work on the Amazon, by Paul Schlener, is available from ABWE.

flight to Manaus in vain, so he waited. Far south in São Paulo, Richard was assured that the engineer had already arrived in the Amazon and installed the radios. With the enormous distance between them, the radio company had not expected Richard to discover the truth. To assist Richard, Hank flew to São Paulo to investigate. It turned out that the radio license had never been approved; the radios had not been sent with a technician, and the company had tried to stall by lying. Hank went to a colonel we had known when he formerly worked in Tabatinga. The colonel kept him waiting for three hours, but when he saw Hank, he assured him that the license permit would be official the next day. Patience and persistence finally paid off. In December 1967, the promised engineer at last arrived with the radios. When Orv Floden and Hank checked out the radios and discovered that they were old, used models, they did the necessary repairs themselves, thankful at least to have the registration and license in hand and radios to begin communication between stations. The missionaries agreed that "a bird in hand is worth two in the bush."

In a written report, Richard said, "I considered it a pleasure to have been able to walk the sidewalks of São Paulo to allow Hank to fly up in the air and on the Amazon where he had, as he said, 'The longest runway in the world.'" Richard and Hank wore out shoe leather over the years as they paired up to get not only the radios, but also legal documents for the Amazon properties, annual license renewals for aircraft and radios, and landing fees that had to be paid in São Paulo. Richard Sterkenburg's self-sacrifice and commitment to assisting our distant Amazon ministry was a great help to us.

Once the radios were operating, 6:00 a.m. and 4:00 p.m. daily contact between stations by single side-band radio, and by ham radio in later years, meant greater efficiency for the aviation ministry. Flight safety improved, and because the pilots were more accessible, their ears buzzed with increased requests for flights.

God tested the pilots' hearts and their willingness to serve others. Terry and Hank learned to divide their time judiciously between transporting other missionaries and the demands of their own teaching and preaching ministries.

ABWE MISSIONARY PILOTS ARE PREACHERS, TOO

The ABWE missionary pilots always took part in some aspect of church ministry, and during 1965–66, the year we filled in for the Blakslees in Fonte Boa, Hank served as interim pastor. Two young men whom Hank baptized that year went on to Bible school in Manaus. Years afterward, the local church at Fonte Boa called a man from among their membership, Hank's namesake, to serve as lay pastor.

Hank rejoiced to see the changed lives of the believers and their enthusiasm to build their own house of worship. The Brazilian men labored, even though it meant standing barefoot in oozing clay, mixing it up and down until their calves ached, packing the sticky mass into brick-sized forms, and then drying them to bake for several days in a furnace fired by wood they had cut down themselves. The women and children helped by stacking the bricks until the Blakslees' return, when construction would begin.

Another crew of Fonte Boa workers helped Hank build an inexpensive floating hangar-workshop to dock on the shore in front of the mission property, so that Hank could keep an eye on the floatplane. The Amazon River current swirled around the bend there, undercutting the high embankment, sweeping away everything within reach in its rush past the town. The floating hangar protected the aircraft from floating debris and exposure to sun and storms.

WHY PRAY FOR MISSIONARIES?

People who pray for missionaries may never find out in this life how important their prayers are. But sometimes they get a glimpse, as did a friend who prayed for us.

While we lived there, Fonte Boa resembled an old-time "Wild West" town. Men holstered pistols and carried shotguns during political campaigns. Drunken mobs tried to take control by force, and those who were ungodly resented and opposed those who followed the Lord. God used these elements to show Hank and me the power of prayer through an incident that happened during the election for town mayor.

One afternoon, the town judge barged through our front gate, clapped his hands to get attention, then, uninvited, opened the door and stepped into the living room. Unhitching his gun holster, he slammed it down on a table nearby. "Excuse me. I have a matter of life and death to discuss with you."

The political situation, he explained, had gone from bad to worse. The local sheriff feared for his life, and a mob was in control. The judge had prepared a telegram requesting federal troops, but before he reached the telegraph office, a mob abducted the telegraph operator and carried him into the jungle. Now the judge wanted Hank's help. "Can you fly me to Manaus to deliver this request in person?"

"I'm sorry, but even if we left right now, we couldn't make it before dark," Hank explained. "Besides, the temporary permit to fly the Cessna has run out."

On the heels of the judge came another man, who was both a church deacon and the father of the mayor. Agitated, he called Hank aside for a whispered conference. "Can you fly my son and his family immediately to Tefe? Their lives are in danger."

Twenty men had threatened to break into the mayor's house to shoot him. The sheriff refused to get involved. Again, Hank explained the plane situation, then offered our 13-foot speedboat (the only one in town) as an alternative. "Take my boat and thirty-three horsepower motor if things get worse."

And, that very day, they did get worse. The mob shot off fireworks and broke into the mayor's office. I was on the other side of town at my outdoor Bible club and had to return through this demonstration being held outside the mayor's office. When I arrived home, Hank was preparing to leave. He and the judge had arranged to sneak the mayor and his family down to the floating hangar. Under cover of growing darkness, they loaded them into the speedboat and, within minutes, the swift Amazon current swept them out of sight and danger. Hank arrived home around 10:30 p.m. and informed the anxious father and the judge, "I got them aboard a launch on its way to Tefe."

We sat down to eat a late supper, but a confused babble erupted at the front gate. First one angry drunken man, then another, yelled, "Where's the mayor? We want him. Where did you take him? You had better tell us or else—"

After banging the gate, pushing and shoving, and blowing a siren every few minutes, the disgruntled mob finally shuffled back toward town, but they returned again and again throughout the night. None of us could sleep. The children, wide-eyed and frightened, crawled into bed with Hank and me.

"Drunk as they are, I doubt their threats will go any further," Hank said, calming our fears as the clamor diminished in the distance.

But then, just as we were falling asleep, we were startled by the sound of a loud bang at the gate, rapid hand-clapping at the front door, and someone shouting, "Senhor Henrique, hurry! We need you. My brother's been shot!"

Hank doubted the reason behind this midnight call for help. Was it a trick to get him outside where the mob could hurt him? Should he go? He dressed and grabbed his medical satchel, but then I watched him hesitate. From the dresser drawer, he removed the small pistol that his friend, a sheriff back in Grand Rapids, had given him for the flight to Brazil, to be used in case of emergency.

Thinking it might save his life, Hank put the gun into his satchel.

But a still, small voice stalled him. "You can't do this. Trust Me."

Hank replaced the pistol in the drawer, then hurried to save the life of the shotgun victim—who turned out to be the mob leader. The drunken men, sobered by the shooting, gathered around their leader.

"Why help a man who threatened your life, Senhor Henrique?" someone asked.

"I'm here to help save men's lives, whether spiritually or physically, just as I saved the mayor's life when he was in danger yesterday."

Guilty heads nodded. Hank grabbed the chance to share the gospel as he cleaned and bandaged the victim's wounded leg. Later on, this man came to Christ.

Months afterward, Hank and I received a letter from a friend in the US who wondered why God had prompted him to pray for Hank around midnight on a certain date. Could Hank or I remember something in particular that had happened that night, he wanted to know. When we went back and checked, it turned out to be the very night of the mob's threat. God reminded us of the unique way He answers prayer, and of how praying friends can make a difference.

SEVEN

CAMPING MINISTRY AND ALLIGATOR MEAT

When the Blakslees returned from furlough we were asked to fill in for the Harrells at their new station in Betania. We were able to continue their work with the Ticuna Indian congregation, and God blessed. In an ABWE prayer bulletin, Hank wrote, "Recently, there has been evidence of real repentance, turning from sin, and leaving the witch doctors. Several have given public testimony in the church, confessing sin and coming to faith in Christ."

That year, Hank and I began a field council camp that served all of our ABWE Amazon churches. Hank agreed to build the new camp and serve as camp director. After clearing the jungle across the creek from Betania, he and his Ticuna crew put up dormitories and an all-purpose building that served as chapel and cafeteria. When it was time for camp to begin, Pastor Oseas da Silva, the camp speaker, and his family, had problems with their flight and ended up stranded in Manaus.

Hank made a nine-hour round trip in the Cessna to get them. When he returned, he quipped, "I already agreed to be camp construction boss and camp director. I had no desire to be camp speaker, as well!"

Before arranging the Silva family's return tickets to Manaus, Hank transported them in the Cessna to the ABWE Amazon mission stations so that Pastor Oseas could speak at services with the various congregations. When Hank offered a bonus for this ministry, Pastor Oseas chose an alligator hunt. They went hunting at night and shot a big one. The alligator tail meat, similar to lobster tail, tasted delicious dipped in melted butter.

FLYING WITH THE GOVERNOR

Following the 1967 camp season, the governor of Amazonas asked Hank to come to Leticia and fly him and his male secretary to all the main interior Colombian towns, so that he could investigate the substance abuse problems of the Indian population. Hank felt at first that he couldn't justify making this three-day trip. Then, Orv Floden, who had begun ABWE's work in Leticia in 1944, reminded him that in the early 1960s, the government had prohibited public evangelical church meetings, and the Flodens had been forced to hold meetings across the border in Marco, Brazil, for over a year. "After all the time our church in Leticia has suffered," Orv said, "this flight could be used to break down barriers and create goodwill."

Hank prayed about it, struggling to find a way to satisfy his longing to leave a gospel witness in these remote towns the governor wanted to visit. Finally, he told the governor, "If you'll give us permission to show a gospel film while you are meeting with the town representatives, I'll agree to fly you." Hank used a Moody Science film in Spanish and Portuguese, knowing it would attract crowds and would give him and Orv the chance to witness or pass out gospel literature.

On the flight back to Leticia after this trip, the governor leaned forward from the back seat to talk to Hank and Orv. "Gentlemen, can you tell me what we've done wrong? I'm perplexed. After all the priests have done to educate, clothe, and teach the Indians a trade, they continue to cause problems. All that expense and time have been wasted, as far as I'm concerned."

"I agree," Orv answered. "All those efforts don't produce a changed Indian unless the Indian first has a changed heart." He explained that a changed heart means the transformed life that comes after believing and receiving the all-sufficient Savior, Jesus Christ.

Hank glanced at the governor and, noting a spark of interest, asked, "We work with the Ticuna Indians at Betania, just east of here. Would you like to see how changed hearts have changed the Ticunas?" The governor agreed, and Hank detoured toward Betania.

Since the governor had chartered the plane for three days, I hadn't expected Hank back home until late and I was surprised to hear the plane buzzing overhead before lunch. Had an emergency brought him home ahead of schedule? Hank detected this question on my face as I arrived, out of breath, to meet them at the lakefront.

"No emergency, Ruth," he said, grinning, "just a friendly visit. I invited the governor and his secretary for lunch, and Orv is here, too." Seeing my distress, Hank added, "Well, I guess it may be an emergency for you, but don't worry about it, we'll gladly eat whatever you have to offer. We'll be back after an hour in the village."

Fortunately, I had mixed bread to bake. A large *ticunaré* (peacock bass) stuffed with onions and green peppers, along with pinto beans, rice, and fried plantains took less than an hour to get on the table, with my daughters pitching in to help.

After dinner, well fed and impressed with all he had seen and heard at Betania, the governor boarded the floatplane with a freshly baked loaf of my bread and the firsthand knowledge that there was a difference between the Indians he visited in Colombia and those at Betania. He listened carefully to Orv, who unfolded God's plan to save lost men and then empower them to change their sinful habits. In later years, Hank often referred to that flight. "We held the governor and his secretary captive in that cabin, and they were bound to hear the gospel. But God knows their hearts, and only eternity will reveal the results of that trip."

Though the governor flew with Hank several times after that, further opportunities to witness never opened up. But several years later, the governor's goodwill toward ABWE missionaries working in Leticia became evident. When Don Fanning settled there in 1971 to begin the aviation ministry, doors opened. Butch Jarvis arrived to partner with Don the following year, and the government granted them both permission to work in La Pedrera, one of the remote Indian villages that the governor had visited in 1966 with Hank and Orv.

BACK TO BENJAMIN CONSTANT

In 1967, we made the fourth move of our second term, back to the mission house in Benjamin Constant. We had agreed to fill the year-long vacancy that would be created when the Bowerses left for furlough. Having an airplane was an advantage for a family that had been assigned to be "furlough replacements" at two different stations downriver, but it was still a challenge to move five children, household belongings, and aircraft tools and equipment every year, though the positive results outweighed the difficulties. At each place, Hank and I left behind part of ourselves in the many "spiritual" children who would grow in the Lord and serve Him in leadership roles in future churches established by coworkers. We also brought with us a new appreciation for those ministries downriver, as well as a determination to better serve our distant partners. Having walked in their shoes, we prayed for them with more understanding.

THE LAYMAN'S INSTITUTE AND THE CONGENIAL CHURCH SPLIT

While Hank and I worked with the military and congregation in Marco, we were also committed to preparing the church in Benjamin Constant to call a Brazilian pastor. Together with Terry and Wilma Bowers, we divided the responsibilities of training leadership. If the church were to become autonomous, its members needed to learn more about practical evangelism, Sunday School teaching, visitation, church polity, and bookkeeping procedures. And if we as missionaries took time to prepare all this training, why not open it up to others? We invited aspiring leaders from all of the ABWE ministries along the Amazon, including those whose congregations were at the stage of organizing and electing deacons and officers, to participate in what we called the Layman's Institute. Pastor Oseas da Silva and his talented wife, Nilda, agreed to come from Manaus to teach the training classes. Downriver, representatives and trainers converged on Benjamin Constant for morning and afternoon sessions, followed by an evening evangelistic service in the church. Three adults received Christ in the evening services, and many laymen returned home to their congregations better prepared to serve the Lord in leadership positions.

Following this training conference, the Benjamin Constant church voted to allow several families who lived a good distance away in Santo Antonio de Benjamin to begin a new work closer to their homes. Terry explained, "During the rainy season, it's hard for these families to take an active part in this church, and it's difficult to convince an unbelieving neighbor to paddle a canoe one hour to attend a church service here in Benjamin Constant." So a congenial "church split" occurred.

Twelve members left with Terry Bowers to begin Sunday services in the home of a believer downriver at Santo Antonio de Benjamin. When the congregation outgrew the house, they moved to a public school building. Terry held weeknight meetings in front of the homes along the banks of the Amazon River. The believers worked to get logs from the jungle for boards, poles for rafters, and thatch for the roof of their new church building. The group continued to grow. Twenty-one prepared for baptism, and, eventually, they organized as the Calvary Baptist Church of Santo Antonio de Benjamin, with an average attendance of 125. Terry and Wilma trained leaders who completed several Bible courses and listened for hours to lessons on cassette tapes. These leaders learned to carry on the work of the church without a missionary or institute-trained leader.

The church in Benjamin Constant was also growing, and

when the congregation averaged 100, it was time to look for a Brazilian candidate to pastor the church. In spite of the ongoing challenge of retaining Brazilian leadership over the years, the church has grown strong. It operates its own Christian school and Bible institute, AWANA clubs, and missionary teams that minister in three villages farther down the Amazon River. ABWE pilots who live and operate the plane ministry out of Benjamin Constant cooperate and serve the Lord in close relationship with the church and the present minister, Pastor Cristiano.

EXPANDING THE FLOATING HANGAR

Throughout November 1969, Hank gathered materials to expand the floating hangar in Benjamin Constant to house two floatplanes. He ordered handmade spikes and hand-sawed lumber and aluminum sheets for the roof, and then he sharpened his tools. Pete Haven, an engineer and Hank's former Sunday school student at Wealthy Street Baptist Church in Grand Rapids, arrived to design and estimate materials for the project.

Then nine men and their pastor from First Baptist Church in St. Johns, Michigan, traveled to Benjamin Constant to reconstruct the hangar, sacrificing their deer-hunting vacations to do so. After being delayed for four days in Bogotá, this crew finally arrived in December, eager to make up for lost time.

On the day of their arrival, they ate lunch, changed clothes, and pitched in immediately, and for the next ten days, our home buzzed like a beehive. From daybreak to dusk, these committed men worked, taking time out only for meals and a midday break. The equatorial sun sapped their energy. Some, seeking relief throughout the day, rolled off the hangar into the river to cool down, then returned to work. They consumed gallons of boiled water, but, other than sunburn, none fell sick. They sometimes tumbled into bed in their work clothes, so exhausted they couldn't drum up the energy to bathe. When tidying their beds each morning, I discovered sawdust, nails, and carpenter chalk concealed in the rumpled sheets.

I hustled to keep ten hungry men fed, sharing my kitchen with two carpenters who were building new cupboards and installing a new cooking range. Aware of the adage "all work and no play makes Jack a dull boy," Hank hired a guide to take the men hunting and fishing in the jungle, which was a memorable fun break for them, and a fill-the-freezer blessing for me.

Hank and Terry were grateful to have a larger place to house both floatplanes, and I was grateful to have a more efficient kitchen. But we were especially thankful to hear how God touched the lives of those dedicated volunteers and led them into further missionary service in other places. One even enrolled in Bible college to prepare for the ministry.

A NEW PLANE FOR THE BOWERSES

Prior to the Bowerses' departure for furlough, Terry and Hank agreed that the Aeronca Sedan, which had served well for two terms, must now be replaced with a larger, more efficient plane. After a cylinder overhaul, the plane was sold to New Tribes Mission. God had blessed the use of the Aeronca Sedan during Terry's first term, as he described in the January 1968 issue of the *Message*:

> During this past term we made 135 evangelistic flights, taking off for 20–30-minute flights to remote villages . . . where we would find people who had never heard the gospel and had no opportunity to hear it except when we arrived by air. . . . A struggling two-week canoe trip to a tribe on a tributary has become just a fast two-hour flight by air. A six-hour trip by launch to hold evangelistic meetings is just ten minutes by plane. A rough all-day trip by speedboat for a missionary to buy supplies is an hour's flight in the floatplane. Five tiring days of river launch travel for a

missionary family returning to their station is a pleasant three-hour ride in the plane.

While on furlough, Terry and Wilma began the process of raising funds to buy a second Cessna 185 floatplane. They used the same method we had used in "Amazon Airlift" in 1963. Once again, God supplied all the funds needed to purchase a 1968 Cessna 185 floatplane, which, when licensed, carried the letters PT-DNY. Hank, who now knew what to expect, repeated all the necessary steps for registration and licensing: the flight from Michigan to the Amazon, the application for the plane's entry into Brazil, and follow-up trips to south Brazil.

REACHING OUT TO COPATANA
During Terry and Wilma Bowers' furlough, Hank flew what had been Terry's monthly supply run down to Fonte Boa and back to Benjamin Constant. On each flight, from high above the jungle, he had his usual bird's-eye view of inhabitants living in small villages along the shores of the various tributaries. Looking for ways to conserve fuel, he figured that he could fit in an evangelistic service either going or returning. On one flight, after he dropped off his last passenger and turned toward home, Hank sighted Copatana, a sizeable riverside village of thatched huts. He noted its location and began praying that God would open the way to preach the gospel there.

Around the bend of the Jutaí from Copatana, he noted a large sandbar emerging as the river dropped in its annual cycle. Hank began to lay plans: *I'll set up an evangelistic outreach on my next supply run and bring the family down for a campout and fishing, as well.*

The children and I enjoyed flying and stopping to visit at the various mission stations on the trip downriver. When Hank took us to Copatana, we had breakfast with the Schlener families, lunch with the Paynes in Santo Antonio do Içá, and then headed for the sandbar on the Jutaí River. The kids saw it first. Excited, Danny

and Kisti squealed, "Can we stop and go swimming, Daddy?"
"First things first. We'll just do a fly-by to look things over
right now. We want to set up a meeting at Copatana for tomorrow," Hank explained. "There will be time afterward to pitch the
tent and go swimming before dark."

The entire town of Copatana turned out to meet us at the
waterfront. Helping hands tied the floatplane to a tree while
Hank, standing out on the float, directed them. Typical river people of the Amazon, with a combined heritage of European,
African, and indigenous Indian strains, crowded around to shake
hands with us. It was hot under the punishing sun, but the multitude insisted that we have a look at their town. We tried to
ignore the stench of open sewers and rotting garbage that littered
straggling rows of thatch-roofed, bamboo-floored huts. Pigs and
children roamed the paths together. Listening to the history of
Copatana and their need for medical help, we perceived not just
their physical necessities, but their destitute spiritual condition as
well. Salvation in Christ could change many of these lives.

The town leaders enthusiastically agreed to welcome us back
to hold a gospel meeting the next day and whenever possible
thereafter during Hank's scheduled monthly supply run. As we
returned to board the floatplane, a throng of friendly kids accompanied Danny, Kisti, Kim, and Linda down the hill, then stood on
the riverbank waving goodbye.

By the time daylight faded at around 6:15 p.m., a gorgeous full
moon reflected its image on the rippling waves that flowed past
our sandy campsite. Kanda, our fifth child and the best camper of
us all, was then a toddler and was already asleep on an air mat-
tress inside the screened tent. The other four children, pajama-
clad, poked sticks in the dying coals of the campfire. "Time for
bed. Last one asleep is a rotten egg!" I challenged as we all ran
toward the tent.

We awoke now and again throughout the night to voices and
the sounds of dugouts grating on the sandbar. Not only the curi-

ous, but also the sick who needed medications, had located us. Around 4:30 a.m. the kids roused, and Hank and I gave up trying to sleep. When we crawled out of the tent, two canoe-loads of curious Ticuna Indians observed our every move. Hank and Danny, grabbing their fishing poles, smiled and waved, but got no response. Hank returned without fish for breakfast, but one kind Indian, who spoke a little Portuguese, beached his dugout and offered to roast his catch and share it with us. Nothing tastes better than fresh catfish roasted over an open fire on the beach. It reminded us of the breakfast Jesus offered His disciples on another beach many years ago. We hoped that kind-hearted Indian, with whom communication was nearly impossible, would someday learn about Jesus' love for him.

Back at Copatana a large crowd waited for us. Under a huge shade tree, someone arranged a table for our Bibles, medicines, and teaching visuals. I unpacked my accordion and taught some easy choruses that our own children sang in Portuguese. Kanda, our toddler, was getting restless, so Kisti played with her to free me to tell a Bible story with visuals. Zacchaeus-like, several boys listened from the tree branches overhead, in the company of a noisy monkey. Since it was probably the first gospel message ever preached there, Hank invited any who wanted to know more about eternal life to speak with him privately.

After distributing Bibles and tracts, Hank dispensed medicine, then went off to look after a few sick people. Around noon, we were thankful for the various fruits bartered earlier in exchange for medicines and Bibles. We were as hungry for them as the folks at Copatana were for the gospel. Over the next half year, continued monthly meetings yielded much spiritual fruit. Eventually, some of these new Christians became part of John and Sylvia Kallin's ministry at the Foz do Jutaí mission station.

After we left Copatana, Ed and Dot Blakslee, forty-five minutes downriver at Fonte Boa, waited for our arrival with their mail and supplies. After Dot's delicious supper of rice, beans, and

Hank, Ruth, Kisti, Daniel, and Kim depart for language school in Fortaleza, Brazil (January 1960).

The Aeronca Sedan ramped at Port of Two Brothers where Orv, Elizabeth, and Helen Floden have just disembarked and are climbing up the steep embankment. Paul Schlener carries their baggage, while his son, Tim, helps the pilot secure the plane.

Above:
MKs from Brazil who traveled with Hank on Christmas break.

Left:
Boarding school parents Ruth and Bill Large with MKs.

A Javarí River preaching point. One of Hank's "Timothys" stands on the float of the Aeronca Sedan.

Above:
The Amazon River, the longest "runway" in the world.

Below:
The first floating hangar for the Aeronca Sedan (Javarizinho River).

Above:
Ruth beside the Scheltema's first floatplane (1962). Ruth took an active part in river evangelism, along with her husband, Hank.

Dedication of the new Cessna 185 floatplane in Grand Rapids, Michigan, with church members and families who took part in "Amazon Airlift."

Above:
Chico, the Dení Indian boy, who was bitten on the arm by a *Jararaca,* a pit viper.

Left:
Terry and Wilma Bowers with their three sons (left to right: Jim, Dan, and Phil) in Brazil (1969).

Orv Floden visits with the governor of Amazonas, Colombia, on the charter flight to investigate substance abuse at Indian villages.

Above:
The five Scheltema children awakened to find curious Indians and Brazilians visiting us at our campsite on the Jutaí River.

Above Left:
Ruth Scheltema and her children at Copatana, teaching the villagers to sing "Crown Him, crown Him, all ye little children . . ." in Portuguese.

Capitão Walquito pins the Peacemaker Medal on Hank's jacket at the military base in Tabatinga, Brazil.

The Colombian Cessna 185-1318P floatplane after crashing in the treetops.

fish, we helped set up benches on their front porch for Bible study and a prayer service. Hank preached and I accompanied the singing on my accordion. We resisted the temptation to stay up late conversing with them; the Blakslees had letters to answer and send with us on the following day, because it would be a month before they had another opportunity to receive and send mail, and we needed to be airborne by 7:00 a.m.

Home at last, I asked the kids, "What did you like best about the trip?" I was surprised to hear their remarks, especially Danny's. I expected them to mention the fun on the sandbar and fishing, but Danny said, "Mom, I got to help Dad tell about Jesus to people who never heard of Him. Like Dad always says, 'Fishing for men is as exciting as fishing for fish.'"

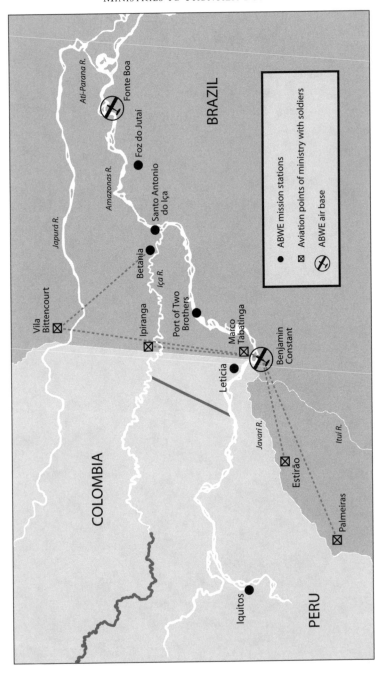

EIGHT

MILITARY MINISTRY

By the time Hank and the children and I moved back upriver from Betania to Benjamin Constant in 1967, God had given us a burden to evangelize at Brazilian military posts. This was impressed upon us one day when military officers clapped loudly at the front door of our home.

Our daughter Linda ran to see who it might be and peered through the screen door at strangers. In English, she yelled, "Mom, some soldiers are at the door. Hurry!" Then she greeted the men in Portuguese and asked them to wait a minute. She didn't understand why the men grinned until she found out they both spoke English.

Their riverboat had broken down on its way to Ipiranga, the Brazil–Colombia frontier military post, which was a day's travel up the Içá River from Betania. The officers asked for Hank's help to repair the boat, and, after Hank consented, the boat was towed to our dock at Betania, arriving at dusk. On-board were the wives of the two officers, their two babies—each under eleven months—three soldiers, and a house maid. And they all arrived in time for supper!

We already had Rosabis and Daví II, seminary students from Manaus, staying with us during school break, so they pitched in to peel and cut up extra plantains to fry. While I scurried to make additional sandwiches with homemade bread, and then to find places to sleep the unexpected company, Hank got better acquainted with them. We enjoyed the conversation and company of these well-educated Brazilians. The guests left the next morning after Hank and the two seminarians helped repair their boat, but the soldiers returned later to explain that they continued to have boat trouble and wanted to get their families home without further delay. Would Hank fly the women and babies up to Ipiranga?

He did so, and this unforeseen contact opened the door for Hank to present the Moody Science film in Portuguese to the soldiers stationed at Ipiranga. The children and I accompanied him, giving me the opportunity to make friends with the officers' wives. The two wives who had enjoyed our hospitality at Betania bragged about my homemade bread to the other women at the post, so besides teaching them to make bread, I also had the opportunity to give my testimony.

This first visit at the frontier post opened our eyes to the need for the gospel among military families. We saw in them an unreached group of people who were isolated from their former lifestyles and in the process of change, so they were more open to the truths of Scripture. Hank and I prayed, and asked supporters to also pray, for God's timing to begin a regular missionary outreach to the soldiers and officers at the various military posts in the Amazon.

The move back upriver from Betania to Benjamin Constant put Hank's landing strip in international waters that belonged to Brazil, Peru, and Colombia. Brazil manned strategic military posts on the various river frontiers: the Solimões, bordering Colombia; the Javarí, bordering Peru at two locations; and the Japurá and Içá rivers, separating Colombia at two locations. All these posts were isolated, making any rescue in a medical emergency infeasible by water transportation.

The ABWE floatplane offered the only recourse in such an emergency. Hank and Terry flew medevac patients for the government and military of all three countries, saved countless lives, and gave a gospel witness as well. Soldiers and civilians alike, eager for reading materials, appreciated the tracts and magazines Hank supplied. Our supporting partners had been praying for us to know God's timing when to begin a church-planting ministry at one or more of the various military posts, and it seemed that now was the time.

TABATINGA

We determined to begin a work at the base in Tabatinga, less than ten minutes by air or thirty-five minutes by speedboat from Benjamin Constant. Hank asked God for a talented local Brazilian believer to partner with him. His idea was to include both low-ranking soldiers and officers together, because if the ministry began with only those in the lower ranks, the officers would take little notice. By March 1968, God answered these specific prayers.

A sergeant and his wife, both Baptists with outstanding testimonies, arrived to live on the Tabatinga base, followed by a lieutenant military doctor and his wife, also fine Christians. Both couples urged Hank to start a Baptist work either on or off the post. They asked the post commander's permission to use the mess hall for worship. The commander agreed, but asked that Hank combine his meeting with an hour of English instruction. "My officers need practice in English conversation," he said, and English became the attraction that drew both soldiers and officers to the meetings.

Evandro Batista, a graduate of the Regular Baptist Seminary of Manaus who was eager to serve the Lord, was called up from the Port of Two Brothers for military service at Tabatinga. Years later, after graduating from Cedarville College, in Ohio, and helping missionary Paul Schlener in Tabatinga, Evandro and his family would go on to serve as ABWE missionaries in Portugal. But in 1968, while he was still a young soldier, Evandro lived with us on weekends and partnered with Hank in the Benjamin Constant church by leading the choir, assisting with youth activities, and preaching and teaching at times. Every Sunday following the morning service and dinner at our house, Hank, Evandro, and I flew to Tabatinga for the afternoon service in the army mess hall.

A good number of soldiers came to Christ, but it soon became evident that to establish a solid foundation for a church, we needed a core of permanent residents, since soldiers and officers were regularly transferred away from Tabatinga. Hank's vision to begin a church there remained strong, and though it didn't happen at the military base, God had a plan for Marco, the adjacent Brazilian town, situated between the military base in Tabatinga and the border town of Leticia, Colombia.

After our return to Benjamin Constant from furlough in 1969, the military continued to use ABWE aircraft for medevacs and official inspections at frontier posts. Whenever possible, Hank would combine an open-air evangelistic meeting along with these flights. At one of these services, in Vila Bittencourt, the military post at the Brazil–Colombia frontier on the Japurá River, a ten-year-old girl named Claudete received Christ. Months later, Hank saw her again, in Marco.

Claudete insisted that Hank meet her parents, who, in turn, invited Hank to teach them the Bible. Their Bible study group eventually overflowed with neighbors and moved from the family's home to their brick factory behind their house. The congregation had a humble beginning, with earnest listeners sitting on rough boards stretched between brick supports. It wasn't easy to hold their attention! A pet dog crawled under a bench, whining for attention, and everyone laughed when a diaperless baby caused a commotion as its mother jerked the baby away from her Sunday dress. Giggling youngsters took turns checking each other for lice, and men occasionally stood up to talk to someone passing by on the outside of the open-air building.

Despite these distractions, God's Word convicted many, some came to Christ, and Hank baptized Claudete, her parents, and a few others. As God's instrument, ten-year-old Claudete had prepared the way for us to get involved in Marco. Years afterward, Paul and Jessie Schlener, and believers from the Port of Two

Brothers, along with Claudete's mother, Teresa, her children, and believers from earlier missionary works, formed the nucleus that would become the First Baptist Church and Christian School of Tabatinga, in the town which was formerly known as Marco.

LIGHT IN THE DARKNESS

Although the Brazilian military obliged Hank to provide emergency service to remote frontier bases, he felt no obligation to carry questionable cargo for them. He monitored his loads carefully, especially because rumor had it that missionary pilots carried contraband jewels or human fat drained from Indians for use as aviation fuel. Once, Hank refused to carry cargo assigned by a Brazilian general, who wanted to take cigarettes and liquor to the frontier military posts to celebrate Christmas with the soldiers.

"The medical supplies can go, but the other stuff stays," Hank advised the soldiers delivering the cargo for the general's chartered flight. "You inform the general and, if he has any question about it, ask him to come see me." He never did, so we assumed he understood, and Hank was able to later give a clear witness of the gospel to this general, who came to dinner at our house to get better acquainted with us.

God didn't always allow Hank and me to see spiritual changes in the lives of those to whom we witnessed, but many of the military majors, colonels, and generals, contacted through a ministry to military bases, were affected in other ways.

During the years between 1963 and 1967, communists attempted to take over Brazil. In response to this threat, the Brazilian military took complete control of the country. Their secret service kept American missionaries and other foreigners who lived on the frontier borders of Brazil under secret surveillance. The government removed other missions from frontier areas, but ABWE's work continued, due, in part, to the plane's usefulness to the military. Hank cleared all flights through the army commander in Tabatinga and registered the names of passengers and the purpose for each flight. When Hank obtained permission to move our family to Fonte Boa, 400 miles from Tabatinga, the commander allowed Hank to submit monthly reports in place of obtaining clearance for each flight. The commander's willingness to lighten Hank's load opened the way for Hank to return the favor.

Commercial airline flights between Manaus and Tabatinga ceased sporadically, for varying reasons. During one of these times, when the commander learned that Hank intended to fly to Manaus to locate twenty drums of gas that had been lost for three months, and to pick up two seminary students for evangelistic services, he asked Hank to take his wife and two children along to visit relatives there.

"There's room in the plane," Hank answered, "but I'll have a layover in Fonte Boa for my Sunday church responsibilities. If they don't mind staying overnight with us, they can arrive in Manaus on Monday," Hank answered. The purpose of the trip was not to transport the commander's family, but since he had room, Hank was glad to help. The plane didn't have enough gas to make the trip, so the commander furnished the fuel, free of charge. His wife and two children heard the gospel in two services, and on several other occasions Hank had the chance to witness to this commander. God used this situation to create goodwill with the military.

When they arrived in Manaus, the full colonel personally thanked Hank for his help, including the many emergency flights he had made to save army personnel. The colonel not only expressed his gratitude, but also was helpful with many of the needs being faced at the time regarding the Brazilian customs department. Once again, God showed His goodness in providing this unexpected blessing.

Several times, high-ranking military officials inquired why ABWE operated aircraft on the frontier. Hank gave a clear testimony of God's call on his life to preach salvation in Christ as commanded in the Bible. "The airplane provides the most efficient way to reach remote areas with the gospel, but wherever and whenever ABWE pilots can fly to help in a life or death emergency, we are also willing to serve the Brazilian military bases along distant frontiers in the Amazon." Hank's preaching trips to the headwaters also facilitated the government health agency's vaccination program. Hank and I vaccinated hundreds against smallpox, keeping accurate records for the government.

THE PEACEMAKER MEDAL

A few years after the attempted communist takeover, Hank would receive a high honor from the Brazilian government. During our furlough in the late 1960s, a telegram from Major Joao Walquito arrived. It requested Hank's presence at Tabatinga, the Amazon frontier base next to Leticia, to decorate him for humanitarian service. This was the first time the Peacemaker Medal, one of Brazil's highest honors, would go to a Baptist or Protestant missionary.

Once he received this prestigious award, Hank used it to good advantage for ABWE. When acting as a mission representative on official errands, he used his copies of congratulatory telegrams, photographs, and commendations from various Brazilian generals and military officers to facilitate necessary mission business. In Brazil, the saying is: "It's not what you know, but who you know."

Hank also used his photo album as a witnessing tool. His photos pictured dynamic stories of many who had been saved through the missionary aviation ministry—physically through his medical knowledge, and spiritually through the Spirit's gift to evangelize the lost in the hard-to-reach headwaters of the Amazon tributaries.

CHANGES AHEAD FOR OUR FAMILY

For the Amazon aviation program, 1970 through 1972 brought significant change. We faced difficult decisions regarding our family situation. As our five children matured, sending them hundreds of miles away to boarding school each year grew increasingly harder. By 1970, none of the children wanted to study so far away from home. I taught all five that year, but home-schooling materials and aids were not as developed as they are now, and I felt incapable of teaching high school subjects. With a teenage son, two teenage daughters, and another daughter approaching that critical period, Hank and I felt we should get them out of the jungle and back into their own culture. We asked the field council and ABWE Board to approve an early furlough beginning in July 1971—in time for our children to start school in the US. We also considered taking a leave of absence until our children were grown.

Interim Pastor Aldeney Cajueiro, serving his practicum from the Regular Baptist Seminary of Manaus, agreed to care for the church in Benjamin Constant after we left. Before leaving for the States, Hank removed the Cessna 185-CJG engine, which was due for a major overhaul, and crated it for shipping to the US. "The old gray mare ain't what she used to be," Hank wrote to our supporters. "The Cessna has 300 tired horses, but you can help revive a horse at ten dollars a head." God blessed and supplied the cost of rejuvenation, and Hank later shipped the engine back to the Amazon to be reinstalled. Meanwhile, Terry Bowers continued flying the newer Cessna 185-DNY.

When we received approval for early furlough and settled in Florida in 1971, the mission invited Hank to serve as a recruitment representative in the US until we could reach a decision regarding our future. Hank entered this new position with enthusiasm as he began to contact pastors and prospective candidates on behalf of ABWE.

2,700-mile air route taken by Dan Fanning and Butch Jarvis to Leticia, Colombia, in the Cessna 185 floatplane in1972. The enlarged area shows where the Project Amazon team from Virginia ministered.

NINE

ABWE AVIATION EXPANDS INTO COLOMBIA

During our 1968 furlough, Hank had met Don and Janice Fanning, ABWE missionary candidates. By April 1970, Don and Jan were appointees assigned to start an aviation ministry in Colombia and were beginning language school in Guadalajara, Mexico. Don, drawn to work with Indians, made arrangements to fly for a week with Hank to learn all he could about aviation in the Amazon. He held the pilot and mechanic licenses and Bible training that ABWE required of missionary pilots, but he lacked sufficient flight time. Although a number of pilots had clamored to copilot on Hank's trip from the US to Benjamin Constant in the new 1968 Cessna 185-DNY floatplane, Don had been the logical choice. He interrupted his prefield meeting schedule to make the five-day trip, which gave him thirty-plus flight hours and experience.

In the fall of 1970, ABWE also appointed Enos (Butch) and Bonnie Jarvis to partner with the Fannings in Colombia. The Fannings arrived in Leticia, Colombia, in 1972, while the Jarvises were still in language school. God had already supplied a Cessna 185-1318P floatplane, and Don began working on the details for its importation. Both Don and Butch had completed their aviation mechanic training at LeTourneau College, in Texas; both had completed Bible study courses at Bob Jones University; now they were teaming up "to preach the gospel, where Christ was not named" (Rom. 15:20). Their goal was to establish a local church in each village within flight range of their air base. Butch and Bonnie were involved in prefield ministry and scheduled to start language study in Costa Rica, but first Butch opted to co-pilot with Don to take the Cessna 185-1318P, which had now been cleared for entry, to Leticia.

It took them a week to fly the plane from Tarpon Springs, Florida, to Leticia, after meticulously mapping out their flight plan by fuel availability at floatplane bases. A flight such as this holds an aura of fascination for the uninitiated, but it always proves to be plain hard work for the pilots.

In the 1972 *Message* article "He Brought It to Pass," Butch described their adventures en route from Lake Tarpon, out to sea over Great Exuma in the Caribbean, and down the chain of the Bahamas to Kingston, Jamaica. Their first overnight lodging was "under the stars on a deserted sandy beach protected by a reef. As the sun was setting, our thoughts of a Caribbean swim were changed when we noticed several five-foot sharks feeding a few feet from shore." At sunup, they took off and arrived late in the afternoon in Kingston, where they intended to clear customs, refuel, and be on their way—but God had another plan. The fuel pump had frozen up, and with low fuel pressure, the plane was inoperable. Don and Butch spent the day dismantling and repairing the fuel pump. Both men were A & P aircraft mechanics, an important factor for safety in places far removed from available resources.

At 6 a.m. the next day, the thermometer read 95°F, and there was no breeze to help give them lift, a critical factor for takeoff with a full floatplane. Though they tried different maneuvers, including rocking, twisting, crossing over the waves in the plane's wake, and changing headings to get a different face into the wind, the plane couldn't get up on the step. They decided to wait until the next morning, hoping for a cooler temperature or at least a favorable breeze.

The Dale Loftis family was serving then in Jamaica with Baptist Mid-Missions, a sister mission agency, and they graciously extended hospitality to the ABWE pilots during their layover. Michael Loftis, who was just eighteen, remembers well that night that the pilots spent at his home. In an interesting turn of events, Dr. Michael Loftis now serves as ABWE's fourth president, and he recently presented the Jarvises with the thirty-five-year Bomm Award.

There was more adventure ahead. After they left Jamaica, they faced a heart-stopping incident as they tried to cross over the Andes Mountains at Bogotá, Colombia. Butch described it this way:

The passes into and out of Bogotá on the south end were both at 10,500 feet; however, the departure pass was socked in and we needed 16,000 feet to clear it by IFR (Instrument Flight Rules). With the floats, the service ceiling was a tad over 13,000, so we chose a parallel pass, which we knew was higher but hoped clearer, and headed up that pass until we were closed in with the rocks of the canyon to the left and below, with clouds above and to the right. When we saw that the "tunnel" was narrowing, we made a 180-degree turn while there was enough space to make it without penetrating any clouds. As we made the 180, the engine burped, sputtered and quit. We were right at 13,000 feet and began an engine-out descent through that canyon back toward the city. At times the base of the canyon wanted to grab the floats but updrafts or ground effect kept us from contacting a single rock.

As we wound down through the canyon, we declared emergency, established our position with the Center of Ground Control at the airport in Bogotá, and as we came down through the 11,000 level, we made another turn. Right in front was the reservoir for the southern part of Bogotá, three miles long, two miles wide, at 9,600 feet—the perfect place to land.

Several years later, when Hank was appointed director of ABWE Air, he would insist on maintaining ham radio contact with his pilots as a safety precaution during trips such as this, but Don and Butch had no such contact now. After landing, they found that the fine micronite filter behind the air box just fore of the firewall was completely clogged by dirty gas. At the altitude demanded, there wasn't sufficient fuel flow to keep the engine running. The floats enabled them to land at the reservoir, and God provided the lake to land on. A good afternoon's work of cleaning and purging the entire fuel system got them running again. To take off at 55 mph, when the plane stalls at 57 mph, shy by almost fifty percent horsepower and the lift needed, was miraculous.

The last 700 miles of the trip proved anticlimatic, but within two days of the engine failure over Bogotá, the pilots moored the Cessna 185-1318P floatplane in her floating hangar on the Amazon River in Leticia, Colombia. Butch then returned to the US to rejoin Bonnie for prefield ministry, and Don concentrated on the inevitable bureaucratic paperwork and fees necessary to get the new Cessna imported, registered, and licensed. Amazingly, the government eventually granted the Cessna free entrance, the first time this had ever happened to an evangelical mission in Colombia.

FINDING THE RIGHT LOCATION FOR THE ABWE AIR BASE

While Orv and Helen Floden were on furlough, the Fannings resided near their house in Leticia. During this time, Don flew numerous search flights, seeking the best place to set up an aviation base and work with the unreached Indian population of Colombia.

One afternoon, while working on documents at his office desk, Don heard the front gate bang and running footsteps approach. Insistent knocking at the front door commanded his attention, and he hurried to see what the commotion was about.

Uribe, one of the old rubber barons that founded La Pedrera, a remote frontier town 200 miles north of Leticia on the Caqueta

River, had died. His daughter and son-in-law (who later became mayor of La Pedrera) were visiting in Leticia when news reached them of her father's death. As family members, they needed to get back home immediately. The man at the door, Uribe's son-in-law, entreated Don, "Can you fly us to La Pedrera?" Don graciously helped the family through their time of bereavement, and this influential family, indebted to Don, formed a friendship with the ABWE missionaries that endured through succeeding years. In return for Don's kindness, they helped the missionaries obtain a sizeable property in La Pedrera alongside the 1,300-meter-long military-owned airstrip, the perfect place for the ABWE Colombia air base. The Fanning and Jarvis families planned to build their duplex on this property, as well. Once again, the Lord had used the pilot and plane, in response to an emergency, to supply a need for His servants.

A PLANE IN THE TREETOPS AND A PLANE IN THE RIVER

In the fall of 1973, a group of sixteen volunteers, led by Pastor Ollie Goad from Immanuel Baptist Church, in Annandale, Virginia, funded a construction trip called "Project Amazon," to build the pilots' duplex in La Pedrera and also to add two additional rooms onto the home of ABWE missionaries Bob and Rita Wright, in Campo Alegre, Brazil.

When the volunteers arrived in Leticia, Don, the only pilot on the field, whisked the first planeload of five "Project Amazon" volunteers away to Campo Alegre, downriver in Brazil. He then flew the second group of ten men and one lady to his family's home at La Pedrera. The teams all worked in steaming tropical temperatures, but also took time to see for themselves, in both of these remote stations, the uniqueness of Indian work the missionaries had told them about. They also witnessed two amazing acts of providence during their stay in South America.

Don had a heavy schedule, twenty-seven hours flying in six days, plus directing the construction of his house. Then, a problem arose—the cement needed for construction never arrived by riverboat as arranged. Under pressure to get the cement to the La Pedrera construction site while the volunteers were there, he flew to Leticia to buy as many bags as he could find. In spite of a drizzle, Don loaded the cement into the Cessna 185-1318P floatplane and started for home.

Ten minutes before touchdown, the engine lost power, back-fired, and went dead. Knowing the river was not within gliding distance, he did all he could to get the engine running again, but finally admitted it was no use; his life was in God's hands to do what He deemed best. Don remembers praying, "Lord, I've given You my life. It is Yours to do as You wish. If You want to preserve it, that would be great, but if not, I trust You." From the earlier panic of the emergency, the Lord gave an amazing peace and calm in the face of inescapable danger.

When he reached an altitude of just 100 feet above the jungle, Don spotted a patch of trees, smaller and shorter than the sixty- to eighty-foot monsters in that area, and headed into it. The bulky floats caught the tree limbs and nosed the fuselage down toward the ground. Don's shoulder harness held; the cargo tie-downs that secured five bags of cement remained intact; the bar-rel loaded with three bags and tied down right behind his seat, buckled around the tie-down straps. But Don, with just a scratch on his arm, was okay. To his amazement, he saw there was little damage to the wings and fuselage of the plane.

When his feet hit solid ground at last, Don first knelt and thanked the Lord, then asked for His protection for the trek he must now make to the Caqueta River. Five hours later he walked into the kitchen of his home to stand before Jan, who could hardly believe either her eyes or Don's story—it was truly a mir-acle of God.

But it was not the end of the story. The "Project Amazon" workers who were downriver in Brazil, as well as those in La Pedrera, still needed flights back to Leticia, in order to catch their plane to the States. How could they manage this with the mission floatplane hung up in a tree?

After chartering a commercial plane to get back to Leticia, Don frantically worked to clear flight permissions from Air Control in Bogotá and from the Brazilian Army, then sent off a telegram to ABWE headquarters requesting insurance for Cessna 185-CJG, the seaplane Terry Bowers had left in Benjamin Constant while he went on furlough. Don then rented a speedboat to Benjamin Constant, where he checked over CJG. Everything was intact; there were no discrepancies in the logbooks or problems with the engine. Run-up was normal. After receiving clearance from ABWE, Don made the flight to the Wrights' home in Campo Alegre, Brazil, that afternoon and waited for morning, when he could take off. A torrential rainstorm hit, and at 4:30 a.m., someone startled Don awake with alarming news, "CJG has sunk."

Don felt sick when he found just one wing and the engine sticking out of the water. If the plane had slipped a few inches deeper into the Amazon, the engine and instruments could have submerged, and a complete overhaul would have been necessary. He learned that during the night several canoes took shelter from the rain under the wings of the Cessna. Ticuna Indians got up on the backs of the floats, sinking the aft end float chambers.

"The Ticunas didn't realize that if the aft chambers filled with water the floats would go under. Both floats sank under the water, and only the ropes securing the plane to the dock kept it from sinking further," Don explained. "The plane should have been pulled up on the shoreline aft or tail first. It never occurred to me to do this since I always moored the floatplane on a floating hangar or shoreline, not at a dock."

God spared the aircraft, though it took seven hours of arduous work to get it floating again. The plane, with the left elevator, flap, and left strut damaged and in need of repair or replacement, was still flyable, and Don arrived at the hangar in Benjamin

Constant, with the five workers from Campo Alegre, many hours later than he had planned. From there, they took a boat to Leticia. The other "Project Amazon" workers in La Pedrera still needed transportation to the Leticia airport. One option remained. Don decided to get the other Brazilian floatplane, Cessna 185-DNY, running; it was still insured because Hank had only recently gone back to the States. Don checked over the plane and decided to use it. The rest of his flights went without problems, and all sixteen "Project Amazon" workers made their connections to the US on time. Don ended his report of these incidents by writing to ABWE, "I am certain that the Lord has allowed this to happen to see if we will really trust Him fully, and by His grace we shall. The Colombian Cessna 185-1318P floatplane will fly again, Lord willing."

DIFFICULT TIMES AT LA PEDRERA

The Cessna 185-1318P that had crashed in the Colombian jungle still rested precariously, nose down, in the trees. The remaining cement needed for the construction on the mission house was inside it. A couple of Yucuna Indians backtracked over Don Fanning's trail, located the plane, and then carried the cement cargo to the construction site. The next week, after a six-hour hike through the jungle, Don disassembled the plane, sleeping at the crash site four nights while volunteers from town carried it, piece by piece, back to La Pedrera. The fuselage alone took seventeen men four days to carry out. It would be more than two years before the plane would fly again.

The "Project Amazon" team from Virginia had dried-in the duplex at La Pedrera, but it was still a shell of a house when the Fannings moved in. The part they occupied had a large open room with few conveniences, not unlike the primitive homes in the village. Jan Fanning and her three youngsters often passed lonely times there, hundreds of miles from another missionary family and always without communication with Don while he was flying. Living and serving in an Indian culture exposed the family to many unhealthy conditions. Dysentery, typhoid fever, tuberculosis, and worms were a few of the diseases common at that time, and Jan paid constant attention to their food and drink. Yet even with the precautions she took, Jan contracted hepatitis. In the summer of 1974, due to health reasons, the Fannings traveled back to the US, where they remained for two years.

REINFORCEMENTS ARRIVE

Meanwhile, Butch and Bonnie Jarvis completed language study and arrived at Leticia to get some orientation before the Fannings left. They were then the only ABWE personnel in Leticia, filling in for the Flodens. When the Flodens arrived back from furlough, the Jarvis family moved on to complete construction on the duplex at La Pedrera and begin the aviation ministry there.

Butch described the two building projects he faced in La Pedrera:

> I finished the walls, put in the floors and ceilings, and built the fireplace in the duplex near the airstrip. For the next two-and-a-half years, I worked to complete the repairs on the Cessna 185-1318P floatplane, which required finding replacement parts, a complicated task in that part of the world. I was also making contact with the Indians and building airstrips in their villages to use once I got the plane back in the air.

Bonnie was a trooper. While Butch traveled on the river, getting things ready for the aviation ministry, Bonnie had the burden of keeping things going during his extended absences. There was no way she and their two toddlers could accompany him on these earliest trips, because his destinations involved primitive, unsafe living conditions.

Butch and Bonnie initiated Sunday school and morning services in the living room of a Colombian man who did carpentry work for them. They taught children who knew nothing about the Bible how to sing of salvation in Jesus. Bonnie's article in the September/October 1975 issue of the *Message* paints a picture of the teaching conditions she faced: "The wind blew the flannelgraph background right off the board and sent kids scrambling to help pick up the pieces; a screeching parrot flew into the room. Disturbing dogs, cats, chickens, ducks, cockroaches, biting gnats, rats and lizards visited us." In spite of the difficulties, many children came to know Christ as Savior. Besides the children, forty villagers attended the morning services that developed into the New Life Baptist Church. Of the 200 Indians living in La Pedrera, 150 made decisions for the Lord.

In 1974, Ed Cone, a friend from High Point Baptist Chapel, in Geigerstown, Pennsylvania, donated a Piper Comanche to the Jarvises' ministry. Since the Jarvises were in Colombia and the Fannings were in the US for furlough, Don Fanning made the contact with the donor and received the plane. Because of the stringent importation requirements, the ABWE pilots and donor agreed to sell it, which provided funds to buy a Piper Arrow Cub (PA-18) airplane on wheels that had already been imported into Bogotá. After Butch modified the plane for bush flying by adding heavier struts and larger tires, he flew the aircraft alone from Bogotá to La Pedrera.

Once the Fannings arrived back from furlough, the pilots didn't replace the Cessna's floats, which had been badly damaged in Don's treetop crash. It was too costly to repair or buy another set, and the pilots found it an advantage to fly the Cessna on wheels. Compared to the one hour and fifty-five minutes in a floatplane from La Pedrera to Leticia, they saved twenty-five minutes of flying time without the drag and weight of the floats. Though wheel-plane flying poses more risks, Tarapaca, a small town on the Putumayo River halfway between La Pedrera and Leticia, provided an airstrip. Tarapaca's location reduced the risk of the long flights over solid jungle between home and Leticia. Don also began evangelistic services there and started a church.

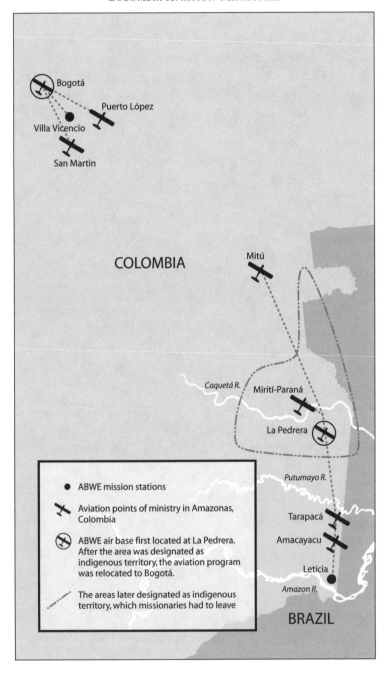

Bogotá

Puerto López

Villa Vicencio

San Martin

COLOMBIA

Mitú

Caquetá R. Mirití-Paraná

La Pedrera

Putumayo R.

- ABWE mission stations

Aviation points of ministry in Amazonas, Colombia

ABWE air base first located at La Pedrera. After the area was designated as indigenous territory, the aviation program was relocated to Bogotá.

The areas later designated as indigenous territory, which missionaries had to leave

Tarapacá

Amacayacu

Letícia

Amazon R.

BRAZIL

TEN

BRANCHING OUT FROM THE LA PEDRERA BASE

Don and Butch ministered to places within about an hour's flying time from La Pedrera, flying over waterways traveled only by dugout canoes. Reaching the nearest preaching points took eighteen hours by canoe; in the Cessna 185-1318P floatplane, it took twenty-five minutes. On one survey to locate an Indian village, Butch spent four days—three on the river, and one on the trail—while Don spent only forty-five minutes by air in the PA-18 land plane to arrive at the same destination.

The airstrips they landed on were out of the ordinary, to say the least. One 800-foot-long strip, the extension of a soccer field, also served as the pasture for long-horned cattle. Before a pilot could land, he had to circle until someone came to scoot the cattle off to the side. After one landing Butch made there, a grazing cow moseyed up to the tied-down PA-18 and horned the wing up through the bottom and out the top. The "skin" on the PA-18, used in place of metal, was a fabric covering of Dacron cloth covered with up to eighteen layers of hardener called "dope," which required careful maintenance. It was this fabric covering the cow had damaged. Butch had to make a patch to fill in the hole on both the top and bottom of the rounded part of the wingtip.

Don and Butch learned that the PA-18 had another drawback—close quarters. Both men were six-foot tall and broad-shouldered. Sitting in tandem, one behind the other, their shoulders touched both windows on either side. They told how an Indian chief guffawed when he saw Don and Butch unfold themselves to get out of the PA-18. When Butch asked why he laughed, the chief answered, "You don't get into that airplane, you put it on like a shoe."

TRIBAL VILLAGE WORK

Work among the Indians required an initial contact to reach each village by boat, then more visits to make friends and get to know the local customs. During the dry season, when the river dropped and sandbars appeared, pilots landed the plane on the beaches in the middle of the river in front of the villages. This "runway" would serve for a few months, until the river rose again in its annual cycle. In each village, they began a Bible study in a home and invited others to attend, then followed this study with an all-village evangelistic meeting. Before they left, the pilots encouraged the men to build an airstrip and to listen to tape-recorded messages until their return.

Butch described a first visit to a tribal village this way:

I had given them three wild pigs that we shot, and the next morning being Sunday, the chief kept me in his house along with most of the men present at the time. The Indians finished a delicious pig stew breakfast, then relaxed with coke powder in their mouths—some still coming out in green puffs. While they talked, the green saliva ran down their lips as the skin sensitivity dulled. Then the chief asked me to conduct a service just like we had at the base church. So I sang some songs and then preached the gospel. They had never heard it before. As a result, most of the men in that group came to know the Lord over the next two years.

The Jungle Bible Institute, set up at the La Pedrera base, opened the way to train young men in each village to preach the gospel. Butch explained, "One of the best ways to get a young man to leave his jungle village for good was to send him to the big city for Bible training, so that was exactly what we *didn't* do."

Butch and Don brought two or three young men from each preaching point to La Pedrera for five days a month, picking them up as they made the rounds to the weekend preaching points, then taking them home the following weekend. During the training, the pilots covered such topics as the importance of personal devotions, how to lead a person to Christ, and how to understand and present the meaning of a passage of Scripture.

Butch said, "By allowing them to live in our town as they did in their homes, and by not being gone long enough to disrupt the slash-and-burn gardening responsibilities to their families, they had no possibility of being spoiled by soft beds and easy living."

FLYING IN GOD'S CARE

Flying over the "green hell" of the Amazonian jungle, missionary pilots experienced unforeseen and life-threatening dangers, including close encounters with flocks of birds in flight, monstrous thunderstorms, blinding rain, or engine or mechanical failure. It was important to stay calm, levelheaded, and dependent on the Holy Spirit for self-control in times of near panic.

Don described an incident that showed God's protective hand on his life in an unusual situation while in the air. Having spent two nights and three days at preaching points, he and a summer intern were flying back to the base at La Pedrera. Don decided to overfly the jungle between the Caqueta and Putumayo rivers, where a primitive tribe was known to live. Several years before, a Colombian had disappeared while crossing into this territory, but as long as they stayed airborne, Don didn't consider it a risk.

After flying a grid search for nearly a half-hour, they spotted the top of a *maloca*, a large thatched house, and then an additional five *malocas*, which indicated that a considerable-sized group had settled this area of the jungle.

Then, while circling at 2,000 feet, the engine quit. Once again, fuel contamination had plugged the engine, in spite of all precautions. Don had installed a kit from MAF (Missionary Aviation

Fellowship) called the Alternate Fuel System, to bypass the carburetor and put fuel directly into the intake manifold, as well as to meter the airflow through two trombone-type controls. When installed, Don could pull the controls back to a stop bolt, pre-set as the maximum power setting for the engine. Before this flight, Don had failed to get the engine to run on the alternate fuel system. Would the system work, now that it was his only hope before crashing?

Flying the plane with his rudder pedals and preparing for a controlled crash, Don fiddled with the fuel system controls. Several times the engine started and then died. He knew the settings were close to position, but time was running out as the plane slipped 700 feet a minute from 2,000 feet, leaving only precious minutes to do the impossible.

Presto! The engine caught and sustained its power, enough to maintain altitude above a stall. But now Don faced another decision. To give the engine the power needed to climb to a safer altitude, which way should he adjust the fuel control—to more fuel, less fuel, more air, less air? All but one would kill the engine. Flying at treetop level, the wrong choice would make the engine die, leaving no time to restart before hitting the trees. Don guessed it needed more fuel, turned the control a quarter turn, and the engine burst into full power.

The return flight to base was uneventful, but the next day, it took over two hours to get the engine to run on that alternate fuel system! Thankfully, when man-made systems are undependable, God can be counted on. A few years later, New Tribes Missions followed up on Don's initial find and planted the gospel among this primitive tribe, which was discovered through the aviation ministry.

Were the results among the Indians worth all this effort? When Don and Butch began work with them, they could not find a single believer. Four years later, they had two established churches, each with their own pastors, deacons, and buildings, and three other villages had a strong nucleus of believers, as well as many others along the tributaries that had heard the gospel message. The two pilots knew that the airplane not only helped their ministry, but actually made it possible.

THE CHIEF'S GRANDSON

Don and Butch often flew emergency cases to the hospital in Leticia and also flew the doctor from La Pedrera to remote jungle tribes, one of which was the Yucunas. One day the Yucunas sent a messenger three days by canoe to tell Butch, "The chief's grandson is very sick. He asks you to fly now to Miriti and help him."

Urgent appeals such as this were common to a missionary pilot in the Amazon, who sometimes learned that an "emergency" was no more than an excuse to get the pilot to visit or to finagle a free ride— "Since you are here, can you fly *so-and-so* back with you?"

Faced with this call for help, Butch wondered if it was an honest emergency. The PA-18 needed repairs, and Butch, who was in the early stage of hepatitis (though he didn't yet know it), didn't feel well enough to tackle them, so he delayed the flight until the next morning. After a test flight, the plane checked out okay. He loaded up the emergency gear and headed for the village, which was an hour away by plane.

The village chief, whose grandson had worsened in the four days since he first sent the runner to get Butch, had become impatient and anxious. He had decided not to wait any longer and had sent the parents with the six-month-old baby to a witch doctor for treatment. Then Butch landed in Miriti, and the chief sent word to the parents to bring the baby back from the witch doctor. Sundown was approaching, however, and Butch, entrusting the baby to God's care, had to postpone the flight to early morning. The next day held several unexpected challenges.

During the night, the baby's condition grew worse. By morning, he was too sick to fly. Butch decided that he must fly back alone to La Pedrera for the doctor and bring him to the Yucuna village. However, a storm moved in to delay his flight until 11:00 a.m., when at last the cloud cover had lifted in places, and Butch felt it was safe to take off.

He had two-and-a-half hours of fuel in the plane, and with an hour of flight time between Miriti and La Pedrera, Butch could opt to fly around the storm, if necessary. But after twenty-five minutes in the air, the weather dropped down to the treetops; he lost sight of the Miriti-Parana River. Even though he deviated to the right—toward the main branch of the Caqueta—then to the left of the persistent rain and fog, he couldn't get through. After checking the fuel gauge, Butch banked the plane and circled back toward the Indian village. By then, the stationary front enveloped the village, the landing strip, and the river. He hovered at the edge, hoping to see a breakthrough, but soon he was forced to weigh alternatives.

Earlier, he had spotted a couple of possible landing sites—one too short, one too hilly, then a sandbar which looked difficult, but much safer than landing in the treetops. Weakened already from the hepatitis, he sensed that he might not have enough strength to climb from the plane or trees, if he even survived such a landing, to hike to the river where someone might find him. Putting this thought aside, he found a sandbar five minutes later. Butch maneuvered the plane down into the canyon of trees, flying the curve of the river to lose altitude. The approach was risky, but after several practices, he felt ready for an emergency landing, if needed. He hoped that the front would move and make a landing at the village possible. He headed that way.

Closed solid, Butch thought. Concerned that he now had only half an hour of fuel time left, he returned to the sandbar. But the storm had closed it off. With only twenty minutes of fuel left, Butch talked to the only One who could help. "Lord, you're going to have to work a miracle to get me out of this situation.

I've done everything I know how to do, and I've never landed in the top of a tree." Despite the crisis before him, Butch knew that God was in control. For ten more minutes, back and forth, he searched for a place to land. As a last resort, he could penetrate the cloud cover and hope that the village strip would be nearby underneath. Watching the sinking fuel gauge, Butch opted to fly into the storm, praying for a break in the clouds. Two minutes later, he glanced down and saw the grass strip. His heart leaped in praise. He spiraled the plane down and landed. Taxiing off the runway, the engine sputtered on its last drops of fuel, and died. Butch breathed his thanks to the Lord for a safe landing, and wondered how the baby was. The milling crowd outside the chief's hut gave Butch his answer. He spied a tiny, crudely built casket on the front porch, and a few hours later, the sickly infant died.

Don, knowing that Butch had been gone too long, arrived the next morning in the Cessna, bringing extra fuel. The baby's father, impressed by Butch's effort to save his child, received the Lord as Savior a few weeks later. The missionary pilot never knows what a flight may entail but, while up in the air, he can fly with confidence under God's control and for His glory.

RELOCATING THE COLOMBIAN AVIATION MINISTRY

When the Jarvis family left for furlough in 1977, the Colombian secretary of foreign relations informed Don that ABWE aircraft and missionaries could no longer reside in, or operate aircraft from, La Pedrera. The entire area around the town had been designated as an Indian reservation. The Fannings packed all missionary equipment and personal belongings, including the Jarvises' things and both planes, and moved to Bogotá.

In 1979, the pilots sold the Cessna 185-1318P to New Tribes Mission; in 1980, the Fannings left ABWE to pursue a master's degree. Butch, however, continued to fly the PA-18 to the Ilanos region, including the towns of Puerto Lopez and San Martin, for weekly evangelism. He helped fellow missionary Bob Trout start the first ABWE church in Bogotá. They also founded the Bogotá Christian Academy, a school for MKs, and Colombia Baptist Seminary, which Butch now supervises.

Between 1981 and 1982, Butch began sensing pressure from the subversive groups operating in Colombia. He said, "Police inspected each flight where we landed. We had to look carefully to determine if they had long hair and rubber boots (which would indicate guerrilla soldiers), or if they were official police. That was the year Wycliffe missionary Chet Bitterman was killed and M-19 took over the Dominican Republic Embassy."*

By November 1983, Johnny Bolin, a graduate of Piedmont Bible College and a missionary aviation affiliate in Winston-Salem, North Carolina, had finished his aviation orientation and checkout with MAF in California. He and his wife, Susan, had completed Spanish language study and arrived in Bogotá eager to fly, but the Piper Cub PA-18 was unavailable. It needed a complete airframe and engine overhaul: there was fabric to strip, tubular framing to fix for rust, new fabric to place and paint, plus a new radio to install. When Butch returned from furlough in 1984, he and Johnny worked together for more than a year to get the plane up in the air before the Bolins moved an hour's flying time southeast of Bogotá to Villavicencio, hoping to share the use of the PA-18. In their first year in Villavicencio, the Bolins began Grace Baptist Church. However, during subsequent years, the drug traffickers and guerrillas began kidnapping missionaries and other foreigners, and it was no longer safe to stay there. Missionary aviation became too dangerous in Colombia, where the guerrillas were targeting planes.

What was Johnny, a frustrated, grounded pilot, to do? Should he move his family to another country, where he could use his

---

*On January 18, 1981, twenty-nine-year-old Chet Bitterman was kidnapped at gunpoint in Bogotá, Colombia, held hostage for forty-eight days, and eventually killed.

aviation training? Should he go with another mission board? Give up and go home? When the situation simply became too dangerous for their family to remain, the Bolins moved back to Bogotá, where they began another church.

Even in Bogotá, however, the ABWE missionaries lived under the threat of bombings and guerrilla activity. Due to the circumstances that developed around that time in relation to small planes, the ABWE missionaries determined that it would be better to suspend the aviation program in Colombia.

Butch later related what had happened to the Cessna 185-1318P, which ABWE earlier sold to New Tribes Mission: "It was the first of forty planes taken by the guerrillas and New Tribes missionary Paul Dye—the first pilot to be kidnapped by the guerrillas—was at the controls. New Tribes produced a documentary of the event and Paul's escape in the Cessna at 1:30 a.m., with only two hours of fuel in the wing tanks. When he ran out of gas, he had to land in the dark, in a cow pasture in San Martin, in the Ilanos region where I had flown for years."

Throughout the dangers—of drug traffickers, increasing guerilla activity, hijacking of small airplanes, and violent slaughtering of Indian believers in the southern section of Colombia where they had ministered—the pilots could see God's hand of protection. There were still many years of service in Bogotá ahead, even though it meant dropping the aviation ministry and selling the PA-18 in 1988. The plane's donor stipulated that the money remain in the Jarvises' account until it could be used in their ministry. In 2001, the Jarvises bought a lot alongside the present church building where they worked, for future expansion of the church.

Near the end of his missionary aviation service, Butch Jarvis rehearsed the past:

> We knew there were not throngs of people in the jungle, but where large cities exist there is generally no need for a

plane ministry. To us the planes were a necessity, not an extravagance. Don and I were thankful that ABWE, though a large worldwide mission, did not write off the small peoples of the world. Many questioned the merits of our work from a monetary viewpoint, but who can place a price tag on a soul? We found that an Animist responds to the gospel like any other lost person. We were grateful for the privilege of being the first missionaries to preach the gospel where Christ was not named in the Colombian Amazon jungle.

The ministry among the almost 11,000,000 in Bogotá challenged us to reach a greater number of lost folks, and we were not frustrated with the change. We had a lot to keep us busy in the Lord's work, but the experiences and stories we gained from jungle flying illustrate and flavor my preaching in a unique way. I thank God for those years.

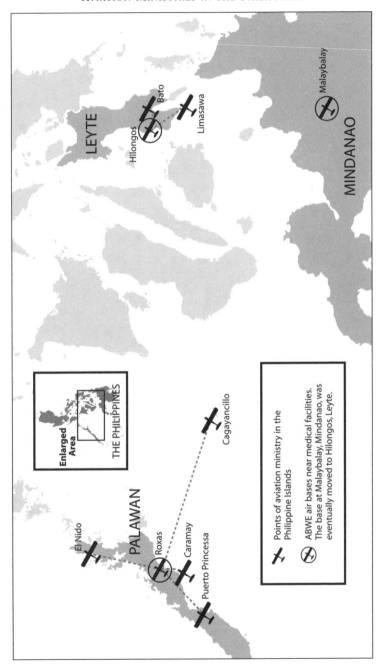

ELEVEN

"COME OVER HERE AND HELP US"

In the early 1970s, "Come over and help us" reverberated in the letters written to ABWE from the Philippine Islands. This cry captured the hearts of those reading "Palawan Calling," regarding new *barrios* (communities) in isolated areas, and written by missionary doctor Ron Esson for the May/June 1972 issue of the *Message*:

> The missionary plane is vital in reaching these places; no road system exists, and other means of transportation are undependable, slow, and difficult. Within three or four years, MAF expects to phase out its work in the Philippines. To continue effective work in Palawan, ABWE must set up its own flight program with a plane and two pilot-mechanics. The need is urgent for volunteers now....

In the Philippines, Drs. Jim Entner and Ron Esson from Bethel Baptist Clinic of Malaybalay, Mindanao, had been hard at work in their medical-evangelistic outreach, flying with MAF pilots monthly to twelve widely separated, remote *barrios*. Now MAF flights would no longer be available.

Then Dr. Link Nelson and his wife, Lenore, reopened the Leyte Baptist Clinic and Hospital on the island of Leyte. During 1974, the doctors recorded over 600 conversions of patients ministered to at that main clinic and its outstations. This work also needed the service of an airplane.

With MAF phasing out its ministry and moving its facilities to Indonesia, the organization offered to sell ABWE its Cessna 180 wheel plane to begin its own aviation ministry in the Philippines. The Mindanao Field Council agreed to purchase the Cessna for facilitating medical work in the Mindanao–Leyte area. However, there were no missionary pilots available.

In another location called Palawan, ABWE's Aero-Medical-Evangelistic Program had begun to develop and operate in 1967. The doctors and team members had partnered with MAF pilots to reach distant areas with the gospel and to establish local Baptist churches. The province of Palawan, spread over an area approximately 400 miles long and thirty-five miles wide, included 100 inhabited islands; some were separated by 180 miles of ocean. Boat travel was difficult and time consuming, even in good weather.

The main island of Palawan had one gravel road that stretched along the shoreline, with a few short dirt roads and trails leading back into interior villages. Reaching villages on the far side of the island entailed several days by boat, or ground travel over 5,000-foot-high mountains. By airplane, the trip took twenty minutes. Villagers willingly built airstrips for the MAF planes. Though doctors and evangelists could only visit the various villages once a month, the townspeople were content to have even that opportunity to hear God's Word and get medical help.

ABWE AIR EXPANDS TO THE PHILIPPINES

In 1973, Larry and Thelma Holman had been appointed by ABWE to the Philippines. From the time he was fifteen, Larry felt sure that God wanted him to be a missionary pilot. After earning his Wings of Gold in the Navy, he graduated from Moody Bible Institute with a Bachelor of Science in Missionary Aviation Technology.

While the Holmans were preparing to work in the Philippines, God brought Lowell Edwards, a World War II retired multi-engine pilot, who volunteered short-term to fly the Cessna 180 land plane. Virginia, his wife, accompanied him. First, the mission required Lowell to train with MAF in California. After his arrival in the Philippines, he was also required to be checked out on the Mindanao circuit by an experienced MAF pilot.

The villagers of Limasawa, a ten-minute flight from the clinic in Hilongos, Leyte, worked for five months with hand tools, prying out rocks to clear a landing strip for the ABWE Cessna. The land was level, with no trees to remove. On September 19, 1973, the strip was ready for Lowell's inspection and he flew alone for this first landing on the untested airstrip at Limasawa. A crowd, gaily dressed in their Sunday best, stood in the shade of the coconut palms beside the strip. Lowell put on a grand performance for them, which he described in the January/February 1974 issue of the *Message*:

> I made a pass over the strip at 70 mph with the wheels just off the ground to get as close a look as possible at the surface! It looked good, so I pulled up and went around. This time I touched the wheels and let them roll briefly on the ground; then full power and around again. This time I let the wheels roll much longer. The next time around, it was full flaps, and as slow as possible—55 mph. The wheels were on the ground and moderate braking brought the airplane to a halt amid a roar of applause and shouts of joy from the crowd as they saw their dream come true.

At last, the medical-evangelistic team would be able to visit Limasawa regularly. Two days later, Lowell flew the first airborne medical team there to conduct the initial clinic at the Baptist Church of Triana.

By the time Larry and Thelma Holman arrived in the Philippines in the fall of 1975, Lowell Edwards had finished his short-term service on Mindanao and the team there welcomed this new pilot with open arms. Dr. Link Nelson and pilots from Jungle Aviation and Radio Service (JAARS) oriented Larry in the routine Mindanao–Leyte circuit of the medical ministry. Larry's experience in short-field landings and takeoffs at Moody proved beneficial at Malabalay airstrip, the most difficult of any he flew. It was a mere 1,040 feet long and had only one unobstructed approach. Density altitudes hovered around 10,000 feet at midday, which had a negative effect on the plane's performance. The Malabalay strip offered a real challenge and little room for error. Because the Mindanao medical program depended on the use of the Cessna 180 land plane, Larry had been willing to begin flying soon after his arrival. But, before long, the Holmans faced a struggle common to missionaries everywhere— seeing obvious needs in two different locations and being able to service only one.

For the Holmans, the two locations were Mindanao, where the medical-evangelistic team had waited anxiously for two years for a pilot to operate their Cessna 180 land plane, which Larry was now using; and Palawan, where they had long felt God wanted them to serve, and where MAF had ceased its partnership of years with ABWE doctors, who were now left with no plane and no pilot.

There was also another conflict. Larry was convinced that every pilot should learn the language before being immersed in the work, which, for the Holmans, meant leaving Mindanao for language school in Palawan. But the Mindanao Field Council recommended that they put language acquisition on hold and continue their aviation service in Mindanao, where the medical ministry was already reliant on them.

What should they do? As first-term missionaries they faced a dilemma. Should they choose contrary to their colleagues' wishes or abandon what they felt was God's direction?

In circumstances such as these, both the missionary involved and the members of the field council must proceed with caution and prayer for God's guidance. The field council must respect a missionary's capacity, when indwelt by the Holy Spirit, to make the decision he believes God has directed him to make, and so the Holman family moved from Mindanao to Palawan to begin language school.

OUTREACH CLINICS

ABWE missionaries Harry and Ann Rogers arrived in Palawan in 1978, before the Holmans left on their first furlough in 1979. Harry, like Hank, had read the life story of jungle pilot Nate Saint, and felt called to be a missionary pilot. The military gave him his start in aviation and the finances to complete his training. Later, he and Ann graduated from Bob Jones University.

The hospital in Roxas, Palawan, opened in 1978, and the two pilots planned to transport its medical-evangelistic team on their outreach flights. The two families purchased property across the valley from the hospital compound, and cleared and prepared it as a landing strip. After furlough, the Holmans built a house near the strip, where they also built a hangar for the plane. And all this was accomplished before the two pilots had a plane!

After searching for a suitable plane at an affordable price, the pilots found a Cessna 180 RPC-384, owned by Weyerhauser Wood Products, in Davao. Harry and Larry bought the plane from the Filipino pilot who owned it, and since the plane needed to be rebuilt, the engine was shipped to the United States for overhaul.

Though Larry Holman and Harry Rogers transported mission personnel who needed quicker, more efficient transportation, they focused their ministry on outreach clinics in remote areas. Typically, their crew included a doctor, a nurse, and the hospital evangelist. Whenever the plane landed, word spread and patients began arriving. They also flew in and out of airstrips in San Vicente, Bato, El Nido, and Cagayancillo, transporting patients in need of further care to other hospitals.

One of the more memorable patients transported was Pastor Quirino Habaradas, an influential pastor in Palawan. At the time of this story, he was pastoring in Caramay, at a church from which many young people went into full-time Christian ministry. Harry described transporting him this way:

In December 1986, while making some repairs, Pastor Quirino fell from the roof of their church building and sustained a head injury. They brought him to the hospital in Roxas. It was not immediately apparent how serious his injury was, but after a day or so, the doctor knew the pastor needed brain surgery.

Pastor Quirino and his wife did not want to travel to Manila because of the expense. We called for the deacons and pastor of the local church in Roxas to come. We anointed him with oil and had a time of special prayer for him.

That evening, the pastor's daughter, Daryl, who was the head nurse at our hospital, said, "You know, it occurs to me that there is a hospital in Iloilo where brain surgery can be done. Could you fly him there in the mission plane?"

They made the flight to Iloilo, and though it appeared that Pastor Quirino would not pull through, God spared his life. Later, after a long recovery that required him to resign from the Caramay church, he went on to start another church.

Larry Holman recorded many memorable flights from Roxas to Puerto Princessa to transport patients being transferred to Manila. On one flight, the patient's blood pressure fell so low that his blood started back up the IV tube at 3,000 feet, and Larry had to fly out over the sea and drop to 500 feet before the IV would work again. On still another flight from the small island of Cagayancillo with ABWE missionary Esther Entner and her son, Tim, pilot and passengers watched a gigantic thunderstorm approach the airstrip where they were to land. By keeping up the speed on their descent from 10,000 feet, they beat the storm to the Roxas strip. But as the plane touched down, cold rain hit. The Plexiglas windscreen fogged over and clouded Larry's vision.

Fortunately, the air strip was over 3,000 feet long, with plenty of room to recover from a high flare-out, the procedure in which the plane levels from its descent towards the runway.

On a different trip, Larry was forced to return to El Nido because of a similar thunderstorm. He spent three days in El Nido, waiting until another missionary, Dan Horton, could get fuel to him by land. The missionary pilots' lives were filled with these unplanned situations, and flexibility helped them and their families to adapt.

While the Holmans and Rogerses were stationed on Palawan, they carried on supportive ministries to churches in various villages, supervised the hospital compound when it lacked medical personnel, taught Theological Education by Extension (TEE) classes, and maintained the airstrip and aircraft.

AVIATION IN MALABALAY, MINDANAO

In 1975, ABWE had appointed another pilot and his family, David and Becky Nelson, to assist David's parents, Dr. Link and Lenore Nelson, in the medical outreach in Malabalay, on Mindanao. As a sophomore at Cedarville College, in Ohio, Dave became burdened to be a missionary, and after a near-fatal automobile accident, he realized that the Lord must have spared him for a purpose. Two years later, he and Becky moved to Tennessee, where Dave took the two-year aviation course at Moody Aviation. By February 1977, they arrived on the field and resumed the aviation ministry that had been carried on first by Lowell Edwards, and then, briefly, by the Holmans.

David Nelson wrote an article for the January/February 1981 issue of the Message describing an unusual Saturday in their ministry. The day started with breakfast at 6:30 a.m. Their three youngsters chattered, and the shortwave radio buzzed as Dave planned his day. He had a sermon to finish for Sunday, and a lesson to type and mimeograph for the afternoon Bible study. The radio caught his attention:

"This is Mambago calling. We have an emergency. A woman began labor at 3:00 a.m. to deliver her third child. She is having complications and is very weak. What should we do?"

A few questions came from a doctor on another set, then the decision was made. "Mambago, this is Dr. Sison. She will have to be flown to the hospital immediately."

Dave picked up the microphone and called, "Malabalay, copy. She will have to come in. I can be in the air in an hour. How is the weather in Mambago now, over?"

Dave lifted off with a stretcher in the plane and his Filipino partner, Dr. Flores, by his side. They knew that at Mambago, a tribal mountain village far from the outside world, an eager group of Christians had asked for a church. Pastor Yambagon responded to the call and had been in that *barrio* for a year. It would have taken two days to reach Mambago by bus, motorcycle, and footpath, but with the plane, it would take only eighteen minutes.

Soon the 300-yard airstrip at Mambago popped into view, next to the river in a bowl-shaped valley with sharp ridges on every side. Dave could see the river gorge and no road in sight for miles. After a soft landing on the small grass field, which also served as Main Street, Mambago, he taxied the plane right to the house of the distressed woman, where a crowd had gathered.

By 8:30 a.m., Dave called Becky on the radio and reported that the patient, Rowena, and her husband were boarded and ready for takeoff. Dave turned the master switch, and as the pastor concluded a brief prayer, the plane climbed to the cooler air above.

By 9:00 a.m., the plane landed in Malaybalay. Dave transferred the woman to a clean operating room at Bethel Baptist Hospital, where Dr. Flores took over. Rowena made it through, but the baby did not survive. The doctor repaired Rowena's ruptured uterus, and she had an opportunity to hear the gospel.

This incident was typical of the responsibilities of the missionary pilot in the Philippines. Medical evangelism softened hearts to the gospel, and new Christians grew as all those involved—whether doctor, nurse, pilot, or evangelist—followed up each one who trusted Christ as Savior. One or the other made sure to disciple and direct the new believer to a local village church.

LEYTE

In 1982, David Nelson transferred the base of operation for the Mindanao Cessna 180 to the island of Leyte. There, Phil and Barb Klumpp, along with many ABWE missionaries in the Philippines, appreciated airplane travel, compared to a seven-hour overnight boat trip, to shop for supplies. Phil said, "It cut hours to minutes for us."

Late in 1985, another approved pilot on prefield ministry, Kevin Donaldson, and his wife, Bobbi, volunteered to fill in for fifteen months for the Nelsons, who were soon to leave for furlough. Kevin carried not only the flight responsibilities, but also installed a new aircraft engine in the Cessna 180 land plane. He also surveyed the Camotes Islands for the field council. This short-term experience better prepared Kevin and Bobbi for their move three years later to open the aviation program in Iquitos, Peru.

THE DOOR CLOSES TO ABWE AVIATION IN THE PHILIPPINES

Although missionary aviation was used successfully to facilitate evangelism in the Philippines for two decades, cultural and economic changes brought an end to this ministry by the late 1980s. Due to policies set in place by Lloyds of London, ABWE insurance coverage eventually required pilots to carry million-dollar liability. Maintenance costs on the planes continued to rise, and government red tape, time-consuming documentation to get equipment repaired in the States, and re-entry processing all became too complex to continue.

At the same time, improved roads in the Philippines diminished the need for private aircraft, and commercial aviation was growing cheaper and reaching more areas of the country. The mission medical facilities became autonomous as capable Filipino professionals replaced missionary personnel. The last ABWE pilot in the islands, Harry Rogers, found that he was flying so few hours that he could no longer maintain his flight proficiency. At that point, the missionaries accepted God's "closed door" to aviation in the Philippines and stepped into other ABWE ministries.

In less-developed countries, however, missionary aviation was still a pressing need, and Hank and I would eventually be very much involved in those ministries. But first, we were confronted with a totally unexpected opportunity.

MAPPING TRIBAL LOCATIONS

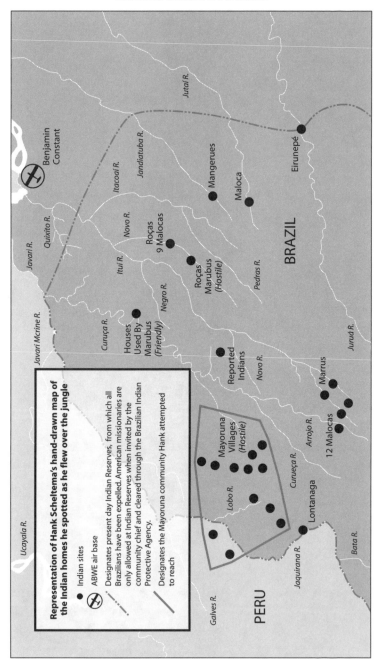

TWELVE

FILLING THE GAP

An old yarn cherished in Holland tells of a young Dutch boy sent by his parents to check the dike, an earthen wall that held back the sea. The boy discovered a small hole in the dike, with water trickling from it. Realizing the danger, he jammed his finger into the gap, plugged the leak, and saved the day.

During the years of 1972 to 2003, God directed Hank, who was also a Dutchman, and I to fill in for various ABWE missionaries who would have otherwise had no one to take over their ministries during their furloughs.

Terry and Wilma Bowers, ABWE missionaries in Benjamin Constant, planned to leave for furlough in June 1972. There was no pilot to take Terry's place, which meant that two planes would be "pickled," or left idle, for a year. But God directed Hank to fill the gap.

If we returned from the States to the Amazon just then, it would mean sending our teenagers away again to boarding school in Manaus. As mentioned earlier, it had become impracticable to teach the higher grades and all five children at once at home in Benjamin Constant, and Hank and I had experienced deep misgivings about sending our children hundreds of miles away to boarding schools where others served as their "parents." But Hank and I agreed with Oswald Chambers, who wrote that if we do our duty, not for duty's sake but because we believe God is engineering our circumstances, then the grace of God becomes ours when we obey.

As we returned from the States to the Amazon to relieve the Bowerses, we found that unique experiences and blessings high-

lighted that year. In August, six college-age missionary appren-
tices, the fruit of Hank's ministry to Bible colleges as an ABWE
representative, traveled with our family of seven and spent two
weeks helping us clean, repair, and paint the house; haul water;
cut down the jungle growth that had encroached on the property; and work on the Cessna 185-DNY. The testimony of these
students left an indelible impression on the youth of the Benjamin Constant church, as well as on our own children.

Meanwhile, Hank spent the month of September in bed, having blood tests and other exams, in an attempt to diagnose a sickness that had started with a high fever, then progressed to painfully
swollen joints—fingers, elbows, knees, ankles, and toes—and
extreme fatigue. Although he followed the Brazilian and Colombian doctors' treatment for what they diagnosed variously as
rheumatic fever, hookworm, or osteoarthritis, Hank remained
puzzled and distressed by recurring symptoms throughout October. In November, he resumed his supply flight schedule, though
we insisted he stay at a mission station on overnight trips because
he was too exhausted to complete the trip in one day. He continued taking oral penicillin for over a year and twelve aspirins
daily to manage the joint and muscle pains. (After years of occasional bouts with these same symptoms and thorough, but inef-
fectual, examinations at several US tropical disease centers, our
colleague Dr. Jack Sorg, who had treated Amazon Brazilians with
similar problems, diagnosed Hank with amoebic cysts of the liver.
His treatment did the trick.)

In spite of this physical handicap, Hank resumed teaching and
preaching at the Baptist church in Benjamin Constant. Ten people came to faith in Christ and were baptized, fifty youth got
involved in weekly Bible study, and thirty enrolled in Bible
courses. From July through December, in spite of illness, Hank
flew nearly 200 hours: forty-two hours in direct evangelism,
twenty-two hours for emergency flights, ninety-five hours trans-

porting missionary families and supplies, twenty-five hours for plane licensing, and thirteen hours of charter flights for the Brazilian Army and Air Force.

The persistent prayers of supporters, along with God's grace, sustained and strengthened him for the work, and he even maintained his sense of humor. Bulletins mailed to us from supporting churches at this time often listed Hank's condition as a prayer request and mentioned the possibility that he had rheumatic fever. One bulletin, however, printed a blooper: "Pray for Hank Scheltema's recovery from romantic fever." Reading the bulletin, Hank laughed and said, "That's one disease I don't want to be cured of!"

During that year back in Benjamin Constant, Hank was again flying over the winding tributaries of the headwaters and areas of jungle thought to be uninhabited. But from his bird's-eye view in the plane, he once again saw the *malocas*—communal thatched houses—of several tribes, scattered throughout the dense, primeval forest, and he thought back to our attempt, several years before, to reach the Mayoruna Tribe.

TRYING TO REACH THE MAYORUNAS

Several years earlier, when army personnel had been called in to investigate a kidnapping up on the Itacoarí River, an army doctor, Dr. Rauto, had requested Hank's help to fly him to the site. On the return flight, over the Javarí River, Hank and the doctor had seen more than twenty of these large beehive-like houses. If this tribe lived as did similar tribes in neighboring Peru, it could mean that more than 100 Indians occupied each house. The tribe was called the Mayoruna, and their isolation from civilization commanded Hank's interest. He could hear in his mind the Lord's words, ". . . to every creature."

At that time, Hank had begun to collect information about the Mayoruna Indians. He had learned that, when traders began traveling upriver to the isolated Indian villages, they carried not only goods to trade, but also diseases that wiped out many of the Indians. Statistics showed that exposure to those from the uncaring "outside" world would open the tribe to devastating colds, measles, tuberculosis, small pox, and venereal diseases. Afraid that their tribe could die off, the Mayoruna had begun kidnapping Brazilian and Peruvian women, as well as children of the isolated rubber tappers and lumber workers who made their home in the jungle.

Various attempts by outsiders to enter the Mayoruna communities had met with death; Brazilians feared their raiding parties so much they withdrew from the area. Eventually, the Brazilian government's Indian Protection Service had declared the area an Indian reservation and began restricting white men who wanted to fish or hunt there. But because of Hank's influence with the military, the government had granted him permission to try to contact the Brazilian Mayorunas. While the government hoped that a missionary would simply teach them to live peaceably with "civilized" neighbors, and integrate them into the outside world, Hank had biblical reasons to try to build relationships with the Mayorunas.

We had also made the acquaintance of two Wycliffe translators, Harriet Fields and Harriet Kneeland, who lived with a peaceful tribe of Peruvian Mayorunas, learning their language and establishing a witness among them. Letters from these ladies had cautioned us to proceed slowly. The Mayorunas in Peru warned the two Harriets that the Brazilian Mayorunas were killers, vicious savages who wanted no contact with the outside world. They practiced endo-cannibalism, seeking reincarnation by eating a loved one after death, believing that the spirit of the dead would continue to live on in a live body. To this end, the bones of the deceased were burned and beaten to dust to mix with their food. Tribal members also painted their nude bodies with a red substance made by mixing powder of the *urucu* nut with water, a custom that had been helpful to us when we tried to locate members of the tribe, because it made them more visible to us against the backdrop of thick jungle vegetation.

God's people back in the States had prayed for Hank to make contact. He laid out a strategy similar to that used by Nate Saint and the four other missionaries who had contacted Ecuador's Auca Indians in the 1950s and had been killed in the process. Following Nate's method, Hank had attempted to make friends with the Mayorunas by using aerial drops of gifts, such as aluminum pans, machetes, and T-shirts.

Fellow missionaries, military officers, and some visitors from the US had flown over the Mayoruna territory with Hank, excited to help spiral down a gift on a rope from the floatplane, CJG. Hank didn't want an engine backfire to frighten the superstitious Indians, so he throttled slowly, reducing power to slip down as close as he dared, then made a gift drop or snapped a photo before gunning the engine to climb out of the clearing.

One day, after Hank dropped gifts, the Indians had responded instead of disappearing into the jungle as they usually did. Two men had held up a hand-woven basket and a clay pot. Another waved a white T-shirt as if to say, "Thanks. Here's my gift to you." This had encouraged Hank to make further plans, along with the Wycliffe missionaries, to set up a camp on a small tributary within trekking distance of the Mayoruna houses. The two Harriets had set up their tent and equipment on June 18, 1968, our sixteenth wedding anniversary, to wait for results.

Included among his daily gift drops, Hank placed a photo of Joe, a Brazilian Mayoruna who had crossed over to Peru, made contact with the Peruvian Mayorunas, and then returned. In the photo, Joe stood between the two Harriets, who had drawn a picture map pointing toward the position of their new camp. Hank rigged a loudspeaker in the cabin of the plane so that the Harriets could greet the Indians in their own language as he made this drop. His hope was that the Indians would get the connection and discern that the red "bird" dropping the presents was Joe's friend.

THE DOOR SEEMS TO CLOSE

Every second day, Hank, our daughter Kim, and I had flown to their campsite to check for news of the Indians. On June 28, 1968, Hank and our son Dan flew over the Mayoruna homes and met with a shock. Four communal houses had been burned to the ground and there was no sign of Indians anywhere.

What had happened? Through their Peruvian Mayorunas, the Wycliffe missionaries heard that the Brazilian group had fled in fear. Their neighboring clan, a day's journey away in the jungle, were fearful of the huge red bird, or spirit, and took steps to eliminate those that were friendly to it.

By July of that year, we had to return to the States for furlough. We felt that God had closed this door temporarily, to give us more time to prepare by studying linguistics and Indian culture. During that furlough, both Hank and I took several courses in linguistics and anthropology at Michigan State, praying that God would open a future opportunity with the Mayorunas.

The two Harriets returned to the Wycliffe base at Yarinacocha, Peru (where they still live and work among the Peruvian Mayorunas today). They provided immunizations and doctors to care for the tribe's physical needs, and with this health care, the tribe grew from forty-two to over 400 Indians. Several other separate, though related, Mayoruna communities, together estimated to have between 500–600 people, were scattered throughout the Brazilian and Peruvian jungles, where they traveled back and forth across the river during the dry season to get food from their fields in both countries. As the two Harriets progressed in learning the language, they began to teach and translate Bible stories and parts of the New Testament. In June 1973, they reported there were 450 Indians in their village. Partnering with other missionaries and volunteers, they stayed at the task of learning the language, as well as continuing with medical and community development. Harriet Fields wrote:

> We do not know of any believers yet. Pray that God's spirit will enlighten their minds and hearts. After I read some passages we had translated to a crippled man being treated, he said, "I do not understand." Thinking the translation was not in good Mayoruna style, I questioned him; but he said, "No, the way it is written is good, but I do not understand these new things." Again and again we must go over the story of Jesus. Women, too, are interested, for which we are thankful.

When Hank and I were given the opportunity to minister in Benjamin Constant in 1972–1973, God renewed our concern for the Brazilian Mayorunas. This came about through an unexpected request from a petroleum company. A helicopter transporting a three-man team for petroleum exploration lost its bearings over the jungle. The helicopter followed the wrong tributary of the Javarí, ran out of fuel, and, without pontoons, sank in the river. The military contacted Hank to make a search flight, and though he found no sign of the helicopter after three days, he rescued the three bedraggled men. It was during this search that Hank again spotted the Mayoruna-like *malocas*, this time on a small tributary, the Lobo, about 100 miles from the Peruvian border.

"Some of the Indians from the previously burned-out Mayoruna houses must be living there," Hank told me, "because someone waved a T-shirt as I passed over."

Since this group of Indians was accessible by water, Hank, accompanied by military officials, flew to the mouth of the Lobo. He tied our aluminum canoe on one float and stored a small outboard motor in the cargo pod. Cruising cautiously up the narrow waterway, they slashed their way through the overhanging underbrush. The travelers pulled up alongside other dugouts staked on a sloping bank. Indian men studied their approach.

The military representatives with Hank informed him that this group of Mayorunas had made contact with the outside world, and Hank noted that the process of "civilizing" this small splinter tribe had begun. Some wore clothing that itinerant traders gave in exchange for Indian wares, animal skins, and crude latex. This indicated the possibility of exploitation: persuading the Indian to take goods on credit, charging inflated prices, and giving less than their value for the jungle products in return. Thinking about this exploitation, and the death toll that often resulted from exposure to the "outside" world, Hank ached to communicate God's love and redemption without delay.

Anthropologists, journalists, and tourists sometimes resent the detribalization and loss of Indian culture that they claim missionary work, no matter what denomination, produces. But with the developing integration and materialism in the Amazon, the Indians need to acquire at least the basic knowledge of reading and writing in Portuguese, as well as adding and subtracting—knowledge that missionaries could provide with consistency. Yet, missionaries in the Brazilian Amazon were soon to be prevented from providing even this service to the Indians.

By 1975, the government Indian Protection Service isolated this headwater region as an Indian reservation, intending to reclaim it from the trappers, hunters, fruit farmers, rubber tappers, and others who had settled there. Only personnel selected by the government, such as teachers and medical workers, would be permitted on the reservation. No missionaries, not even a Brazilian fisherman, hunter, or tradesman, would be allowed without official agreement. By the time we were able to return again in 1976, the door to reach the souls of the Brazilian Mayorunas for Christ had slammed shut in Hank's face.

Hank and I prayed for this work among the Mayorunas over

many years, collaborating financially with Harriet Fields and Harriet Kneeland to print portions of the New Testament for the Mayorunas, many of whom eventually came to Christ. To the glory of God, the Mayoruna New Testament translation was dedicated on April 17, 1994.

THIRTEEN ✈

ANOTHER CHANGE FOR THE SCHELTEMAS

Nearing the close of our fill-the-gap assignment, a confidential letter arrived from ABWE President Dr. Wendell Kempton, with a challenge to consider a position as the first ABWE Southern Representative. Hank and I had been praying for God's direction for our family and future service. We had received various offers from churches and Bible schools, and had even considered secular employment.

Hank responded, "Not one of these offers rings true; that is, not one would be utilizing our full potential, talents, and experience for God's glory. Missions is the burden on our hearts, and we are thrilled to challenge others to become involved, too. We would like to remain with ABWE and hope someday, Lord willing, to return to our aviation ministry in the Amazon."

The decision to fill this gap in the southern US also solved the problem of our teenagers' education. Our family would remain together, involved in recruiting foreign missionaries and acquainting churches with ABWE, and we would maintain our missionary status until our return to Brazil, after the children were established in college or married. When the ABWE Board approved Hank for this position, in August 1973, we relocated to Atlanta.

For the next few years, Hank contacted churches throughout the South that could financially adopt ABWE appointees on prefield ministry. He spoke in chapel and missions classes at Bible colleges, universities, and Bible institutes across the nation, interviewing interested students, personally and in group sessions. Many were applicants for summer AMP (Assistant Missionary Program) positions, but a growing number desired full-time service. At the commissioning service for Tim and Nancy Pierce, at Alto Baptist Church, in Alto, Michigan, Hank praised God as he read Nancy's testimony:

> At the age of eleven, my family and I attended a missionary conference in which Hank Scheltema was the speaker. The Lord used him to burden my heart for missions and to call me to be a missionary. I entered college and during my junior year, the Lord reaffirmed my call through a chapel speaker who was the very same person God had used to speak to me many years before—Hank Scheltema.

When Hank showed Nancy's testimony to me, I thought, *If only this one person responded to God's call after listening to Hank speak, it is worth all his days and weeks of being away from home and family.*

MKs, as well as furloughing and prefield missionaries, crisscrossed the Atlanta area in their travels; they soon dubbed our home "Hank's hangout and Ruth's restaurant." The phone would ring and we would hear, "I have nowhere to go for spring break or between quarters. Can you fit me in?" It thrilled our family to continue contact with kids Hank had flown back and forth to mission school in Brazil and Peru, or with MKs who had been at boarding school with our own children. Hospitality was an unforeseen ministry, an added blessing in our work as Southern Representatives.

Another blessing of this special year was the birth of our sixth child, Kay Leanne, born in January 1975—almost 12 years after the last one.

LOOKING AHEAD

Late in 1975, ABWE commissioned Hank to contact all ABWE field councils worldwide to determine the potential for future aviation ministries. The following January, Hank and Dr. J. Don Jennings, then ABWE International Director of

Enrichment and Evangelism, traveled together to several South American fields. Hank surveyed Paraguay and Peru by request of the field councils there. He was excited about the prospect of reaching the gospel-starved interior sections of the country around Asunción, Paraguay. Ninety-five percent of the population there lived with unpaved roads that had to be closed down after rain to protect travelers and were accessible only by motorcycle or horseback even in good weather. But there were airstrips in every remote town.

Hank reported the survey results for Paraguay and Peru to the ABWE Board: "To my knowledge no other country is as wide open for this type of ministry; that is, regarding aircraft and pilot licensing. I recommend that ABWE, as soon as possible, open Paraguay to a plane ministry to support evangelistic outreach, facilitate missionary transportation to interior towns, and encourage the formation of airborne medical teams."

Hank surveyed two different areas in Peru—Iquitos and Coastal Peru, which were separated by the Andes Mountains and hundreds of miles of jungle. A missionary pilot working with the Iquitos Field Council would need a Cessna 185 floatplane or a Cessna 206 amphibian to coordinate with river evangelism for Theological Education by Extension (TEE), in which pastors remain in their home villages to work while they complete their courses. A six-place plane could also transport five students from the Iquitos Bible Institute to initiate church plants and to participate in evangelism and follow-up. A plane to supply ABWE boat-ministry missionaries with mail and food would save hundreds of hours and gallons of fuel in travel to Iquitos.

The Coastal Peru Field Council expressed interest in basing an airplane and pilot in the towns of Ica or Arequipa, from where they could fly to the Andes Mountains towns. Travel into the mountains by motor vehicle had become so difficult for missionaries that outreach to the Quechua Indian villages had to be discontinued. Don and Vivian Bond in their GMC Step-van had worn out themselves as well as their motor home, traveling at 10,000 to 15,000 feet above sea level over one-lane, rough dirt tracks. Lightweight aircraft built to fly the heights would be faster and far less wearing on the missionary. Although the Peruvian counterpart to the US Federal Administration of Aviation would expect our pilots to fulfill stringent, complicated requirements and documents, and to build airstrips as well, the need for the gospel to reach these isolated mountain towns outweighed the inconvenience.

Dr. Kempton often quoted Matthew 9:38 and said, "The recruiting center is in the prayer closet." Praying friends implored the Lord, in His time, to send missionaries and aviation personnel to fill these needs in Paraguay and Peru, and He answered. Paraguay was opened to missionary aviation within four years, and Peru within six.

While these changes were under way, disturbing news came from the Amazon. Terry Bowers continued to suffer with an undiagnosed stomach disorder, then with typhoid fever. He began experiencing blackouts, and no longer felt capable of flying, especially on extended flights or in tight places. Forced by his illness to apply for a medical leave of absence, Terry faced a difficult decision that permanently removed him from flying. The Bowers family returned to the Amazon for a time after their 1972–73 furlough, but Terry did not serve as pilot. Instead, he and Wilma served a term as church planters in Minas Gerais, Belo Horizonte, Brazil. His physical problems persisted until, in July 1991, after a time of teaching mechanics to prospective missionary pilots at Piedmont Baptist College, he died of pancreatic cancer and passed into God's presence.

The Bowerses' sons followed in their parents' footsteps. Jim and Philip, along with their wives, served with ABWE in the Amazon, and Daniel, after fourteen years with American Airlines, served with Mission Sports, an organization that sponsored athletes from Bible colleges in summer missionary ministry.

BACK TO THE AMAZON

By 1976, with two Amazon airplanes (one that had not been flown and had needed repairs since its sinking in 1973) without a pilot, the situation in the Central Amazon Field looked grim. Downriver missionaries had no plane service and no radio communication from the base station in Benjamin Constant. The floating hangar and equipment there were unattended, and there was no one to supervise properties at other stations vacated because of missionaries' health problems.

Once again, Hank stepped in to fill the gap. Our three older children, enrolled in colleges, remained in the States; Linda and Kanda attended high school a thousand miles downriver at Manaus, and two-year-old Kay, of course, lived with Hank and me in Benjamin Constant.

Our former home in the tropics, vacant for a couple of years, had deteriorated. Pastor Ollie Goad, who was now ministering at our sending church, Wealthy Park Baptist Church of Grand Rapids, along with twenty-one eager workers from the church, journeyed to Benjamin Constant to help us put it back in shape. This crew volunteered to help raise the roof on the Baptist church in town and also assisted other missionaries at their stations. God used this experience to burden Bill Spoelhof, one of these volunteers, to return with his wife, Susan, to serve in the Central Amazon as career missionaries. Pastor Mason and six men from Berean Baptist Church, in Ogden, Utah, arrived to wire the house for electricity and to help Hank overhaul and repair both floatplanes. These volunteer groups saved Hank countless hours of physical labor. However, there were times when Hank had no one to help in strenuous situations.

Hank found that he had to stay physically fit to push, pull, lift, and paddle a 1¾-ton plane against strong currents. Sometimes he had assistance, but more often he had to do these things alone, and even pilots who keep themselves in good shape, as Hank did, can face health problems as a result of these demands. Years earlier,

Terry Bowers had suffered a triple hernia, and a subsequent operation in the US, and now Hank also developed a hernia, which required immediate attention. God brought to mind Dr. Jack Sorg, a fine intern-surgeon back in the States. By way of ham radio contact, Dr. Jack advised Hank to come to Atlanta for an operation, and when he did, he shared with the Sorgs his burden for a doctor to serve in the Amazon.

Dr. Sorg would later explain, "We had been called to medical missions but didn't know where God wanted us to serve. By Hank's initiative, we were invited to survey the upper Amazon River in November 1977 with him. Through that survey, God led Sandy and me to join ABWE with the intention of starting a medical ministry in Santo Antonio do Içá."

SNAKE STORIES

During prefield ministry, Dr. Jack and Sandy and Hank sometimes gave joint church presentations on missions in the Amazon. The Sorgs appreciated Hank's sense of humor and ability to liven up a presentation, usually with a snake story. Jack later described the results (which Hank and I were completely unaware of at the time) of one such snake story:

"The children listened intently with open mouths, and when Hank suddenly unrolled an eighteen-foot-long snakeskin down the center isle, there were some screams, and a little boy in the front row burst into tears and wet his pants."

Over the years of ministry in churches and colleges, Hank became famous for one particular snake story. He told it this way:

One day, my son Dan came running to the house yelling, "Dad, Dad! Come quick! Come quick! There's a great big snake out on the island."

"Oh Dan," I said, "it's probably just an old log washed up on the shore."

"No, Dad, it's a snake. I saw it."

At the hangar in Roxas, Palawan, Larry Holman, his wife, Thelma, and two daughters work together to paint Cessna 180 RPC-384.

Above:
David Nelson and short-termer Kevin Donaldson prep Cessna 180 RP-413 for a medevac flight.

Below:
Hank arrives at the ABWE Airbase in Concord, Georgia, in the donated A-36 Bonanza. The ABWE Cessna turbo 210 is on the apron at the hangar.

The Mayoruna Indian settlement the Scheltemas tried to reach.

Beverly Fogg teaches Paraguayan children beside the Cessna 185 at the landing strip in Mbuyapey.

Right:
Kim, Reneé, Peter, and Al Yoder. The baby is Regina, whose life was saved when the family was able to fly from the interior town of Itaberra to a doctor in Salvador.

Below:
The 18-foot anaconda of Hank's snake story.

Hank Scheltema, holding "Andy" (the skin of the 18-foot anaconda), tells his famous snake story to a Sunday school class at First Baptist Church, St. Johns, Michigan.

Above & two photos at left: The Javarizinho River, where the floating hangar is tied to shore in front of the missionary pilot's residence, fluctuates 50 feet in its annual cycle. The drop in the river from August to October is a yearly threat to the hangar.

David Zemmer packs the plane for a trip to Ubiraitá, an interior town where David and his Brazilian team were starting a church.

Tom Peace performs a 100-hour inspection on the Cessna DNY floatplane, which is ramped on the floating hangar at Benjamin Constant.

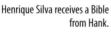

Henrique Silva receives a Bible from Hank.

Right:
Randy Bielfuss, an experienced mechanic on PA-12 repairs, came twice from Anchorage, Alaska, to weld the tubular structure that had been damaged by the tornado. Randy and many other volunteers repaired, reassembled, and covered the plane's frame with fabric, then doped and painted it.

Left:
Ruth, Kay, Hank, and Phillip arrive at the Iquitos Airport after the long, two-aircraft flight.

So I grabbed my shotgun and we headed down to the canoe. We had heard from some of the Brazilians that a little boy had gone missing from the riverside, so Dan and I figured this big snake was the culprit. We paddled to the island.

"You lead the way, son. You know where you saw the snake."

The grass was as tall as Dan and after we had walked awhile, he turned to me and said, "Don't you think you should go first, Dad? You've got the gun."

We looked all over the island, but the snake was nowhere to be seen. We did find where it slithered down the bank to the river and, by its track, it was a big one.

I looked at Dan and seeing that he was so anxious to get the snake, I decided to wait. After a while I said, "Who knows how long it'll be before we'll see it. Anacondas can stay underwater a long time. We might as well go back home."

"Can't we wait a while longer?" Dan asked. "It sure would make a nice trophy, Dad."

At this point, Hank usually unrolled the 18-foot skin and asked the audience, "Don't you think it's a nice trophy?" before he continued:

Of course, while Dan and I sat there waiting, we recalled all the stories we had ever heard about anacondas: How they can stay underwater for hours at a time; how they lure their prey in close by remaining camouflaged; how they grab on, wrap a few loops around their prey and hug 'em to death, then swallow 'em whole.

After a couple of hours, I said, "I don't think it's coming out. Let's go." I nudged Dan and we started back up the path. Then, I saw it—and froze. Perched on a branch in a tree right above Dan was the biggest snake I had ever seen, its head cocked and ready to strike. The snake slithered down the tree, hit the ground, and moved toward us.

"Hurry, Dan! Back to the river." The snake had us trapped with no way to escape except for the river. Knowing that anacondas are most at home in the water, I decided against it. I yelled, "Quick, Dan. Up in the tree over there." In the rush to give him a leg up, I dropped my gun, but followed him up anyway. "Climb up as high as you can."

I glanced down. The snake hit the tree trunk and its head went up and over the first branch. I pulled out the little knife that I always carried in my pocket, opened the blade and held it ready. The snake stared at me with its beady eyes, flicking its tongue back and forth. But when I looked at the head on that huge snake and back down at the three-inch blade in my hand, I put the knife back in my pocket.

In the jungle I wear big knee-high rubber boots to protect me from snakes—but not the size of this one! I decided what to do. When it lunged to strike, I would kick it as hard as I could and break its snout. So I waited, poised and ready to kick.

But I forgot one thing. What does a snake do when it strikes? Opens its mouth. And when the snake struck, its mouth flipped wide open. My foot went in and the snake began to pull on my leg—just like I'm pulling yours!

Hank's stories carried a spiritual application, just as this one did. Hank and Danny did get an eighteen-foot anaconda, but how they accomplished it was embellished at the expense of the listener.

"Satan, too, tries to deceive by wrapping a lie partly in truth. Only he doesn't do it in fun; it's for keeps," Hank told his listeners.

NEW RECRUITS

All things work together for good (Romans 8:28). As a result of that 1976–1977 fill-the-gap ministry and Hank's illness, God called not only the Sorgs, but also two other families into missionary aviation with ABWE, Dale and Beverly Fogg, and Clifton and Hannah Jensen.

Clif Jensen recounted how he came to visit the Amazon:

> I first met Hank at a Moody Aviation mission conference. His upbeat and positive outlook was motivating for me. Through a former college friendship with Dave Nelson, I was inclined in the direction of the Philippines for a field of service.
>
> After finishing Moody's program . . . as things slowed down during the winter, I contacted Hank about the possibility of visiting the field to get a taste of mission life. . . .
>
> After a two-week visit to Brazil while Hank and Ruth were filling in for a year, I remember arriving back in Florida and telling my wife, Hannah, something to the effect, "I think we should seriously consider Brazil as a field of service. They really need help there."

Before Dale Fogg came to serve six weeks with us, he and Beverly had completed Bible and aviation training at Piedmont Bible College; they had been accepted by ABWE and appointed to the Central Amazon aviation team. After an eighteen-month effort, they had not yet been granted visas for Brazil, and it seemed unlikely to happen at this point. Because they had their full support and no place to serve, Dale felt he should survey the needs in both Peru and Paraguay before making a decision.

When Dale requested a transfer, his report to the ABWE Board read, "With the realization of God's leading through blocked and open avenues and trust in His sovereignty and perfect time, we have asked and received a transfer to Paraguay." God, working behind the scenes and in answer to prayer, had begun in this way to provide the pilot and plane for the challenging new field of Paraguay.

Dale and Clif, who came to Hank for flight training and short-term field experience in the summer of 1977, in turn assisted him in the floating hangar shop, cleaned tools and equipment, and organized them for the Brazilian Department of Aviation's inspection. God's assignment for Hank during that 1976–77 year of filling the gap included getting the hangar approved as a certified repair station. This accomplishment meant that all government-required inspections on our aircraft except the 1,000-hour inspection could be done in Benjamin Constant, saving pilots a fifteen-hour flight to Manaus for every 100 hours of use on the engine. Thanks to Clif Jensen, Dale Fogg, and another missionary apprentice, Glenn Goodman, Hank was able to write "mission accomplished" across his annual report.

Another new couple, Thomas and Beth Peace, believing that the Brazilian visa situation would be resolved soon, were also appointed to the Amazon aviation team. They were both graduates of Omaha Baptist College, now Faith Baptist Bible College in Ankeny, Iowa. Tom completed his commercial pilot and mechanic licenses, and, in 1975, a year into their prefield ministry, he went to Moody Aviation for his flight and mechanics evaluation in preparation for flying in the Amazon. The Peaces studied at language school in Fortaleza, Brazil, while Hank and I stayed in Benjamin Constant, awaiting their arrival.

FOURTEEN

INITIATING ABWE AIR

By 1977, ABWE had six aircraft and eight pilots serving in three countries. This growth brought about various predicaments and highlighted aviation concerns for which field councils, pilots, and other missionaries wanted answers and guidance from ABWE headquarters.

The pilots needed someone to provide current aircraft advisory news and technical information, including factory maintenance updates, safety bulletins, and insurance coverage. The men on staff at ABWE headquarters did as much as they could, but they were without sufficient knowledge and expertise in aviation. It was necessary for the pilots to maintain their proficiency in flight and mechanical skills, and someone was needed to monitor this.

Missionary pilots everywhere also encounter various pressures from those whom they serve. There is sometimes a lack of understanding about how much weight and how many passengers a plane can carry. Pilots are asked questions such as, "Well, this doesn't weigh much. We can take it, can't we?" without realizing how delicate a balance the pilot must constantly maintain.

A separate issue arose concerning missionaries who were licensed private pilots. Missionaries sometimes questioned why such pilots couldn't fly ABWE aircraft when an approved pilot was unable to fly because of health, absence, bad weather, or other prescheduled responsibilities. This unresolved issue put pressure both on missionaries who needed immediate aviation service and on the pilots who couldn't fulfill the missionaries' expectations.

The need to address all of these issues, along with the need to develop consistent policies and guidelines, especially in light of the expansion of aviation into other fields, caused Dr. Kempton and his field administrators to look for an experienced man to supervise the mission's aviation program.

In the fall of 1977, Dr. Kempton asked Hank to pray about serving as the Director of the Aviation Department, in addition to his work as ABWE's Southern Representative. Though Hank had sensed that this offer was coming, he could hardly believe it when it came. He felt humbled to be asked, knowing that the job of coordinating ABWE's expanding aviation department would demand more than his capabilities. Yet in the strength of the Lord and with His enablement, Hank grew confident of God's plan and direction.

In May 1978, the mission Board officially appointed Hank to the position of International Administrator of Aviation. He would continue recruiting, but now he would also screen prospective pilots and maintain files on their flight certificates, proficiency, and mechanical skills, both before and after their acceptance as approved ABWE pilots.

One of the first things he did was to clearly outline the aviation requirements: a commercial and instrument license, an airframe and powerplant mechanic rating, 500 flight hours before departure to the field, and final screening and mission field flight training by competent aviation personnel.

I worked alongside Hank in our office at home in Atlanta to handle correspondence, keep files in order, and assist in billing, accounting, and shipping replacement and repair parts to the fields. Hank was responsible to encourage effectual, efficient, and safe aviation service to mission personnel who were involved with evangelism and church planting in remote areas. As safety director, he kept abreast of safety advisories and recommendations for both personnel and equipment. ABWE Air began to coordinate aviation efforts around the ABWE world, answering specialized questions and dealing with logistical situations. Hank also began the practice of staying in close touch with ABWE pilots by ham radio. Contact was an integral part of safety, especially in flight-following. More than once during many years of using ham radio, his twice-daily contacts with ABWE pilots saved lives and aircraft.

A long-standing concern common to all of the ABWE pilots needed attention: resolution of aircraft liability insurance coverage. After one pilot faced the difficult situation of seeing an emergency patient die while waiting for insurance to be transferred from a mission plane that had broken down to one that was air worthy, he wrote:

> As you know we do have Brazilian insurance on the planes, yet we cannot fly the planes here with passengers unless we also have the insurance that ABWE requires with Lloyds of London. This can be a touchy situation for us here since the officials know that we have the Brazilian insurance on the planes, and yet we can't fly emergencies because of lack of stateside insurance.
>
> Our ABWE missionaries have their own life insurance, health insurance, the Brazilian plane insurance, travel insurance, and now Lloyds of London. Why all this insurance? The cost of flights will soon be too high with these insurance requirements. Can someone study the situation and come up with a solution?

Hank investigated insurance rates around the world and corresponded with all the pilots to get their suggestions and compare the results of their research, but years passed before the issue could be resolved completely, with ABWE finally agreeing to allow the pilots on each field to find the needed insurance coverage for the mission plane, whether from within the country or through another agency in the US.

PASSING ON THE VISION

The year 1978 proved momentous for us in other ways, also. Hank began teaching missions courses at Carver Bible Institute and College, in Atlanta. Teaching both African-American and international students would become a twenty-year plus ministry for us. I was to pinch-hit as a teacher when he traveled. I would also work in the library and sometimes assist in the office at Carver.

"But it isn't enough to just teach missions," Hank said. "A vision of the field must be caught." So Hank and I trained and took to Brazil several teams from Carver to see missions in action. Among those who went along on a two-week trip to Brazil was Mrs. Earlene James, who later served as a missionary in Kenya.

With assistance from Carver student Ronald Swift (who presently serves with Dr. Charles Stanley at First Baptist Church in Atlanta), we used our home to launch a neighborhood Bible club with African-American children and a Bible study with their parents. Several neighbors came to Christ that year, including one named Bernice Parham, who eventually took over teaching my Bible club after Hank and I relocated to the new air base. For several years in the 1980s, Bernice Parham's club had the largest attendance of any child evangelism club in Georgia.

NEW WINGS AND A NEW AIR BASE

Before our last return to Benjamin Constant to fill in, Hank had sold the plane he had used as Southern Representative and was now without wings. He felt crippled. "I sure would like a plane," he told me, "and it would be nice to have it sufficiently equipped to make the survey flight down in the Andes." (Of course, he also asked the Lord and informed God's people.)

In 1978, the Lord supplied funds and, in September, Hank took delivery of a 1975 turbo-charged, six-place Cessna 210 (T210). He used this aircraft in ministry for over twenty-six years, flying across the US to scheduled meetings, offering rides to award winners in mission conferences and camps, and flying to and from South American countries to survey new fields and serve missionary pilots and their work.

Flying an airplane enabled Hank to travel more economically and return home sooner; it also gave him contacts among other pilots and mechanics employed by airlines in Atlanta. These Eastern, Delta, American, Republic, and Northwest Airline mechanics and pilots wanted to help missionaries by using their technical knowledge and supply sources. Hank studied ways to use their help in the various plane ministries of ABWE.

At first, Hank kept the T210 tied down at the South Fulton Airport, not far from our home in College Park, Georgia. But after a tornado-like storm damaged several airplanes, we felt we needed a hangar, a more secure location for the mission plane. After speaking to the Christian Airline Pilot's Association, Hank met Lewis Rabbit, an Eastern Airline captain and Phillip LaBerge, a Delta captain, two pilots God sent to be Hank's special friends and invaluable co-laborers over the span of many years. Phillip and his wife offered their Meadowlark Airport, a 2,700-foot sod airstrip, between Zebulon and Concord, 32 nautical miles south of Atlanta on 178° radial, for Hank's use.

Through Phillip's recommendation, we bought property next to this airfield to build a hangar for ABWE and a home for us. We named it the ABWE International Airbase. Volunteers, friends, and supporters helped Hank build the 50- x 60-foot hangar, and then our home, with ample room to offer hospitality to pilots and mechanics-in-training, and to volunteers who worked on the aircraft.

Men experienced in metal work, fabric repair, and stripping and painting, came from as far away as Alaska to help Hank rebuild planes at the air base, often assisted by their wives. Sherman Baughman, longtime friend and aircraft mechanic honored in the Eastern Airline Hall of Fame for building specialized repair tools in his work for Eastern, used his God-given ability to build or adapt special aircraft tools for mission aviation. These self-sacrificing men, women, boys, and girls are too many to mention by name, but God has recorded each one, and someday accolades will be given for labor done in His name and for His glory.

IN SEARCH OF PLANES

Another of Hank's duties as Director was to find planes to equip various ABWE fields. When planes were needed for the South American fields he had surveyed in 1976, Hank asked God to provide aircraft, then researched, advertised for, and checked out planes that could be used.

God supplied numerous aircraft through unexpected circumstances. One was a damaged Cessna 180 donated by Lee Talladay from Milan, Michigan, and carted back to the Georgia air base by Hank and his friend Orlin Bestrom, of Grand Rapids. Another was a Cessna 206, an ex-drug-runner that Hank purchased from a sheriff's auction in New Mexico. Hank and I disassembled and carted that plane by truck and trailer across the country from Carlsbad, New Mexico, back to Georgia.*

He scoured the US to find a Cessna 185 floatplane or a Cessna 206 amphibian aircraft for the plane ministry in Iquitos, Peru, when the Donaldson and DeWitt families were gearing up to go to this field. At the same time he was searching for this plane, Denny Washer was in language study in Togo and also needed an airplane. The red tape and international communication difficulties involved weighed heavily on Hank's mind.

Jerry Horne from Holland, Michigan, who wanted Hank to have a safe, well-equipped plane to fly for more effective ministry, had donated a streamlined Beechcraft Bonanza A-36 in top condition. We deeply appreciated this gift, but the plane was very

---

*The complete story of the ex-drug-runner is told in Chapter 26.

expensive to insure and operate. After several years of flying the Bonanza, Hank got permission from the Hornes to sell it. He used the proceeds to rebuild and modify the ex-drug-runner, to buy a damaged Helio Courier, and to purchase new floats for the Iquitos floatplane. And he still had $20,000 remaining to help purchase a Cessna 206 for Togo.

Following the tornado-like incident at South Fulton Airport, Hank purchased a storm-damaged 1947 Piper Super Cruiser, reduced to a jumble of parts stowed in several baskets, for $1,000. At the time, he didn't know why God provided this "basket-case," but he would later rebuild and adapt it to fly the heights of the Andes Mountains in Peru. Many volunteers worked on this project with him. Randy Beilfuss, an experienced PA-12 me-chanic from Alaska, and his wife arrived to help. When Hank had spoken at Word of Life Bible Institute and Piedmont Bible College, he had enlisted student aviation-mechanic volunteer Andy Braun to help, and he was assisted by ABWE missionary Glenn Budd (the pilot designated to fly this aircraft), Glenn's friend and supporter Jim Donaldson from Republic Airlines, and several others. They were busy restoring the PA-12 for many months, during which time "Ruth's restaurant" and "Hank's hangar" had wall-to-wall occupants.

God brought ABWE Air planes from many different people and some interesting situations, but He faithfully supplied each plane we needed.

PARAGUAYAN AVIATION MINISTRIES

FIFTEEN

EXPANSION PLANS

Expansion was part of Hank's plan for the aviation department. During that memorable year when Hank became Director of ABWE Air, our daughter Kimberly graduated from Piedmont Bible College, in Winston-Salem, North Carolina, and married Allen Yoder the following year. Al completed aviation mechanics and commercial flight training, then applied to ABWE to initiate the aviation-church-planting ministry in Bahia, in southeastern Brazil.

Dennis and Diane Washer, who were appointed to Togo, planned to use an airplane as a tool in planting churches there. That same year, the Foggs transferred to Paraguay to pioneer the aviation-church-planting program Hank had envisioned. And the following year, ABWE appointed Jon and Kathy Griffin, who partnered with the Foggs for two years.

Dale Fogg's preparation for an aviation and church-planting ministry had taken years, including the frustrating wait for Brazilian visas, which helped the Foggs be open to accepting the challenge to initiate the aviation program in Paraguay. They completed Spanish language study and, in August 1980, began acclimation and acculturation in Asunción, Paraguay.

Dale said, "The only familiar things there were the faces of our family. We were thrust into a trilingual experience in a semi-tropical land, where the only thing that happens quickly is sweat!"

It took Dale a year to obtain the documents needed to remain and work in Asunción and to import the Cessna 185 ZP-TVY that Hank had purchased from an Atlanta dealer. Through the very generous donations of two specific businessmen, many of the

Fogg's supporting churches, and numerous interested individuals, funds came in to purchase, refurbish, and equip the Cessna.

SURPRISING BEGINNINGS IN PARAGUAY

Once he arrived in Paraguay, several overland survey trips occupied first place on Dale's agenda as he sought a location for their initial aviation evangelistic church plant. He and Bev first targeted Villa del Rosario, an interior town with an airstrip and a population of around 5,000. It took a twelve-hour road trip to get there, but could be reached by air in twenty-five minutes.

The Foggs knew that the Paraguayan constitution provided religious freedom, leading them to conclude that they could hold an open-air meeting in Rosario. After handing out several hundred invitations to the meeting, they waited at the airstrip for the crowds that would show up. After a three-hour wait, thirty to forty people appeared.

Following Dale's gospel presentation, an armed escort invited the Foggs to accompany them to the office of the Chief of Police. Dale later described their experience at the Police Department:

> "Who are you?" the chief demanded. "Give me your documents. What are you doing here?"
>
> We told him we had come from the capital to hold an evangelical service on the airstrip, to which he responded, "You can't do that." (Which meant, not without his permission.)
>
> We responded, "We already did." (Which he already knew.) Then we apologized, begged his forgiveness, and explained that we were new in the country. After being sternly informed that henceforth any such action should be brought to his attention for his approval, our documents were returned to us and we were allowed to leave.

This vivid experience taught Dale the protocol he observed in every town he visited thereafter. However, not long after the police summons, the Foggs were summoned to the mayor's office.

The missionary team had started meeting regularly in the humble home of the Cuellar family, outside in their yard when it was warm, or inside with all the doors and windows open when cold, because the law prohibited closed-door meetings. Following one service, the summons came from the mayor.

"You cannot continue to meet at the Cuellar home," the mayor stated.

"Why? Have we broken a law?" Dale asked.

"You should have your own church building." Dale nearly fell backward when he heard this, but the mayor had more: "I have the perfect piece of property you can build it on, and the municipality is willing to sell it to you."

"God used the mayor's political motivation to provide the property for a church in Villa del Rosario," Dale recounted. "When we returned to the capital, I made three phone calls, and within six weeks, the money for the land and church had been supplied and the church constructed. 'Ain't' God good!"

"And I want to tell you how God orchestrated an answer to prayer in this," Beverly added. "The Cuellar family had a married daughter, a Christian, named Agripina, who no longer lived in Rosario. She visited her family infrequently, and a long time after we started meeting at her parents' home, we finally met Agripina. Imagine how thrilled and humbled we felt when she told us how she had prayed for years for God to send a missionary to her family and to start a church in Rosario. The entire Cuellar family served the Lord in various places and ministries throughout Paraguay, and it was a blessing to see fruit that not only remained, but reproduced."

LORD OF THE WEATHER

Flying in the interior, the Foggs never knew what to expect, especially since Paraguay was famous for rapid and violent weather changes, the cause of frequent aircraft accidents. Many years after Maranata Baptist Church in Rosario got its own Paraguayan pastor, Gregorio Segovia, the Foggs and ABWE church-planting assistant Laura Fouser flew up through a beautiful, clear sky to help Pastor Segovia in an afternoon youth rally. The weather changed around the time the meeting began. The sky grew black, the wind velocity increased, and finally the rain came drumming down on the metal church roof and sheet metal sides. Ultimately, the noise grew so loud the people could only hear if they stood right beside the person speaking.

The service ground to a halt as the racket increased with the din of quarter-sized hailstones, and while the church *oohed* and *aahed* at the phenomena turning the ground white, the three missionaries were *oh-noing* and praying for God to protect the Cessna 185 ZP-TVY. Just a few months earlier, Dale had finished major repairs on the airframe, and he could only imagine the damage the hail must be doing to the plane. When the storm passed, Dale still had to preach, and God gave him peace of mind and clarity of thought to deliver a strong evangelistic message. At the invitation, six young people came forward to trust Christ as Savior.

Heartsick, yet knowing he must assess the damage to the plane, he mustered the courage to get a ride to the airstrip. But when he arrived there, he couldn't believe his eyes—there was not one dent or dimple! Sighing with relief, Dale turned to an approaching woman who lived next to the airfield and asked, "Did it hail here?"

"Did it ever!"

Dale smiled broadly as he walked around the plane several times, running his hands over the cowling and flaps. "It might have hailed at your house, but it didn't hail here. God's hand covered and sheltered this airplane." He ended the telling of this incident with his typical dry humor: "And three little missionaries went *wow! wow! wow!* all the way home, rejoicing at God's protection."

BEARING FRUIT

During their twenty-two-plus years in Paraguay, the Foggs flew regularly to seven remote towns to minister and establish congregations, four of which developed into indigenous churches. None of this could have been accomplished without the use of the airplane.

As Hank's initial survey of Paraguay in 1976 had shown, the country was peppered with airstrips. The Foggs chose numbers of them, depending on how close the airstrips were to the people, for evangelistic outreach. On these flights, Dale usually took along a team of believers—to instill a burden and vision for their own people's souls—or had his family accompany him. He flew to a targeted town, made low passes, raced the engine, did pull-ups and dragged main street, all safe aerial maneuvers designed to attract the people's attention. Then he landed and waited for his congregation to arrive. He or a Paraguayan preached through a portable PA system hung beneath the wing of the airplane. In places without an airstrip or with an airstrip in disrepair, the team dropped hundreds of gospel tracts above the center of the town, and the people snatched them up joyfully.

At one such meeting in Horqueta, Paraguay, only fifteen or twenty spectators showed up. Among them was a young man on a bicycle with a strange-looking box tied onto the back with strips of old inner tube. He asked for, and was given, permission to tape record the message being preached. The team proceeded to preach the Easter message of Christ's purpose in coming, His death, burial, resurrection, His pardon for sin, and free gift of salvation.

Dale's team, though disappointed at the small attendance, had other towns to visit that day, and so they prepared to leave. When the bicycle boy asked where they were going, Dale answered, "Somewhere else, to do the same thing we did here, but we hope more people will attend."

"Don't be disappointed at the small turnout," the young man replied. "In fifteen minutes, all of Horqueta will hear the message you just gave. I work for the local radio station, and I plan to air the tape I just recorded."

God is not willing that any should perish, but that all should come to repentance (2 Peter 3:9). God's Word is powerful, sharper than any two-edged sword. It will accomplish many times over what a child of God can imagine.

Once Dale underestimated the results of a few Bible studies he held with a man in southern Paraguay. A Paraguayan pastor working with a small nucleus of believers in Ayolas had asked Dale to hold a Bible study with a contact person there. Dale was able to hold only three studies before losing touch with the contact person, but years later, while ministering in another town, Dale encountered that same man and heard amazing news from him. The Bible study group had continued to meet; it now had property, a church building, and a Paraguayan pastor. When Dale accepted the invitation to preach a three-day conference there, he found 150 members. What a blessing to see what God had done after just three Bible studies!

MINISTERING TO THE INTERIOR

In the Foggs' second term, God provided funds to build a spacious hangar on land at the Silvio Pettirossi International Airport in Asunción. They developed plans to spearhead church plants in two new interior towns by holding evangelistic campaigns and making regular trips to Mbuyapey and Capitan Bado to disciple new believers. These two locations had a nucleus of believers with which to begin weekly services. ABWE missionaries Chuck and Jan Robinson, along with a Paraguayan couple, moved to

Capitan Bado and worked for two years to teach and train leaders. Their contribution and dedication brought stability and continuity, which resulted in a strong, indigenous church, Iglesia Bautista Independente Fundamental.

The interior town of Mbuyapey challenged Dale and Beverly. Time and again, they thought the ministry to be hopeless. Someone there had punctured all three tires of the airplane while it was tied down on the local airstrip overnight. But they knew the Lord wanted the people of this town to be saved, so they persisted and a church was started. The congregation renovated a house next door to the Betel Baptist Church building, in hopes that a Paraguayan couple could move in to pastor them. Over the years, the believers grew discouraged when two different attempts to get a Paraguayan to lead this flock failed. In God's time, a Chilean couple, graduates of the ABWE Bible Institute in Santiago, Chile, arrived in Paraguay looking for a place to serve as missionaries. The Foggs helped them move into the house next to the church in Mbuyapey. While Satan's tactics to thwart the ministry failed, the Foggs' God-given persistence paid off in spiritual dividends.

One of these "dividends" was Delia, whom Beverly led to the Lord and who had been discipled and baptized as a teenager in the church plant at Mbuyapey. One day, Delia came to Beverly in tears. "I don't know what to do. Everyone at school makes fun of me because I don't dance and drink *cerveza* (beer) anymore."

Beverly thought, *It has to be hard for her to overcome temptation. The only entertainment in this town is drinking and dancing. So many girls end up pregnant. Oh, Lord, help me console Delia and say the right words.* Beverly found that Delia had only her cousin, a young man who was also a member of their small group, to be her friend at school, and she realized how lonely Delia must be.

Beverly prayed with Delia and encouraged her to understand that all believers go through rough times for the Lord's sake, that Delia's time in high school was only a temporary phase, and that, as God's child, He had a special plan for her life. "Don't give up following the Lord for a time of sin that you will regret in later years," she advised. As the difficult years passed, Delia remained faithful. She enrolled in Bible college, met her husband (who is now a pastor), and is still serving the Lord with her family in another remote town in Paraguay.

When the Foggs returned for their third term, with their children now on their own in the States, they asked God to help them build their own home rather than having to pay exorbitant rent again. God provided the exact piece of land they desired, across the road and up the hill from the ABWE hangar. Their home became a center for their ministry of hospitality, a witness to neighbors who came to their Bible study and to a saving knowledge of Christ. During their fourth term, this home Bible study came under the direction of ABWE missionaries John and Ronda Lennon, who rented a storefront nearby and began weekly services. That nucleus of believers grew into the Esperanza Baptist Church and eventually overflowed into their own larger building.

REJUVENATING THE CESSNA 185

Despite regular maintenance and inspections, hours of flying the Cessna 185 took its toll on the engine and airframe.

"Just about all of the essentials are worn slap out!" Dale wrote in his usual colorful way.

Thinking ahead, he tried to anticipate all the problems and situations he would face in overhauling the plane. Repair parts would have to come from the US because they were unavailable in Paraguay. He would then need to find someone to transport the parts to Paraguay, but that would still not guarantee he'd have all the needed parts on hand as he began the overhaul. However, if he accomplished the detailed and extensive 1,000-hour inspection in the US during his furlough, he would have telephone access directly to the manufacturers and suppliers, as well as their technical assistance and consultation. He determined to get ABWE's permission to do the job in the US.

Dale and a pilot friend, Dan Donovan, ferried the Cessna to the States on an eight-day trip. Dale's trusted mechanic friend, Larry Belton, at the Bob Jones University aircraft shop in Greenville, South Carolina, waited for Dale's arrival and go-ahead to begin the projected work. Dale squeezed in time to assist him between scheduled meetings at supporting churches. Delta mechanic Tom Holmes and his son, David, fitted the much needed cargo pod to the airframe, completing the modifications for operational safety and increased ministry capability.

At last, only the return flight to Paraguay remained. Dale flew the plane from South Carolina to the ABWE Airbase in Georgia to pick up pilot Dan Donovan and mechanic Tom Holmes, who would help him fly the plane back to Paraguay. In February 1991, the three taxied the renovated Cessna 185 down the runway in Georgia and headed for South America.

En route, Hank talked to Dale by ham radio every hour on the hour or at the half-hour agreed upon. Flight-following enabled Hank to pinpoint Dale's location, give weather forecasts, and receive Dale's report on the performance of the overhauled engine and propeller. On every climb, Dale noticed that fuel pressure fluctuated slightly, but stabilized when the plane reached level flight. He suspected a particle of dirt—something that would clear up on its own. But while flying at 9,500 feet with a four-hour leg over the ocean ahead, the pressure fluctuation began to concern him. He mentioned it to Hank during a ham radio contact.

"I agree with you," Hank commented. "Sounds like a problem somewhere with the spider (fuel distributor). May be insignificant, but then again, it might be vital. For safety, I'd check it out before long."

When they landed at Grand Turk Island, Tom Holmes, looking through the opening in the cowling, announced, "I see the problem! It's an easy fix."

Once they were airborne again, Dale reported to Hank on the ham radio, "The locking nut on the fuel pressure line from the spider to the gauge came off, and when the airplane angled in a climb, the nut jiggled on its seat. Once we leveled out, the wind pressure, no doubt, jammed it solidly against the seat and stabilized the indication."

Tom had positioned and tightened the locking nut, a simple matter accomplished without removing the cowling, and the three men rejoiced that God had spared them from a potential engine compartment fire. After helping Dale get the plane home, Dan and Tom returned to the US on a commercial flight.

CAAMINDY

Following the trip from the US, Dale resumed his evangelistic flights to the interior with the newly overhauled plane. Paraguayans came to Christ by other means as well. After listening to Dale's witness for four years, Silverio, the hangar guard, accepted Christ as Savior and became a vibrant witness to others. Subsequently, his wife came to Christ, and together they traveled to the interior to Caamindy to witness to his wife's relatives. Spending Christmas there, Silverio returned and told the Foggs the good news. "I led my father-in-law to the Lord. There are others waiting there with open arms to hear you preach. Please go."

The fruit in Caamindy was ripe for picking. Silverio and Lidia had been testifying of what God had done in their lives. Nine people came to the Lord on the Foggs' first visit, and each subsequent trip saw more saved, attending discipleship classes, and wanting to be baptized. The Foggs, soon to return stateside because of health concerns, worried about leaving this flock without a shepherd. But God answered prayer.

Once again John and Ronda Lennon helped, this time in Caamindy. Out of the church that had grown from the Foggs' neighborhood Bible study, the Lennons handpicked leaders to go each month to Caamindy, to train leaders to hold their own meetings and carry on the ministry by themselves.

As Dale would say, "Ain't God good!" Indeed, God had orchestrated these circumstances and opened the way for Dale and Beverly to consider making a transition to a different ministry.

A CHANGE OF MINISTRY FOR THE FOGGS

Hank received a letter from Dale, dated August 1, 1998, asking us to pray before answering his question, "*If* we did come back to the States, would there be a place for us in ABWE Air?"

Perhaps Dale wrote this in premonition of what developed two weeks later. Two Paraguayan doctors found an abnormality in Dale's heart and recommended catheterization. The Foggs returned to the US for this procedure, and on October 10, 1998, the attending physicians found four blocked arteries, two with only a trickle of blood passing through. In November, Dale had six by-pass surgery. In January 1999, the Foggs returned to Paraguay with questions about the future, but trusting God to guide and provide answers. And they were encouraged. God was preparing the way for Mike and Sharon Thompson and their two sons to join the Foggs in the aviation ministry.

Both Mike, a New Yorker, and Sharon, a South Carolinian, had Christian parents and had received Christ as children; both had surrendered their lives to the Lord as teens; and after Bible college and marriage in 1989, they both knew they wanted to pursue foreign missions. God used Elisabeth Elliot's book *Through Gates of Splendor* to show Mike how missions and flying airplanes complemented each other. He completed his Bachelor of Theology and Aviation degrees at Piedmont Bible College, and in 1996, ABWE appointed them to serve with the Foggs. After flight and mechanical clearance at the ABWE Airbase, the Thompsons completed language school in Costa Rica and arrived in Asunción on June 15, 2002.

The Foggs spent their last six months in Paraguay helping the Thompsons with obtaining their documents, orientation to the culture, and introduction to the aviation community. By 2003, Dale and Beverly moved into their new job as Associate Director of Aviation Ministries Worldwide and Associate in Church Relations in the Southern Region of the US, while the aviation ministry in Paraguay passed into the capable hands of Mike, Sharon, and their two sons.

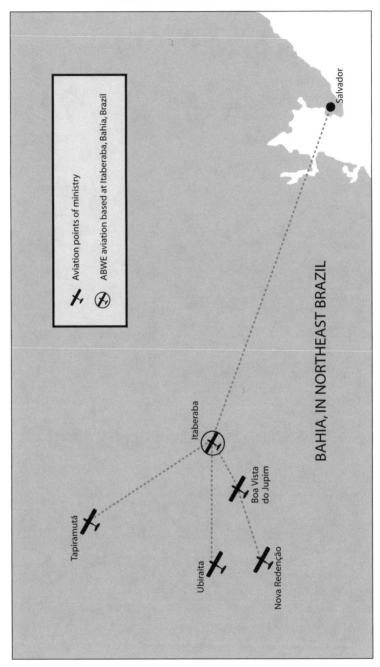

Aviation points of ministry

ABWE aviation based at Itaberaba, Bahia, Brazil

Salvador

Itaberaba

Boa Vista
do Jupim

Tapiramutá

Ubiraita

Nova Redenção

BAHIA, IN NORTHEAST BRAZIL

SIXTEEN

ABWE AIR EXPANDS

By this time, ABWE Air was operating nine aircraft on seven fields. There were fourteen approved aviation church planters— nine on the field and eight non-flying-status missionaries, five of whom were still in prefield—yet to be evaluated and approved for aviation ministries. Hank communicated with pilots on five of the seven fields via ham radio at least one to two times daily. (The other two fields were out of range.) Four of the nine aircraft were being overhauled, which meant that Hank stayed busy ordering and sending engines, propellers, and maintenance directives. Now and then, he put aside his tasks in Georgia to visit the Philippines, the Amazon (Brazil and Colombia), Paraguay, and Bahia fields, hand-carrying aircraft parts as needed.

Back at the air base in Georgia, Hank continued his varied duties. Besides recruiting helpers to work at the air base, he was also enlisting prospective missionary pilots at several of the aviation training schools across the country. During this time, he initiated a long-term correspondence and relationship with Herman Teachout, who would later play an important role in ABWE Air. Their correspondence began while Herman was single, and continued after his marriage to Tami. The Teachouts volunteered for several short-term aviation assignments on various fields, which were excellent preparation for what God planned for them in the future.

AVIATION SAFETY

Hank also established an aviation safety program using the services of Missionary Safety International (MSI). MSI provided a quarterly publication on safety issues for all ABWE pilots, including incident/accident reports for guidance in preflight inspections and maintaining and improving aviation skills and knowledge. MSI team members scheduled visits to overseas locations and offered safety seminars. Hank often had the safety team visit ABWE personnel to evaluate shop habits, maintenance of aircraft, and safety alertness.

After receiving MSI's reports, Hank himself traveled to the various aviation fields to check on these things. There is wisdom in using a multitude of counselors, and Hank consulted with safety experts to keep sharp himself and to encourage accountability from our mission pilot-mechanics. MSI's publication, *Safety Net,* provided published conclusions as taught by the Federal Aviation Administration, showing how procedures and human behavior interrelate in aviation safety, the major reasons for human error, and hazardous thought patterns that lead to mission aviation accidents or incidents.

One of Hank's objectives as the safety supervisor was to make these materials available to ABWE pilots. Reading, studying, and applying this material fell on their shoulders. The pilot-mechanics had their hands full, not just with aviation and mechanical jobs, but also with evangelism and discipling. Ensuring the safety of their passengers and aircraft was a tremendous responsibility and demanded the pilots' personal, disciplined thinking and planning. One of the many articles Hank mailed to each pilot was "Complacency," written by Edward Gluklick and published by the *Aircraft Owners and Pilots Association* (AOPA) magazine. The article emphasized that too many pilots, including missionary pilots, consider their license and ratings to be self-perpetuating. Prime factors contributing to accidents are flying infrequently, but not enough to stay sharp, and sloppy maintenance on the aircraft. The sticky job of checking up on his pilots' flight performance, proficiency, and maintenance skills fell on Hank's shoulders.

Sometimes Hank's visits to various fields were for longer time periods in order to fill a gap, as he frequently had in the Amazon. There he flew personnel to and from the Santo Antonio do Iça hospital construction site, to Brazilia to follow up on the missionaries' permanent visa situation, and to check out new pilots in floatplane flying. Hank, our daughter Kay, now nearly a teenager, and I also spent three months in Kenya to survey for a future ABWE aviation ministry. While there, we taught at the Karatina Bible Institute to relieve Dave and Elwanda Fields for a short break. Hank taught evangelism, and Kay and I taught the MKs for six weeks.

To keep the ABWE Board abreast of new developments and changes, Hank reported to them two times a year and also participated in Candidate Classes, where he interviewed aspiring aviation church planters.

OPENING THE FIELD IN BAHIA

Hank's vision of using aviation church planters to reach the interior of Bahia, Brazil, began to develop in 1980 when, after Candidate Class, Allen and Kim Yoder were appointed to Bahia. They had served there earlier as AMPers and had been challenged to help plant churches in the interior of that state. Enthused about the opportunities, Al soon laid out a strategy for aviation ministry. He designed a plan to plant multiple churches per term, training "Timothys," or potential leaders, to take over the newly established works, while he would move on to initiate ministries in other places where transportation is difficult.

Another couple, Tom and Sue Jertberg, were also new members of the Bahia aviation team, although Tom still lacked flight hours, prefield training, and final approval by ABWE Air. Tom's parents, Frank and Doris Jertberg, had served several terms as ABWE church planters in Pernambuco and then in Bahia. Having grown up in that region, Tom was also enthusiastic about using a plane to reach interior, distant areas of the state. He hoped to fly as co-pilot during his first term, then complete ABWE Air requirements during furlough.

The Jertbergs completed prefield ministry and arrived in Salvador before the Yoders. By the time Al and Kim came in September 1982, the Bahia Field Council had already worked out a methodology and plan for aviation church planting.

The team plan, although different from the one Al designed, was a good one. It included a four- to-six-year period for the pilots to work together to start a strong mother church, targeting the more educated middle and upper classes of people in a large town, such as Itaberaba. Field council members believed that working with educated folk would produce a solid base for reproduction. If a church were started with predominantly lower class, uneducated members, then the next phase—training leaders in TEE classes and working with those leaders to plant churches in surrounding towns via the aviation ministry—would be more difficult.

By 1986, they expected Tom to be ABWE-approved and ready to help Al take trained leadership from the mother church in Itaberaba to assist at aviation outreaches. Plans for phase two, scheduled to begin around 1989, included another pilot and a second plane purchase. Though Al believed that the aircraft's potential would be unfulfilled in following this strategy, he agreed to it.

A PLANE FOR BAHIA

Through many faithful churches and individuals, the Lord provided $15,000 for Al to purchase a Brazilian-made and Brazilian-licensed 1976 Embraer Corisco, referred to by the missionary pilots as the Piper Arrow because of its similarity to that US-made model. Buying the plane in Brazil would save importation work, cost, and a long flight to transport it from the States to Bahia. But there was danger involved in carrying the large amount of cash necessary for the purchase.

In December, Hank flew to Bahia with $15,000 in small bills hidden in pockets I had sewn by hand into his T-shirt. He and Al flew Varig Airline from Bahia to São Paulo to complete negotiations to get the plane. At the hotel, both felt uneasy about the cash they were carrying. Hank locked and barred the door with a chair; Al closed the wooden shutters and locked the windows. At one point, Hank peeled off the money-padded T-shirt and handed it to Al.

"Here," he said. "I've worn it two days; it's your turn!"

Needless to say, they both sweltered all night in that tightly closed, non-air-conditioned room, but they kept the money safe and made the transaction the next day.

INVESTIGATING ITABERABA

During a break from language study, the Yoders scheduled a flight in the Piper Arrow to investigate Itaberaba, the town the field council had suggested for the strong mother church mentioned in phase one of their plan. After an hour airborne, Kim, who was in the passenger front seat, leaned over to catch Al's attention. "How much longer to Itaberaba? I've got to land soon." She had picked up a "bug" from the previous meal and stomach cramps gripped her.

"We're about fifteen minutes out, but there are no buildings. It's just a paved strip eight kilometers from town in the middle of the *sertão* (semi-arid scrub-tree terrain). I don't know what to tell you." Once the strip came into sight, Al pointed, "Look, I'll land and taxi into those tall weeds off the apron so you can hightail it off into the brush." Kim jumped down from the cabin before the propeller stopped. Her childhood experience of flying with her father in the Amazon had taught her how to meet such an emergency.

Meanwhile, the curious airport guard ran over to the Piper to check things out with the pilot. "Why did the lady jump from the plane and run off?" he wanted to know as he tried to peer around Al's side-to-side posturing and attempts to shield Kim from view.

By the time Kim reappeared, Al had distracted the guard. His name was Louro (Blondie). Why this name should be given a black-skinned, black-eyed, black-haired man posed an interesting mystery, but even more interesting was the result of that first contact with Louro. Al hired him to guard the Piper Arrow while they went into town to complete their survey. A few months later, when the Yoders and Jertbergs settled in Itaberaba, Louro guarded the ABWE plane and property at the airfield. Through Al's persistent witness, he came to Christ, along with his wife and daughters. Louro and members of his family then became some of the earliest members of the church in Itaberaba.

MOVING TO THE INTERIOR

When language study was completed, both the Yoders and the Jertbergs moved from the coast to Itaberaba, an interior town of 35,000, to begin their church plant among the upper middle class. Every other Sunday, the Yoders, and sometimes Tom, also traveled over two hours by van to Tapiramutá, a small mountain town without an airport, in order to help an existing congregation there. They left home around 10 a.m., their van packed to the gills with equipment, Bibles, and a potty chair and walker for the two Yoder toddlers. Kim reserved the back of the van as a place for the kids to sleep (although sleep was next to impossible on that bumpy road) on the way home after midnight.

The Yoders would arrive in Tapiramutá by 1:00 p.m. and would visit door-to-door, ending up at the home of their co-workers, Brazilian missionaries Gildete and Suely, who became good friends with Al and Kim. These ladies received support from churches in Salvador and carried on ministry between the Yoders' biweekly meetings. Following Sunday afternoon visitation, Al held a Theological Education by Extension (TEE) Bible study and baptismal class while Kim attended to the children's nap. Kim brought pre-baked meatloaf and other foods from Itaberaba to add to their coworkers' potluck meal before the evening service. Electricity was undependable in Tapiramutá, and when it failed, Al preached by candlelight. God blessed, and the attendance grew.

In the first several years in Itaberaba, much was accomplished to lay a good foundation for the budding aviation ministry. Besides assisting with the struggling congregation in Tapiramutá, the Yoders and Jertbergs were able to purchase property at the local airport in Itaberaba and oversee the construction of a hangar that they planned to use not only for storing the airplane, but hopefully for the establishment of a certified repair shop where most, if not all, of the aircraft maintenance could be performed. A non-profit foundation called "The Hope Foundation" was organized with goals, bylaws, and a constitution. Many hours were spent in getting the Brazilian government to recognize the foundation and obtaining the required documents to register it as a non-profit. The Brazilian churches would then be able to use this foundation as an "umbrella" to build a multifaceted ministry which could include camps, Bible bookstores, radio outreaches, a seminary, and a national mission board.

Children's Bible clubs, a weekly radio program called "The Voice of Hope," a Bible bookstore called The Hope Bookstore, and other informal outreach ministries were also initiated. The bookstore was opened not only as an outreach, but with the thought of providing some income to a future Brazilian pastor's wife, as she could take over the operation of the store and be paid a salary from its profits.

In order to stagger their furloughs, the Jertbergs returned to the US on furlough first. Tom expected to complete his requirements to be approved by ABWE Air during this furlough. However, the Lord had other plans, which became evident when Susan developed medical problems that barred their return to Bahia.

A FAMILY EMERGENCY

Though Al wasn't using the plane as a means of evangelism because of the field council plan, he did fly to transport missionaries and, in times of emergency, saved many lives. Among them was Regina, his own newborn daughter.

Regina was born at the hospital in Itaberaba, and five days after birth, her skin and eyes grew very yellow. Kim grew concerned because she knew from experience with her first two babies that jaundice indicated high biliruben levels in the blood, which can affect reflexes and may cause brain damage. Al and Kim insisted that the local doctor run a blood test. The doctor, who was inexperienced at treating jaundice, minimized its significance. After he made multiple attempts to draw blood with no success, Al and Kim decided that they must take Regina back to Salvador, where Dr. Washington, who had delivered their son Peter and treated him for jaundice, would know what to do.

Al dropped Kim off at home to pack for the trip while he hurried to preflight the plane. He phoned missionary colleagues in Salvador to arrange for ambulance transport from the airport to the doctor's office. Within the hour, they were airborne. Examining her little daughter's face and movements, Kim prayed, *"Lord, help us be in time . . . but give us grace to accept whatever happens."*

Dr. Washington, an experienced pediatrician trained in the US, met them at the airport in the ambulance. He took one look at Regina and said, "Take her right to the hospital. I'll call ahead to make arrangements. She needs an immediate blood transfusion."

There was a mad scramble to find a reliable blood donor. It was next to impossible to find one with type A positive, but God provided Jerry Neuman, a fellow ABWE missionary colleague. When the transfusion was completed, the doctor reported, "We nearly lost her twice. This procedure put a lot of stress on her tiny heart. It looks like she's going to be okay, but after a couple of days under the biliruben lights and then reflex testing, we'll have a better idea."

Kim and Al were grateful for God's provision and counted their blessings: the life-saving flight, the knowledgeable doctor, the blood donor, and, of course, their daughter's life. They gave special thanks when further testing revealed that all was well.

THE BAHIA MINISTRY GROWS

Building a hangar alongside the Itaberaba airfield and making improvements on the aircraft took time; but sandwiched between these duties, Al continued to operate the weekly half-hour radio program, "The Voice of Hope." As a result, many received Christ as Savior and joined the Yoders' home Bible studies, which had grown to a good-sized core group of new believers. Working alongside Al, Kim headed up a Bible correspondence course for about twenty-five students who lived in surrounding areas. She also held a weekly Bible club for neighborhood children and initiated an AWANA club. Witness and lifestyle evangelism to new Brazilian friends in the upper class brought few of them to Christ, but results among the poorer classes encouraged the Yoders to include them in the services of the new congregation.

Even though their ministry to the poorer class in Itaberaba was a diversion from the original plan for the church plant, the Yoders saw much fruit in the last year of their term. In September 1985, Mark Cuthbert, a Brazilian MK who directed a twelve-student Cedarville College choir, offered to participate in Itaberaba's first citywide evangelistic campaign. They rented a gymnasium, set up an overhead projector, passed out gospel tracts and invitations, and made valuable contacts with city officials. The choir concert attracted hundreds, and Mark's preaching impacted many. Later, when the missionaries rented an old warehouse in the center of town (paid for by the ABWE program People Advancing Compassionate Evangelism [PACE], which contributed $5,000) and began regular Sunday meetings, attendance mushroomed. Before the Yoders went on furlough, they held their first baptism service, which was the beginning of Hope Baptist Church. The

Jerry Neuman family, gifted church planters, moved from Salvador to Itaberaba to take up the responsibilities for this church.

When the Yoders left Bahia for furlough in 1986, Al was discouraged. Yes, he praised God for progress in phase one—Hope Baptist Church in Itaberaba and the advance in Tapiramutá; those who had come to Christ; funds to buy the Piper Arrow and build the hangar—but all this had been accomplished without doing what he defined as real aviation church-planting evangelism. Nor would he be able to do this until phase two kicked in. He left the field with little sense of fulfilling what he thought God had called him to do; however, he was committed to trying again next term. He looked forward to partnering with Dave Zemmer, who had been appointed in 1984 and hoped to be in Bahia when the Yoders returned from furlough.

Dave, the son of missionary parents, had been open to missions during his college years. After he graduated with a Mechanical Engineering degree in 1973, he spent nine months in Israel working on a kibbutz and learning Hebrew. Dave writes, "That was a defining time in my life in which I determined to fear the Lord above all else."

He then went on to serve as a church intern in Lapeer, Michigan, where he met Patricia Neely, the pastor's daughter, and they were married in June 1976. Three years into his engineering career, the Lord showed Dave and Patty how they might serve Him in missions. After Dave took seminary training in missions at Grand Rapids Baptist Seminary, along with flight training at Grand Rapids School of the Bible and Music, he and Patty applied to ABWE Candidate Class and were appointed to partner with the Bahia aviation team. Dave completed his A & P aviation mechanics license and two months of further field aviation training with MAF in Redlands, California, and the Zemmers arrived in Salvador, Brazil, on March 16, 1987. They enjoyed two visits to Itaberaba, where they planned to work with the Yoders, before going on to Fortaleza to begin Portuguese language study. But at the end of this year, the Bahia Field Council members, the Yoders, the Zemmers, and Hank, as Director of ABWE Air, faced an unexpected development that took us all by surprise. It began at a conference in Benjamin Constant.

SEVENTEEN

THE CONFERENCE IN BENJAMIN CONSTANT

For years, mission pilots in South America had protested the exorbitant costs of double aircraft liability insurance. Al, along with Dick Buck, a missionary colleague from Bahia, took the opportunity to press Hank and Bill Pierson, ABWE treasurer, to meet with the pilots to resolve this ongoing problem. Without such resolution, their aviation ministries would shut down for lack of funds. Hank commented, "Satan is doing his best to keep aircraft down when the need to speed the Light is imperative."

Since Hank and I planned to take four Carver Bible College students to minister in Amazonas from May 14 to June 1, 1988, Mr. Pierson and all South America aviation personnel agreed to congregate in Benjamin Constant to discuss the insurance dilemma.

The Zemmers were still in language school, so Al Yoder represented the pilots from Bahia. His family accompanied him on the long commercial flight to Tabatinga, where veteran ABWE missionaries Paul and Jessie Schlener met them. While waiting to take the ferryboat down the Amazon River to Benjamin Constant, the Yoders listened to Uncle Paul's and Aunt Jessie's entertaining stories of Kim's younger years when she flew the headwaters with her daddy, Hank. To Al, Kim's smile said, "It's so good to be back again."

Then Paul got serious. His stories depicted the many facets of their former work downriver at the Port of Two Brothers, the challenge of church planting in Tabatinga, and the Bible teaching he provided for the Ticuna Indians who looked to him for training. As he listened, Al got a glimpse of the vast distances between mission stations and the hardships missionaries endured in travel.

Some downriver stations were depleted, with the missionaries gone stateside because of health problems.

When they arrived at Clif and Hannah Jensen's house in Benjamin Constant, Al listened as Clif reported the precarious condition of the aviation ministry and its great needs.

Late that night, after everyone had gone to bed, Al couldn't sleep. Thoughts and impressions whirled and spiraled in his mind. By daybreak, he was wide awake, sitting up and pulling on his trousers. He leaned back against Kim and whispered loudly.

"Kim. God wants us to work in the Amazon."

"Oh, Al!" Kim sighed, then went back to sleep. She figured it was a passing fancy; but as Al persisted, she had to grapple with his conviction of God's guidance. It wasn't that Kim didn't want to return to the Amazon—she had grown up there and loved it—but she didn't want her feelings to influence this decision. She wondered how Al could be so convinced of God's will so quickly. It would take time to convince and assure her from God's Word.

Besides addressing the insurance situation, much interaction went on between pilots during the meetings. The times when things go wrong in an airplane are more exciting than when things are normal, and pilots tend to remember and to talk about those experiences. Much of that kind of conversation was exchanged, but Al and Clif Jensen also discussed other matters.

A VITAL CONVERSATION

Unlike the Foggs, who had switched to working in Paraguay rather than wait indefinitely for the remote possibility of getting permanent visas from Brazil, Clif and Hannah had opted to start Portuguese language study while they waited for their permanent residence visas to be granted.

Clif told Al, "During our first term, we were in Manaus for two years, mainly due to language school delays with the birth of Ethan and school schedule issues with the other four kids. And since we had only a temporary visa, I had to renew my pilot's license every time we renewed the temporary visa, about every ninety days."

"And that meant a trip to Brazilia to take the test, right?" Al asked.

"Yes, for the original pilot's license. After that, someone from Wycliffe did the legwork in Brazilia every time the visa was renewed," Clif explained. "But after several renewals, the authorities became suspicious about the process and said, 'No more.' But that worked out, too. We ended up going on furlough in June 1985—but still without permanent visas."

"Did you get a chance to do any river evangelism with Tom Peace by plane?"

"No. Both planes needed a lot of maintenance. We had to change the engine on DNY, and it was down for some time. CJG had a damaged float, and needed metal repair, but neither of us had funds to do it. But thanks to volunteer helpers, especially the two short-termers, Pete Wing and Herman Teachout, we installed three separate cylinders on DNY and got it airborne again. Then, after Tom and Beth Peace left for furlough, the visa situation grounded me."

"I don't know about you, but I felt frustrated with so little chance to use the plane for ministry my first term," Al stated.

Clif agreed. "With me it wasn't only visa and licensing problems. There were constant repairs on the floating hangar and both planes, time-consuming trips to Leticia to help out missionaries downriver, and the weekend demands of the church here in Benjamin. We had a good prospect for a Brazilian pastor, but until then, I filled in as preacher, trainer, building superintendent—you know how it goes. My goal to visit previous works and begin one or two new locations on the river never materialized. When Hannah and I and two of the kids came down with hepatitis, we wondered what God was trying to teach us."

"How's it going *this* term? Did you get your permanent visas?"

"Not yet, and we're already into our second year." Clif chuckled. "I haven't flown anything—not even a kite—for months, so even if it wasn't so humid here, I'd still be rusty. And who knows what happened to our licensing papers. I hope they're in Brazilia."

"What're your plans when you do get your licenses and the Peaces get back from furlough?" Al wondered.

Hank, who was listening in, interjected, "Both planes look like they need painting."

"And cylinder overhauls and float repair in order to pass inspection," Clif added. "You know that better than we do, Hank. CJG is twenty-five years old and DNY is twenty."

"And when they're both flying again, then what?" Al persisted.

Al showed such interest that Clif described in detail the pressing need for additional help to utilize the potential of two floatplanes in the Amazon.

After listening to Clif, Al said, "If the Amazon Field Council expressed their need of my help to the Bahia Field Council, I would be willing to come for three or four months on loan to relieve the situation here, at least until the Peaces return. Of course, Kim would have to agree to it."

A CHANGE OF DIRECTION

As an old expression says, Al's offer opened a can of worms.

Having the Yoders on loan for four months to the Amazon field would indeed benefit the work there. Al wanted to get both planes flying by rebuilding the two engines and repainting both planes. It was urgent to reverse the decay to the floating hangar by ridding it of termites and repairing structural weaknesses. He wanted to help establish a strong youth program in the Benjamin Constant church. Most of all, he wanted to begin weekly evangelistic preaching points with the airplane—to get the aviation program back up in the air. "I didn't have the opportunity my first term, but now I want to fly and use the planes to their full potential. I'm still convinced my multiple-church-per-term plan of aviation church planting will work."

But what about the aviation program back in Bahia? Would the Zemmers be prepared to complete phase one and initiate phase two without the Yoders' help? And what if the Yoders decided to remain permanently in the Amazon? Would it be a mortal wound to the ministry in Bahia? Was this development God's way to test the commitment of missionaries to Himself and to His purpose, or was it Satan's ruse to thwart God's plan?

THE BAHIA MINISTRY EXPANDS

Back in Bahia, God gave grace to work through the details step by step. By January 1989, Al completed weeks of flight orientation with Dave Zemmer in the Piper, and the Yoders fulfilled their responsibilities to Hope Baptist Church in Itaberaba (now grown from three to twenty-five members). Jerry and Lynda Neuman returned from their furlough to partner with the Zemmers and take over at Hope Baptist Church. Following months of prayer for God's direction, Al and Kim transferred permanently to the Amazon.

Meanwhile, in a letter dated June–July 1989, from Bahia, Brazil, the Zemmers wrote:

> It is with joy that we write this letter to you. The first week in May, Dave went to Rio de Janeiro to visit the government office responsible for granting his pilot license. He took with him every document that he might possibly need. . . . In May, he received the needed license and is now able to fly the Piper Arrow that is a part of our ministry here. THANK YOU FOR PRAYING! Dave has been in the air again. . . .

Since the Neuman family had arrived to take the leadership of the Itaberaba church ministry, the Zemmer family, excited to begin outreach to small towns nearby, was able to fly to Ubiraitá to make contacts. Ubiraitá, an interior village with a population of around 2,000, boasted streets traveled more by horses than by the outdated cars driven there. The airstrip was nine kilometers outside town, and there was no reliable ground transportation to and from the plane. A broken-down car or horse-drawn cart might get them partway, but usually the evangelistic team of four members from the church in Itaberaba walked ninety minutes in the hot noonday sun before the meeting. Weather dictated their Sunday flight to Ubiraitá, which was located on the far side of a mountain. On drizzly Sunday mornings, they had to wait an hour to see if the clouds would clear so that the Piper could fly safely over the mountain. Cows met Dave on the runway and he often had to circle twenty minutes, waiting for a rancher to herd his cows off the strip.

Dave described their first meeting room:

> Located off the main area of the weekly Sunday market, it was a grain storage room where bags of grain and starchy food supplies were kept. There was room enough to duck the head on entering and stand in the small opening cleared of sacks, now pushed to one side and behind the low counter. With a makeshift pulpit, the first meeting got under way and the Word of God was presented to a few people, some who were hearing it for the first time.

After a move to a more suitable room, which held two rows of three benches and some chairs, Dave experimented with a small amplifier and microphone, but it didn't function correctly. He discovered that, though the microphone had a short in the grounding circuit, as long as he wore tennis shoes while holding it, all went well.

During one service, however, a *shocking* experience occurred when a barefoot drunken man, holding out his hand, walked down the aisle toward Dave, who received him with an extended hand. No sooner had the drunken man grabbed Dave's hand than he let out a very healthy shout! This unusual opportunity to give the gospel was one of many that opened up for Dave, and within a few months, he saw five men and two ladies make decisions for salvation.

Zuka was one trophy of God's grace. A spiritist, deep into the magic of Candomble/Macumba, he kept his books on spiritism hidden under his bed. Valdinei and Edma, two of Zuka's eight children, received Christ during the Bible school that members of the ministry team held during the preaching service. They began praying for their dad. A few months later, Dave led a weeping Zuka to the Lord in the presence of these two who had prayed for their father.

Between thirty and fifty adults attended services every two weeks. Twenty-five adults and older young people enrolled in evangelistic Bible studies by correspondence. During two weekends in October and November, Dave and a fellow missionary from Salvador held Bible conferences.

Patty Zemmer, busy home-schooling their two boys, took an active part in the Itaberaba church, teaching Bible classes, discipling ladies, and presenting musical programs with a clear gospel message. At Christmas she directed an eighteen-member choir presentation at packed programs in Ubiraitá and Redenção, as well as at Hope Baptist in Itaberaba.

As Dave looked forward to furlough in May 1991, he wrote:

> Hope Baptist Church (Itaberaba) has called a Brazilian pastor and his wife. They will be here the week before we leave. Their coming enables Jerry Neuman to continue the preaching point of Ubiraitá by car while we are on furlough.

The Neumans would cover the Zemmers' ministries during their absence, but what about the Piper Arrow? Due to its design, an unused aircraft engine is susceptible to corrosion and rust, even more than an automobile engine. Without doubt, a plane left in its hangar for a year would also have parts stolen, not to mention the damage rodents would do. Al Yoder, flying in the Amazon, was also concerned about the Piper Arrow, PT-NCC. He suggested a solution to which Dave and Hank agreed.

Al wrote Dave, "I'm willing to keep the plane with me. I'll fly in a commercial airline to Bahia and we can fly PT-NCC back to the Amazon together. I can check on it, fly it, and have the engine overhaul done and ready for you to fly back to Bahia after furlough." With a little ingenuity, the pilots fabricated a cover for NCC from a net intertwined with cloth strips. This cover served as an excellent protection from the equatorial sun during NCC's time in the Amazon.

TRAINING FAITHFUL MEN

Dave Zemmer was a goal-oriented, aviation church planter. From the beginning of his missionary career, he begged his prayer partners to ask God for men with leadership gifts to be saved and added to the church where he ministered. In his progress reports toward ministry goals, Dave mentioned how God was answering this heart desire.

The Neumans transferred to another field shortly after the Zemmers arrived back from furlough in 1992, so Dave partnered with Pastor Moises at Hope Baptist Church in Itaberaba. Dave and Patty concentrated their efforts on discipling and training church leaders there, men who could help evangelize and strengthen the works in Ubiraitá and Boa Vista, which were still in the embryonic stage. By the end of his second term, Dave reported that trained teams of mature men were helping him evangelize, lead, and teach in all three ministries without his direct supervision. "In spite of this positive growth, Hope Baptist Church lacks some essential ingredients to be a self-sustaining, mature church," he wrote in 1995, and continued:

> The church is growing but is unstable financially. The sooner Hope Baptist Church can assume full financial responsibility for their pastor, the better. We trust that through the salvation of some and the growth of others, God will provide this financial and leadership ability within the next year. We see this hope through the eye of faith. What can we do together to prepare for this provision of the Lord?

Dave came up with a plan. The cost of housing Pastor Moises' family took the greater share of the pastor's salary. Why not build a church parsonage to ease this financial burden? Ortonville Baptist Church in Michigan and Clearcreek Chapel in Ohio both sent teams to build this parsonage; three individual families and four churches contributed money to pay for it. To God be the glory for a great labor of love and sacrifice! As a result, the pastor's family had a home and Hope Baptist could afford his salary.

NEW MINISTRY IN BARREIRAS

Achieving financial and leadership stability for Hope Baptist Church in 1996 made it possible for the Zemmers to begin a new ministry in a blossoming region of Bahia. Barreiras, a major center of development sometimes referred to as the most promising breadbasket of South America, with a large and growing population, challenged them to establish a sound Baptist church there.

"We need another pilot here in Bahia, Hank," Dave wrote. "I would be pleased to supervise the aviation ministries which will probably include evangelism and TEE, but I won't have the time required to develop the aviation aspects of this ministry. To carry out the legwork of this new aviation ministry, we need another pilot to fill my place."

The Zemmers, after moving from Itaberaba, began an aggressive ministry in Barreiras, distributing thousands of tracts, invitations to services, handing out gospel literature, and canvassing door-to-door. Just before furlough, they began holding regular meetings for the new Berean Baptist Church. In their absence, ABWE missionaries Dick and Mavis Buck continued to develop the ministry until the Zemmers' return in 1999.

But because of the location of this new ministry, Dave no longer used the Piper Arrow for evangelistic aviation outreach. The aircraft, hangared for several years at Asas de Socorro (the Brazilian counterpart of MAF), was finally sold in 2004 because ABWE had no pilot-mechanic to resume the aviation ministry in Bahia.

Did the need and challenge of the vast area surrounding Barreiras, ideally suited to be reached by an airplane ministry, diminish over time? Was that the reason why ABWE Air had no pilot-mechanic to continue the aviation program in Bahia? There are too many Scripture passages that prove otherwise. ABWE Air is looking for applicants to reopen this ministry. *Pray ye therefore the Lord of the Harvest* . . . (Matthew 9:38). The need is great; where are the missionary pilots?

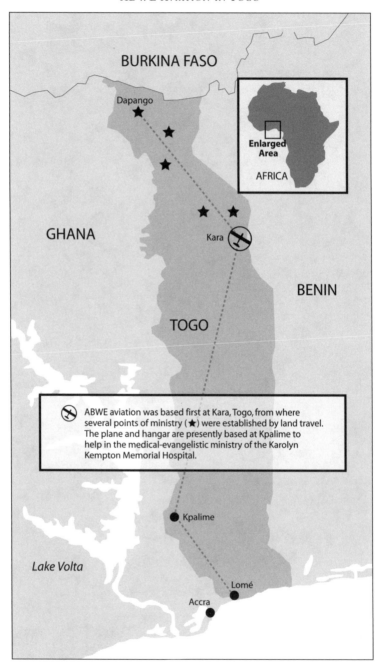

ABWE aviation was based first at Kara, Togo, from where several points of ministry (★) were established by land travel. The plane and hangar are presently based at Kpalime to help in the medical-evangelistic ministry of the Karolyn Kempton Memorial Hospital.

EIGHTEEN ✈

ABWE AIR EXPANDS TO AFRICA

In 1984, Hank and Dennis Washer began looking for a place to put an airstrip adjoining ABWE's Karolyn Kempton Memorial Christian Hospital, in Togo, West Africa.

One day, as they inspected what appeared to be an ideal site, Dennis found himself wondering: *How in the world can we afford to pay the Togolese for each one of those palm nut trees and then uproot them to clear the airstrip?*

After their brief talk about the cost facing the aviation program in Togo, Hank could read Dennis' thoughts. "Yep, that's the problem in a *palm* nutshell, Dennis," he said, laughing. "But you and I know who owns the cattle on a thousand hills. If He wants us to get that land for an airstrip, He'll open the way—all in His own time."

God's provision came many years later. The Togo Field Council, after lengthy negotiations with indecisive owners, obtained the property. After numerous starts and stops, including a riotous military coup, Togo's Civil Aviation Department approved the site for an airstrip. Ralph Gruenberg, ABWE Executive Director of Projects, and his crew of volunteer laborers, arrived with modern equipment to design the grades, crowns, and drainage. They cut, filled, and completed the sod strip late in 1995, and a church in Indiana funded the construction.

Both Dennis and Diane Washer had been reared in Christian homes, and Dennis' parents, Dallas and Kay Washer, also served in Togo with ABWE. Dennis and Diane had each come to Christ at an early age and committed to serve the Lord as a missionary. Both attended Bob Jones University, where they met. Late in

1982, they arrived in Kpalime, Togo, to begin language study.

Dennis, like most approved pilot-mechanics with ABWE, was eager to get back to flying, but there were the usual delays for licensing, documentation, and getting an aircraft. He received a donated Cessna 182, already in Africa but badly in need of repair, to initiate his aviation ministry. Because the plane was in Lome, seventy-five miles away on heavily rutted roads, Dennis had few chances to work on it; yet by the time language study ended, he had finished an overhaul of the cylinders and was waiting for the first official inspection to get it registered.

From the beginning of their ministry, the Washers concentrated on a village ministry. In a year-by-year report given to the ABWE Board, Dennis described how God blessed:

> The second year, we concentrated on building up the visitation program as a vital part of the week's schedule and starting a men's Sunday school class. We prayed for rain to fill up our baptismal creek and it was our joy to be able to baptize thirteen, including our son, Michael, in August 1984. Several weeks later we baptized another three. During this year we saw our attendance on Sunday morning climb to 125. We were also privileged to hold the funeral services for a dear old lady who was saved as a result of Diane's visiting with her.
>
> Our third year, we concentrated on getting our young men some sort of Bible Institute class; four of them completed General Epistles. Diane and Annette Williams started a women's class—a real challenge, as the national ladies are prone not to think on their own, but to accept what is told them. Men accepted more responsibility within the church, leading music, giving announcements, even preaching the Sunday morning message. In spite of—or perhaps because of—Satan's attacks, our church family grew the most during this third year.

The airplane had been grounded most of the year before the Washers' furlough, waiting for parts and radios to be repaired in the US. Before they left, Dennis removed the engine and propeller to ship to Florida, where he planned to overhaul them during furlough.

Frustrations bombarded the Washers during their year in the US. Complications delayed the Togolese registration on the Cessna 182; the Togolese government seemed more favorable to the use of a helicopter than an airplane; and insurance costs had skyrocketed. Togolese regulations required that the Cessna be kept in a hangar on a government-approved airstrip, and this caused indecision about where the Washers should locate for their second term. Dennis wrote to his coworkers, "We believe there is potential for the airplane, whether it is located south or north. In other words, we're throwing it into your laps. You decide where you want us to fit in. With airplane or without, north or south, let us know what you're thinking so we can plan accordingly."

Because of the obstacles encountered, Dennis had yet to prove the worth of the aviation ministry to his colleagues. The Washers anticipated using the airplane more in their second term, even though direct evangelism of the smaller villages would be hampered by government-imposed regulations. Takeoffs and landings were restricted to approved airstrips, and there were only five in all of Togo, each located in a large city. But just fifteen miles north of Kara, where the Washers settled after furlough, Sarakawa had an approved field where the plane could be tied down.

It is claimed that in aviation the hardest service a plane can get is *inactivity,* and that the only thing costlier than flying a plane is *not* flying a plane. Cylinders, for instance, can rust to the point of no return in just a few months. Dennis found quite a bit of corrosion on the fuselage of the Cessna 182, so he planned to strip off the old paint and repaint it. All seemed to be proceeding well. He installed the overhauled engine, as well as the radios he purchased during his first term, but had never installed. By the end of March 1986, when the annual *harmattan* (an extremely dry wind that forms over the desert and carries great quantities of fine dust) settled, the plane was operational.

NEW HELPERS ARRIVE

When Dennis' parents, Dallas and Kay Washer, were on furlough, their testimonies had impacted a young couple named Randy and Jeanette Alderman, both graduates of Bob Jones University and open to go wherever the Lord directed. When they went before the ABWE Board in 1982, they chose to serve in Togo as partners with the Washers. Jeanette was a registered nurse and Randy was a pilot-mechanic, trained at Piedmont Bible College. By the time they completed prefield ministry, French language study in Quebec, and aviation-evaluation training with Moody Aviation, and then arrived in Kara, Togo, it was August 1989. New developments had materialized, making it evident that Satan had launched vicious opposition against getting an aviation ministry in Togo off the ground.

Dennis and Diane Washer had resigned from ABWE for personal reasons, leaving the airplane and budding congregation in Kara to the Aldermans. An African pastor came alongside to help Randy adjust to using a translator in three different language groups, while Jeanette and the four children had their own adjustments to make.

"Mama, are we the only people who aren't black?" four-year-old Erin asked one day. The church met on their front porch and the children soon felt right at home, taking on the new language, eating new foods, climbing palm trees, and chasing stray goats.

Randy finally got his Togolese license to fly, but the Cessna 182 had once again been idle for some time, and after Randy did a thorough inspection, he wrote Hank to share a burden. "We think Togo needs a different plane. The 182 is only a four-seat aircraft and has more corrosion than we can repair, cost-effectively. We would like you to start looking around for a 185 or 206." It was agreed that the Cessna 182 would be sold and that Hank would begin searching for a replacement.

Meanwhile, God blessed the Aldermans in their church ministries. To accommodate the increased numbers in attendance, they doubled the size of their building (they held church in the airplane hangar) and built twenty new benches.

"These kinds of church problems I do not mind," Randy commented in a letter to praying friends. "We have finished a building for our Lama and Kpindi churches and we are looking for a motorcycle to buy so we can send one of our young men to teach there each week. The two churches at Dapong are in the infant stage with many new believers."

Besides caring for their children and their home, Jeanette also put her nursing skills to work. "Guess what one of my patients told me today when I treated her pinkeye?" she asked Randy as she bustled between the stove and the dinner table. He knew that Jeanette had been busy home-schooling two of their kids and working for several weeks with the epidemic of pinkeye rampant in Togo. "The witch doctor calls pinkeye *apollo*. He told her that when the Americans went to the moon with Apollo 11, they brought back the disease from the moon!"

"That's probably why she came to you. The witch doctor couldn't cure her and no doubt told her that since Americans brought *apollo* from the moon, and you are an American, only you have the cure."

After one exhausting automobile trip to the interior, Randy described his latest experience to the family. "With all the rain, the roads are impassable. Sure wish I could fly to Dapong. Can you guess why I'm late?" he asked.

"You had a flat tire," J.J., the oldest, guessed.

"I wish!" Randy winked at his wife and continued. "No, the car got stuck in the mud and the African AAA and I worked from five o'clock until after ten last night trying to get it out." He didn't want to stop and explain to the kids what AAA meant, so he hurried on with the story. "We gave up and slept in the bush."

Incredulous, Erin squealed, "Really, Daddy? You slept in the dark without Mommy?"

Randy nodded. "And I took a bath in a mud hole like the Togolese do. The nearest well was a mile away."

"Randy, did you have to say that? Little pitchers have big ears!" Jeanette objected.

Randy continued, "It took twenty-five guys to lift the car out of the mud, but we did it, and here I am." Beaming, he said, "The best part was that I got to share the gospel and five of the guys promised to come to Bible study."

Six months before their furlough, the Aldermans were seeing tremendous growth in their church plants despite great opposition and persecution from unbelievers, especially in the church at Dapong, where the parents of the church young people refused to feed their children for days because the children would not deny that they believed in Christ as Savior. Twice the congregation made mud bricks, only to have them destroyed by people who opposed the church. Randy was also involved in the construction of two other church buildings. Even without the capability to travel by airplane, God blessed their labors.

ROADBLOCKS TO AVIATION

Although Randy pursued every avenue possible, government rules and restrictions barred his getting to interior villages with an airplane. The political situation worsened, deterring progress, and he was unable to get permission to construct an airstrip at the hospital. Because of government restrictions, he couldn't put the Cessna 182 up for sale until August 1991. The funds were to be deposited with ABWE, reserved toward its replacement; but by this time, the field council had divided opinions about the usefulness of an aviation program in Togo. As their first furlough drew near, Randy and Jeanette went over and over the issues facing them, trying to make a decision regarding their future. They did not approach a change in ministry lightly, but they desired to use Randy's skill as a pilot to unreached remote villages. The airstrips where Randy intended to land had to be regulation length and width in order to meet the Togolese government's requirements, but these requirements would restrict his points of aviation evangelism to only the larger cities of Togo where transportation wasn't a problem.

During their furlough, Randy and Jeanette faced the age-old struggle to wait on the Lord after praying "to be filled with the knowledge of his will in all wisdom and spiritual understanding," from Colossians 1:9. Should they pursue the aviation ministry in Togo or transfer to another field? A year of furlough and distance from the work on the field would help them determine what to do. They asked for wisdom to discern and the patience to wait.

In July 1993, near the end of their furlough, the Aldermans determined that God wanted them back in Togo. They trusted God to supply a Cessna 206 airplane and the additional ministry funds for its operation.

During this time, Hank and his volunteer mechanics at the ABWE Airbase in Georgia had repaired and modified Cessna N25F, the wrecked tail dragger (a plane with a third wheel on the back) donated by Lee Talladay. ABWE pilot Scott Dewitt had been flying this aircraft in San Diego, California, while on furlough from Iquitos, Peru, and planned to fly it cross-country back to Georgia. To help Randy keep current in flight skills during his furlough, Hank encouraged him to get to California, have Scott check him out in the Cessna N25F, and fly it back to the air base. The extra time Scott and Randy spent practicing stalls, approaches, and various landing procedures helped to sharpen their skills before returning to mission field flying. This donated, damaged aircraft, returned to useful service by God's servant mechanics and those who supplied the money, symbolized God's many gifts to build the ABWE worldwide air ministry, a monument to His marvelous grace.

In March 1994, the Aldermans announced the further gift of a 1964 Cessna 206. Through his many contacts, Hank located the plane and made inquiry on a Monday; on Tuesday, he checked on the title search and mechanical condition; on Wednesday, Hank and Randy flew to San Antonio, Texas, inspected the aircraft, and purchased it for less than what they expected. With funds from the sale of the Cessna 182 in Togo, funds raised through the Aldermans' supporting churches and individuals, and funds from the sale of the A-36 Bonanza which had been donated earlier by the Hornes, the needed money was in hand.

By phone, Randy told Jeanette, "It's air worthy, but Hank will be making some modifications for Togo flying, and will probably strip and paint it. But, Lord willing, we'll have it finished, dismantled, and crated to ship in May."

At the air base, Hank and Randy had several assistants to get the 206 equipped and shipped to Togo. Clif Jensen, who now worked with Hank in Georgia, and Randy hauled the plane on a trailer to Jacksonville, Florida. As they unloaded it from the trailer down a board ramp, one of the boards slipped off the blocks and the front of the plane landed on Randy's shoulder, pinning him between the plane and trailer. In the emergency room, the doctor found no broken bones, but a badly bruised shoulder and back. Later, however, back in Togo, the ABWE missionary doctor discovered a torn cartilage in Randy's chest.

A UNIQUE HELPER

Hank anticipated that Randy would appreciate having an airplane mechanic to help reassemble the Cessna 206 in Togo, so he sent ABWE short-termer Bryan Wilson. Bryan was a student at Moody Aviation and an invaluable pilot-mechanic, and he had been traveling from field to field to help in aircraft maintenance. AMPers—short-term missionaries with special abilities and the gift of helping and serving—are greatly appreciated, invaluable to missionaries, and sought after for various ministries. Bryan was unique, with a sense of humor a mile long. He worked on six of our ABWE aviation fields and accomplished much within a two-year span. Following is an excerpt from a letter Bryan wrote to the pilots about his two years with ABWE:

First, I will start with "the inventor," Hank. Man, did I learn a ton about how to make things work, how to fly a small plane internationally and all the paper work involved, even how to catch a catfish on a trout line. What I admire most about Hank is that he can keep all you guys pretty well supplied on the technical end, run the hangar, be involved in ministry at Carver Bible College and church and still take time to show guys like me how to land a Taylorcraft.

Second, "the Sunday school class." I think normal people call them the Jensens? For me, their house was the "basement bed and breakfast." Man, I had a good time with these soccer fanatics. There was always a freezer full of ice cream and a dinner table full of laughs. Clif taught me about patience and how to stick with a task until it is finished and done right!

Third, "the petting zoo," or at least that is what I was when David Budd would sit in my lap and pet my beard like I was a chimpanzee. Perseverance. That is what I learned from the Budds. They have been starting an aviation ministry for two terms, and struggling through all sorts of things to get the aircraft into the mountains. Stick-to-itiveness is what the Budds have!

Fourth, "Mr. Dedicated," Randy Alderman. After eight years, he finally got an aircraft in Togo. Randy taught me that an awful lot of groundwork has to be done before you can get an aircraft imported. He also taught me how to drive around potholes at sixty miles an hour without spilling your iced tea!

Fifth, "the Donaldson's Amazon Inn." If you are in Iquitos, you have to stop in. Make sure that you don't give them more than twelve hours' notice, though. And if you stay there you have to go for a ride on the back of Kevin's 125cc motorcycle, in the rain, carrying two aircraft cylinders in old cardboard boxes. It's tons of fun! They taught me true hospitality.

Finally, no discussion of ABWE pilots would be complete without "crazy Al" Yoder. I am not sure I ever saw Al during the day. He was always moving so fast I just caught a slight breeze as he blew by me on his way to get the duct tape. Al taught me how to do ten things at once, and how to fly across the Caribbean without stopping in the Bahamas. I think I also must have learned another 110 uses for duct tape, as well as three good ways to kill yourself behind a ski boat.

After Bryan finished his degree at Moody Aviation, the Lord directed him to join Flying Mission (FM) and work in Botswana, maintaining and flying their six mission planes. Bryan is presently the Senior Aviation Manager for FM in both Botswana and Zambia.

TOGO'S FIRST MEDEVAC FLIGHT

Kay and Dal Washer worked together as missionaries in Togo from 1974 until Dal's death in 1989. Kay continued the work alone, and she returned one day to her home near Kpalimé from a trip to Kenya. She stepped up on the terrace, lost her balance, and fell backward. Loud snaps sounded as first one bone, and then a second, broke in her lower leg; the impact of the fall also broke her upper arm and shoulder.

Friends temporarily splinted Kay's broken leg with pillows and got her to the Karolyn Kempton Memorial Christian Hospital— an agonizing hour-long ride over pothole-ridden roads—but the missionary doctor there knew that the surgery needed to repair Kay's broken leg would have to be performed in the States. The only airline that would agree to transport her in this condition flew out of Accra, Ghana.

Knowing that Kay faced long hours and days of travel to the US, the hospital staff in Togo got her into a fifty-pound cast and designed tie belts to hold her in a standing position while she moved from plane to plane and down the aisles. In spite of the pain, Kay and a nurse colleague, Ann DenUyl, who went along on the trip, practiced in the hospital how Kay would travel on the plane. The first step would involve lifting Kay up into the airliner's cabin with the food service derrick.

"Oh, well," Kay said, swallowing her pride, "I'll try not to think about how I'll look!"

Once the hospital staff in Kaplimé had Kay ready for transport, the next hurdle was getting her to the airport in Accra, a trip which, just two months earlier, would have meant an eight- to ten-hour drive over more bumpy, pothole-ridden roads. Instead, the new airstrip at Kpalimé was now available, cutting travel time to Accra to just an hour and forty minutes by air.

While Randy removed the back seats from the Cessna 206 in order to get Kay on board, he asked, "Who would have dreamed, Grandma Kay, when you told me in 1980 how an airplane was needed in Togo for medical evacuations, that you would be the first to need it?"

Kay nodded, "God knew before we did how much we needed this medevac capability."

After taking a minute for prayer and goodbyes, the missionaries watched Randy taxi the plane to the far end of the airstrip, rev the engine, pick up momentum, and surge upward to the sky. The flight took forty minutes to Lome, then another hour across the border into Ghana to Accra, where Kay would be transferred to British Air.

Looking up at Randy from the stretcher on the tarmac in

Accra as the ambulance crew settled her, Kay affirmed, "The trip by road would have killed me. I couldn't have made it without you and the plane."

Randy nodded. "Thank the Lord for His provision. I'm glad I was here to help."

After airline transfers at London and Atlanta, with Ann DenUyl at her side to boost her morale and give her medical support, Kay was taken by van to her home in Greenville, South Carolina. After surgeries and painful, extensive therapy, plus a scare with a brain aneurysm, she recovered and has even returned to Togo twice on ministry trips.

Following this lifesaving event with the plane, Randy's flights kept him busy up in the air, and also on the ground with aircraft maintenance. His ministry to several village church plants demanded his attention and guidance before his upcoming furlough in 1998. It was a great loss when the Aldermans decided not to return to Togo with ABWE following their furlough.

NINETEEN

A RENEWED VISION FOR TOGO AVIATION

In that same year of 1997, Matt Cropsey, the son of ABWE missionary doctor Robert Cropsey of the mission hospital in Togo, and an aviation student at Bob Jones University, contacted Hank about aviation ministry. Matt spent the summer in Georgia as an ABWE short-termer, living in our home and assisting Hank at the air base, gaining hands-on mechanic experience and building flight hours. He tried to explain to me Hank's method of teaching:

> I was a new A & P and Hank asked me to put the engine baffles on the C-182 that he was converting over to a float-plane. He showed me the pile of parts supposed to go back on the engine and suggested that I sort through them and figure out where I thought they fitted. He left me to my own devices while he went to work at the house. An hour or two later when he checked in, he could see I couldn't make sense of the baffling. He told me enough to get me started and left again. Time passed and he reappeared to help me figure out where the next piece went. At the end of the day, the baffles were done. Hank encouraged me to always use my mind and think through things to come to a correct conclusion. He was a patient teacher.

During Matt's short-term service, Hank chose him to accompany Al Yoder to fly the Cessna floatplane CJG from Brazil to the Georgia air base for extensive overhaul. In this way, Matt could build flight hours and experience as co-pilot.

Matt and his new bride, Amanda (Mandy), wanted to restart the aviation program in Togo. In May 1998, Matt wrote: "Uncle Hank, the Togo Field Council members all agreed to give the aviation ministry one last go."

And in June, all three station councils voted to invite the Cropseys to Togo for one to two years, to see if an aviation ministry would fit with their latest goals and strategy. The following March, the Cropseys, Herman Teachout, and Hank traveled to Togo to review the possibilities of bringing the aviation ministry back on line. Matt and Mandy attended ABWE's 1999 Candidate Class, received their appointment, and launched into prefield ministry.

As an MK from Togo, Matt hoped to join the Togo team by the year 2001. However, he knew that the Cessna 206 in Kara had deteriorated after three years without use. It should first have a thorough inspection. In March 2000, Mandy's brother, Darrell Wood, and Joe Austin from Duncan Aviation, in Battle Creek, Michigan, volunteered to accompany Matt to check the Cessna's condition, make repairs, and list parts to replace.

After this inspection, other matters came up. Matt and his father, Dr. Bob Cropsey, met with a group of Togolese pastors to strategize how to incorporate medical/aviation evangelism with their goals for reaching Togo. They worked on a design for a hangar next to the hospital airstrip, digging footers in the hard, solid, red clay, laying all the rebar to support the structure, as well as pouring some of the concrete in the ground. A fellow missionary, John Teusink, would continue to oversee its completion, working alongside Ralph Gruenberg and a crew of volunteers.

During prefield ministry, while Mandy continued to teach in their church Christian elementary school, she also studied French, prompted by Matt, who was still fluent in this language. At the same time, Matt continued working full time at Eagle Aviation, Inc., in Columbia, South Carolina.

At the Tabatinga airport, the Piper Arrow is protected from the Amazon sun with the unique covering fabricated from a net intertwined with cloth strips.

Randy Alderman anchors the dismantled Cessna 206 to the trailer to be hauled to Jacksonville, Florida. From there it would be freighted by container to Togo, where it was reassembled for service.

During Hank's twelve weeks in a pelvic sling and leg boot under traction, he carried on his responsibilities, with Ruth's help, as director of ABWE aviation and professor of missions at Carver Bible College.

Glenn Budd and the PA-12 with the mountain dwellers of Pechuquiz, Peru.

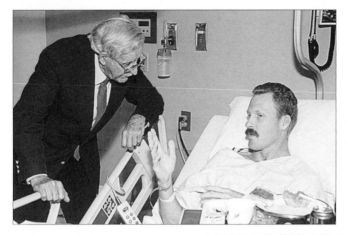

Hank Scheltema debriefs Kevin Donaldson at the hospital after Kevin and his family were transported from Iquitos to the US.

Below:
Papua New Guineans gather under the wing of the Cessna T206 on a remote mountain one-way strip in the Simbai Region. Herman Teachout listens to the excitement of the local folks while Bill Tobias translates.

Above:
Hank Scheltema inspects the Cessna 206, a former drug-runner that had been damaged in a forced landing.

After repairs and modifications on the drug-runner and other planes were completed, Melvin and Beverly Crowell came from St. Johns, Michigan, along with Melvin's brother and sister-in-law, to strip and paint the planes.

Tim Gainey, the beloved "Bird of Paradise," surrounded by the men at Bundi where he was filling in until Steve Aholt arrived from furlough.

Al Yoder and Matt Cropsey replace the damaged cylinder on the Cessna floatplane CJG after their forced landing on the Cuyuni River.

Al Yoder (left) and Matt Cropsey (right), stranded on the Cuyuni River, were rescued by Guyanian helicopter pilot Colonel Charles.

In March of 2000, a team of eleven men and one lady from Grace Baptist Church of Kankakee, Illinois, arrived in Benjamin Constant to build a floating house-hangar, for which they had raised over $22,000.

Left & Below:
Hand-sawed eight-inch-thick *maçaranduba* (ironwood) boards, over forty feet long, were nailed with three-foot-long spikes to the foundation of floating *açacú* logs, which resist decay even when immersed in water.

The floating house-hangar, completed and floated down the Amazon River to its new site on the Camatiã River, the gateway to a vast Ticuna Indian Reservation. Al and Kim Yoder live onboard and reach out to evangelize and disciple Ticuna believers in several communities.

A DIFFICULT DISCOVERY

In June 2000, Matt was loading an aircraft engine onto a truck and pulled muscles and ligaments in his back. After extensive physical therapy without progress, x-rays disclosed an hereditary condition in his back. Spondylolistheses leaves the overall structure of the back weak, and when muscles that keep the vertebrae in place are pulled, the vertebrae shift. The orthopedic back surgeon recommended several months of physical therapy, hoping that Matt could strengthen the muscles and correct the condition. An MRI, followed by a myelogram, showed two ruptured discs in Matt's lower back, which were the cause of his extreme back pain and would require extensive surgery. The ten-hour surgery involved entering from the front to remove the two ruptured discs and fuse the lumbar from L-4 down to S-1. The surgeon rolled Matt over to perform the same process from the other side. To stabilize the spine until the fusion became solid, six screws, two in each vertebra, and two rods along the fused vertebrae were inserted. Fusion material consisted of cadaver bone and pieces of Matt's hip bone.

Postoperative x-rays showed that the last screw inserted had pushed part of a bone graft out of place, so the whole surgery was redone two days later. Afterward, physical therapy continued for the next year and a half until Matt was able to go back to work. The therapist's assessment of Matt's capabilities limited him to lifting no more than seventy pounds. A week later, Matt experienced a setback and had to go back on painkillers.

Throughout the ups and downs of the next months, Isaiah 58:11 spoke to Matt. *And the Lord shall guide thee continually, and satisfy thy soul in drought, and make fat thy bones: and thou shalt be like a watered garden, and like a spring of water, whose waters fail not.* He testified that the Lord had placed him and Mandy in a desert where they found the Oasis, Christ, from which to draw life-sustaining water.

Prefield ministry had to be postponed because of the pain

Matt experienced riding in a car. How could they do the job in Togo, when Matt was in pain just trying to complete prefield? Complications indicated further surgery, but after more therapy with a pain clinic, Matt improved. By December 2002, Mandy gave an update on his situation:

> Matt has experienced some improvement since the pain therapist had him begin wearing a supportive belt daily. He still has leg pain, but the exercises have helped. We are not sure when he sees his surgeon again and believe that upon his surgeon's approval, he will be released. The cold weather is difficult for him since it causes his back and legs to hurt more. Thankfully, Africa has not historically been a cold field!

By mid-June 2004, the Cropseys and their two children, Matthew and Anna, completed all of the required shots, acquired passports, and got their airline tickets to Togo. They expressed their appreciation to churches and individuals who backed them through their "desert" experience by believing that the Lord still had a plan and purpose for them in Africa.

> After much prayer and consultation with the ABWE-Africa administrator and my parents, we decided to go back to Togo for a short term . . . to go through the airplane again and fix those items we had shipped parts out for. The plane had been relocated by truck in 2002 down to the hospital. It had been disassembled for the trip and needed to be put back together.

In November 2004, Matt reported that he had been able to tackle repairs at the hospital and, with his friend Joe Austin, piece the airplane back together and complete the engine work. Joe promised to work on getting his company to help refurbish interior items, while Matt installed an engine monitor and fuel flow system, along with an oil filter system. Matt worked to get the hangar doors in place so that the airplane could be locked inside the hangar when they left Togo.

His short term was not without spiritual fruit. Several of the hospital maintenance men with whom Matt held Bible studies were saved or recommitted their lives to Christ. On one occasion, he held a preaching and film night at the hangar. Over 200 villagers attended from the valleys surrounding the airstrip. The challenge of ministry in Togo thrilled his heart as he and the family returned to the US in time for Christmas and to continue prefield ministry in 2005.

Things thought to be life's greatest trials or tragedies are found to be God's way of bringing about something better. This chapter on ABWE Air ministry in Togo cannot be completed yet, and we trust that days of "something better" are ahead. Matt is presently on health leave of absence until doctors clear him to return to Togo. During this time, he is serving as Associate Pastor at his home church.

In September 2005, Matt traveled to Togo for two weeks with Ken and Ellen Fuss, who were seeking God's will as to where to serve, since the aviation ministry in Iquitos was closed. During their time in Togo, God burdened Ken's and Ellen's hearts to restart the aviation ministry there, and they are currently making plans to attend French language school in preparation for this ministry.

TWENTY

THE AMAZON—SPECIAL FLYING CONDITIONS

Flying and living in the Amazon revolved around water—either too much or too little. After two weeks without rain, the Javarizinho River, which flowed in front of the missionary residence at Benjamin Constant, Brazil, dropped more than fifty feet below its peak level. As the river emptied, the floating hangar had to be resituated two or three times a day to keep it afloat. The Javarizinho, landlocked because both the source and the mouth were blocked by silt, endangered the hangar that straddled the dried-up riverbed. Tom Peace, Clif Jensen, and Al Yoder, in turn, watched this phenomenon each year. Since they were unable to take off or land the floatplanes during the several weeks when the river was too low, they used that downtime to make repairs on aircraft or hangar.

When it rained, it poured a translucent curtain of water that made flying VFR (Visual Flight Rules) impossible, and we did not have the capability to fly IFR (Instrument Flight Rules). If caught in bad weather with a general thick overcast, the pilots flew low above the water or landed on the river to wait out the rain. It sometimes meant tying up alongshore to spend the night.

Tom Peace related two bad-weather experiences that were common to missionary pilots on the Amazon:

> On a flight from the hospital to Fonte Boa, I had to land on the river and wait it out. Brazilians and Ticunas came by in their canoes and lingered by the plane. This gave a good opportunity to witness and give them a tract. Life for river people moves at a slower pace and something new like an

airplane is worth investigating. Then the weather cleared and I was able to fly on.

Another flight I made with Paul Schlener. We left on a Sunday morning with heavy clouds, but had no problems and arrived at Santa Rita, had the morning service and great fellowship. Paul wanted to get back, so we took off right after the services. We ran into a bad storm and had to land in the middle of the river. We drifted until we got into the weeds by the shore and anchored there about three hours. We thought we might have to spend the night in the plane, but arrived home at 4:30 p.m.

Al Yoder also had stories about flying in Amazon rainstorms. He was once detained until after lunch to load and transport five summer missionaries (AMPers), students from various US colleges, back to Benjamin Constant from Iquitos, Peru. Thunderstorms built up in the afternoon; he wished he could have left earlier.

At the far end of his flight, Al knew trouble was brewing when he spotted a boiling, black wall ahead, ablaze with flashing lightning. He climbed higher to check the storm's height. *Too high,* he thought. *Can't get around it. Gotta get under it. Gotta keep the river in sight.* One thought after another moved him to act as he turned to land on the Peruvian side of the river. The AMPers were reading or dozing, unaware of what Al faced, until a prestorm updraft blasted the plane and their heads banged the roof. Then the wind at the floatplane's rear pushed it down to a splash landing and across the choppy waves toward shore.

Al pointed to the storm and yelled over his shoulder. "Get the paddle and rope ready, guys. I'm heading for that cleared area ahead. We've got to move fast to get the plane tied down before the storm hits us."

Within minutes, the pilot and passengers moored the plane and climbed back into the cabin, out of the blustering wind. The violent waves tossed, rocked, and bounced the plane in every direction, while the five AMPers leaned forward to listen as Al tuned in the amateur radio secured above his head. He explained, "It's time for radio contact," then put the microphone to his mouth. "PP8 ZKY. PP8 ZKY. Are you in there, Kim?" Al waited and tried Kim's call letters again.

Hank's voiced boomed loud and clear, "WA4 VSP reporting in."

Al smiled over at Joel Jefferis, one of the AMPers. "Good old faithful Hank."

"PP8 ZPA. Here's WA4 VSP. I'm not picking up Kim either, Al. I'll give her another try. PP8 ZKY. PP8 ZKY. Here's WA4 VSP. Are you in there, Kim?"

There was a pause.

"Nothing heard, Al," Hank said.

"Must be her electricity's gone off. Same old problem in Benjamin Constant."

"What's going on? Is everything okay?" Hank asked. "Shall I give Kim a call on the land line? Do you want me to let her know not to look for you before tomorrow morning?"

"Sure. Tell her to check in at 6 a.m. radio time. I hope we'll be airborne and be there for breakfast. Hey! Here comes the rain. PP8 ZPA. Going clear."

By now, Al faced a new dilemma. The violent wind had loosened the once taut rope that secured the plane. One wing bumped against a thorn tree, and the branches clawed and scratched the recent paint job.

"I'm going to cut us loose to drift, Joel," he told one of the AMPers, who had his private flying license. Keep your feet ready on the rudders!" He pushed out of the door and walked forward on the float. Reaching to yank out the paddle used to anchor and tie up the plane, he lost his balance, leaned against the thorn tree, and fell off the float into the seething river. Two AMPers scrambled to pull him out and get him back in the cabin.

Al, drenched and shivering, let the swift current take over while he steered with his feet on the rudders. Joel took pity on him and worked to pull the stout thorns out of Al's head, shoulder, and arm. In between "ouches," Al informed the AMPers of his next move.

"The floats are taking on a lot of water. I'm heading across the river to the windward side where the trees will help shield us and the waves will be less damaging." His hand on the throttle, he peered through the curtain of rain, checking the distant shoreline for a clearing. It all looked the same—a solid tangle of vines and overhanging tree limbs, poised to puncture the wings or damage the fuselage. Al gritted his teeth, pushed the throttle, kicked the right rudder, and shouted, "Well, here goes. We have to anchor this baby soon and get the floats pumped out."

By the time the plane had been moored again, Al's teeth were chattering. Hypothermia had set in. The two girls, the only passengers with extra clothing, offered Al a clean, dry T-shirt and jeans. All six, weary and apprehensive, scrunched down in their seats to pass the night.

At last the storm passed, the wind quieted, and it got hot inside the cabin. Two of the guys climbed up and slept on the wings. Al felt responsible for the five young people and the mission plane, exposed overnight in terrorist waters and what was known as "drug-runner's alley."

Dawn brought another hard-earned lesson for Al. The guys were pumping out the floats before takeoff, and as one AMPer climbed out to help, the pump was accidentally kicked. It landed in the swift current and sailed out of reach. Without a spare pump, they had to figure out how to take off with excessive water weight in the float compartments.

When Al tried to take off, the engine groaned as it strained to plow through the water without breaking free. "Lean forward as far as possible," Al yelled above the roar. "And when I pull on the yoke, rock back and forth with the motion of the plane. We've got to rock and roll in order to break free of the water's drag to get up on the step."

Al was sweating profusely from the exertion but, at last, a slight breeze gave some lift—just enough. A sigh of relief was heard as the floatplane picked up momentum, slid across the rippling waves, and went airborne. From then on, Al stored an extra float pump in the plane and made every effort to schedule flights early in the day to avoid the afternoon weather.

MORE CHALLENGING THAN THE WEATHER

Different challenges faced new aviation missionary Michael Chiano. Michael had majored in missionary aviation at Grand Rapids School of the Bible and Music and a summer in the Amazon as an AMPer before he applied to ABWE and received appointment in 1979. He met and married Teresa Boice, a former missionary to the Amazon, and in mid 1985, after language study, Michael, Teresa, and Jeremy, their adopted Brazilian son, arrived in Benjamin Constant.

Although Michael arrived ready to fly the Amazon floatplanes, he met with disappointment. With no pilots on the field, the Brazilian Amazon aviation program was immobile. The situation was frustrating for Michael—even more aggravating than having to fly around thunderstorms.

Hank had advised Michael of the scenario awaiting him. Clif Jensen had left for furlough earlier than originally planned, and Tom Peace had been delayed in the States because of his wife Beth's emergency back surgeries. Because of this, Hank flew commercial airlines from Georgia to Benjamin Constant, gave Michael his flight check in the floatplane, and listed directions for Tom, as senior pilot, to help Michael build proficiency. Before Tom returned from furlough, Michael had obtained his Brazilian flying license. Taking PT-DNY up one day, Michael smelled a fuel leak and aborted his takeoff. Removing the cowling, he located a fuel leak due to a leaking O-ring on the fuel gasculator. It was a serious leak, and he had no O-ring to repair it. That was the last time Michael had DNY up in the air because the plane was no longer air worthy. From then on, Michael's contribution to the aviation program would lie in his abilities as a mechanic.

By the time Tom returned to the field, both twenty-year-old planes needed top overhaul—that is, the engine cylinders would have to be removed and rebuilt before official inspection and clearance to fly could be received. But the pilots waited for months for the float struts to be delivered. Exasperated, Tom finally started to reorder them when he received a telephone call. "The plane struts are *where?*" he exclaimed. "In the customs office in *Bogotá?*" The shippers had addressed the struts to Bogotá instead of Leticia, and wanted US $1,500 in duty tax, although Tom had paid only US $1,100 for them originally. Tom eventually sorted out the situation, but not until the struts were returned to the factory and reshipped to Leticia. It required a lot of patience, paper work, and persistence.

Finances to pay for the needed replacement parts on the planes became an issue, as did getting those parts to the Amazon. By December 1986, Michael, frustrated and disappointed that he could not fly, explained to his praying friends that the planes were still inoperable:

> . . . we haven't been able to fly for many months due to a gasoline leak and need of some new bolts. They have been ordered and shipped but we don't know where they are. We hope they are not "lost."

Another letter dated March 1987 stated:

> I woke up today as usual before 6 a.m. to give myself a few minutes to clear my head before talking to one of our single missionaries by radio. We do this every day (no tele-

phone service worth using) to see how she is doing and to pass messages and bits of news. Ordinarily we would use the plane to visit her and the other missionaries if there existed a problem or emergency but since the plane is unusable because we still need a few parts, we could only pray.

Before their furlough in April 1987, Michael wrote:

I'm still hoping to put our plane back in shape before furlough. Teresa has stepped out of her Sunday school class in anticipation of our leaving and I am using my boat with another Brazilian brother to visit a town one hour away where years ago he and another pilot were beginning to establish a work.

In 1981, during prefield ministry, doctors had diagnosed Michael with familial polyposis, a hereditary condition. They found 200 polyps in ten inches of intestine. Almost the entire colon was removed, and after checkups, the number and size of polyps existing in the remaining portion of colon decreased. The doctor cleared Michael to serve in Brazil, but on his furlough, a medical exam in June 1987 revealed another polyp. Then doctors discovered that their son, Jeremy, had a heart murmur. Although these trials alone did not lead them to consider other options for their future, the Chianos, after a year's leave of absence, tendered their resignation from ABWE.

A FIELD LACKING WORKERS

Until Clif Jensen returned from furlough, Tom needed a second pair of hands to make repairs on the planes, especially with riveting. One day, Beth agreed to help him fix a hole next to the battery box. Tom filed the hole, cut the aluminum for the patch, and called Beth to hold the "bucking" bar.

"Watch it now," he warned her. "Get a good grip on it, because this bar may be an innocent looking piece of metal, but it lives up to its name when the rivet gun hits it."

Beth gripped it with both hands and held on tight, but it still took awhile for her teeth to quit chattering when they finished the riveting. What would missionary pilots do without their spunky wives? Beth, like most pilots' wives, wore various caps, over and above the usual call of duty.

By September 1987, with repairs sufficient to get them airborne, the Peaces flew CJG downriver for a prearranged VBS at several Ticuna villages. Afterward at the floating hangar, Tom noticed oil on the plane's belly and tore into the engine to find a couple of oil leaks. He had to replace a broken muffler where a previous weld had not held. Locating what was broken wasn't a problem; getting its replacement was.

Clif, who had arrived back from furlough, got on the amateur radio and located a muffler in São Paulo, 3,000 miles southeast of Benjamin Constant. They waited two weeks to get the muffler by mail, then found they had insufficient money to pay for it. Since the other floatplane, DNY, was still down for repairs, the pilots confiscated its muffler to put on CJG in order to keep one aircraft airborne. Opportunities opened to fly to preaching points where several received the Lord and were baptized.

At this time, liability insurance was still draining the pilots' work funds. But Tom, an optimist, wrote to praying partners, "Please pray for the funds needed to keep these planes working. Our funds keep going down but we are *looking up!*"

Where else would one look in times of great need? *I will lift up mine eyes unto the hills, from whence cometh my help. My help cometh from the Lord* (Psalm 121:1,2a).

TWENTY-ONE ⊬

HELP ARRIVES

June 1988 rolled around—and God sent help. In fact, circumstances had begun to change on that unforgettable night during the conference in Benjamin Constant, when Al whispered to Kim, "God wants us to work in the Amazon."

By January 1989, the Yoders moved from Bahia to Benjamin Constant, Amazonas, during the time that the Peaces were on furlough. The Brazilian pastor had left for another church below Manaus, leaving the ministry in Benjamin Constant once again in the missionaries' hands. Al and Clif preached every other month at Benjamin Constant and held services at river preaching points. Al expanded the youth work to include retreats and camps. The pilots agreed to build a youth center on the mission property located on the Javarizinho River. Al did the major part of building this center with the help of short-term teams, including one from Shawnee Baptist Church in New Jersey.

The Yoders had occupied the mission house on the Javarizinho and were using the Peaces' household furnishings while they were on furlough. So when Tom and Beth returned, both families lived together in one house for six weeks, while the Peaces gathered their belongings to move 160 miles east, to Santo Antonio do Içá, where the Amazon Baptist Hospital was short on staff and in need of their help.

At the same time they were packing to move, they also packed separate suitcases for their sons, Lloyd and Philip, who were heading off to boarding school. Tom arranged boat travel for the boys from Benjamin Constant to Manaus, and from there by commercial airliner to Fortaleza—thousands of miles away from home. Years later, after Bible training, both Lloyd and Phillip would be appointed, along with their wives and children, to ABWE missionary work in the Amazon. Lloyd is now training to fly one of the floatplanes his father once piloted.

Once the Peaces settled near the hospital in Santo Antonio do Iça, Beth helped by using her nursing skills, and Tom, an all-around mechanic, had lots of equipment, boats, and houses to repair and maintain. Tom hoped to build a floating plane hangar near the hospital property in a protected river port on a tributary of the Amazon. Both Tom and Beth were involved in multiple responsibilities in Santo Antonio do Iça, and also ministered at two river towns, each within two hours by speedboat. The response at these two towns, in works started by hospital person-nel and Brazilian evangelists, blessed them: 100 attended at one place and about sixty at the other. Many came to Christ, and the Peaces taught and encouraged them.

The plan to base a plane in Santo Antonio do Iça never mate-rialized, and Tom and Beth withdrew from active participation in aviation. However, God continued to bless and use them in their work at the hospital and in their ministry to the Ticuna Indians at Betania, through the boat ministry from Santo Antonio do Iça to small settlements up and down the Amazon.

LICENSED TO FLY

By this time, Clif Jensen had finally received his Brazilian pilot's license, and wrote:

> Since that happy day, we've poured many gallons of avia-tion fuel through the chamois filter to keep our Cessna 185 seaplane in action. One flight was to medevac a victim of an alligator attack to the hospital in town. Each Sunday for the past month, we've been holding meetings fifteen minutes away where forty folks are gathering with us for worship and Bible teaching.

Clif was also discipling Jacó, a faithful young man from Benjamin Constant who went off to the ABWE seminary in Natal and returned after graduation to pastor the Baptist church in Santo Antonio do Iça. Clif and Al finished repairs on both floatplanes and got them relicensed after official inspection. Only the aircraft mechanics that came from the States to help can appreciate the astronomical job this was, working twelve-hour days to rebuild the floats. Clif wrote:

For the past twenty-one years the aluminum hulls of these floats have made hundreds and hundreds of takeoffs and landings on the Amazon and its tributaries. As much as we pilots try to avoid it, a stick of wood or a barely submerged log will appear in the path of the plane. Each bump and thump against the bottom of the floats affects the performance and safety of the plane until it becomes necessary to replace the metal "skin." What a fantastic time we had with Jim, Buddy, and Tom (Delta Airline mechanics) as we drilled, pounded, cut, riveted, and painted these twenty-one-year-old "canoes" and gave our Cessna PT-DNY a new lease on life. They perform great!

Stripping paint and dismantling doors and propeller for a complete new paint job on PT-CJG progressed at the same time as a major reformation of the twenty-seven-year-old floating hangar. A crew of Brazilians removed flooring, replaced beams and joists that held the huge floating logs together, and dismantled and rebuilt the entire maintenance shop so that it was ready to relicense as a Brazilian-approved aircraft repair station. During this time, Al also obtained his Brazilian Inspection Authorization (IA). Taking these steps would save the money and time consumed in the six-hour flight to Manaus for annual aircraft inspections. The pilots would be allowed to repair the planes, and Al and Hank could sign them off as air worthy. Due to federal regulations for a licensed shop, these steps also affected many former, relaxed customs regarding the use of the floating hangar. Brazilians and missionaries alike, who had once used the hangar to store boats and lumber, do laundry, take baths, and swim, now had to be restricted so as not to hazard losing the hangar's shop status. Everything had to be in continual readiness for the discriminating federal inspectors.

FUEL PROBLEMS

Constant over decades, the problem of fuel acquisition encumbered the Amazon aviation ministry. Even the military base in Tabatinga received only limited shipments of aviation gas, and frequently only after a six-month wait. Only specially-licensed boats were permitted to transport fuel, and by the time the fuel reached Benjamin Constant after a 1,000-mile river trip, the cost per fifty-gallon drum was out of reach. Each pilot stocked his own barrels and ordered fuel months in advance. This meant the pilots needed to raise large deposits of money to pay these expenses. Whereas in the 1960s and 1970s, Hank and Terry Bowers had required flight costs to be paid in aviation fuel, now, because fuel was so difficult to get, payments had to be in cash. Drug traffickers, who hijacked small aircraft, now stole filled barrels from the ABWE storage shed or siphoned gas from the wing tanks on the floatplanes. After each flight, the pilots took care to secure the airplanes with a prop chain, a throttle lock, and locks on gas caps. Hi-tech alarm systems had to be installed to safeguard the fuel supply and the floatplanes from the traffickers.

After the Yoders left for furlough and before the Jensen's arrival in May, 500 gallons of ABWE's aviation fuel, valued at over $2,000, was stolen, and Clif had to ration the remaining fuel. He squeezed in a flight to pick up a Brazilian pastor ministering in Indian villages about forty-five minutes downriver. On the same flight, he brought a snakebite victim to the hospital. But the fuel situation continued to worsen, as Hannah reported in her letter of January 1993:

> The fuel for the planes is almost gone and there is still no response on the request Clif made to buy more. Permission must be given from the government each time we buy fuel. He resubmitted the request so hopefully something will be done about it soon. There is one barrel for sale next door in Peru for a very high price. Who knows, maybe it is the gas that was stolen from us in May! It's more than likely "hot."

The missionaries questioned whether it was wise to store a large stock of fuel. It seemed to put the ministry at risk, in light of the drug trafficking in that area. Benjamin Constant was located on the river which had become the highway for speedboats running drugs between Peru and Colombia, and aviation fuel was in demand to process cocaine. Would it be best to relocate the planes to a different and safer area of ministry? Hank and the Amazon pilots searched for answers, but it was an ongoing problem.

Hank not only received information from Mission Safety International, but also from the International Association of Missionary Aviation (IAMA.). Al Meehan, of IAMA, supplied regular updates on risky areas in the world where missionaries need to be informed of crime, terrorists, guerrilla fighting, and drug activity. Hank felt that the Amazon aviation program needed a security contingency plan, and he began to work on it.

MORE CHANGES AHEAD

Hannah Jensen had been busy hosting short-term helpers from the US, both airplane mechanics and those who came to help build a camp and a cement game court for youth and AWANA in back of the church. The Jensens had designed and built an apartment adjacent to their house where Hannah hosted their guests and home-schooled all five of their children.

But now, David and Sarah Jensen would be seniors in high school following the Jensens' upcoming furlough. Hannah and Clif, concerned about their children's future, considered the various options commonly faced by missionaries in similar situations. In the end, the Jensens departed for furlough in June 1990, content to wait on the Lord for guidance, which came when the ABWE Board agreed to extend their furlough a year so they could see David and Sarah through high school graduation. (The Yoders, to give the Jensens this freedom, opted to remain on the field a fifth year.) In May 1992, the Jensen family returned to the Amazon, but David and Sarah, who had enrolled at Moody Bible Institute, stayed only until August, when they left for college.

While Clif left for Manaus to get the medical exam required for his pilot's license, Hannah and the children settled back into their house to get ready for a large youth team (composed of over twenty people) from Johnson City, Tennessee, which was due on June 13. This group came to minister to the Benjamin Constant church and other ABWE stations with music, puppetry, and films. Though the Jensens were unaware of it, God was working behind this event to direct them to their future ministry, three years ahead.

Meanwhile, the Jensens were still grappling with their most difficult decision—how best to care for their children. Daily they grew more confident that God was directing them to leave the Amazon. Another factor in their decision was Clif's belief that the church in Benjamin Constant needed to be more independent. If he stayed, the church would continue to rely on him. So the family returned stateside, trusting a sovereign God to guide them.

By August 1993, the Jensens completed the transition from Brazil to an expanded ministry in the aviation department at the air base in Concord, Georgia. Clif served as Aviation Ministries

Specialist to assist Hank in servicing ABWE pilots by procuring and providing aircraft replacement parts, visiting fields to evaluate ministries and provide pilot substitution, and helping to rebuild and modify aircraft for needed fields. Since Clif was a certified flight instructor, he was available at the air base to give pilots their refresher training and evaluations.

Hank had work outlined for Clif and himself—a trip by commercial airlines to Brazil. A salvage company in Griffin, Georgia, sold a Helio Courier, damaged in Port Velho, Brazil, to ABWE, but someone had to fly there, repair it, and fly it back to Georgia. God cared for Hank and Clif on that grueling assignment—five days to repair the Helio for the thirty-hour flight and five days with a tail wind speeding them back home. In order to get it back to the US, Hank had to negotiate its release from the Brazilian military and inspect the plane for flight ability.

During this experience, a Brazilian Air Force sergeant, Henrique Silva, who had been unjustly imprisoned, was released just to help get the Helio through the clearing process. This time with Henrique gave Hank a chance to witness. In a letter written in September 1993, Henrique commented on his encounter with Hank:

I know tonight the dark thinking of suicide will come again, but I encountered an extraordinary old man who told me the truth and gave me a Bible as a good-bye present. It eased those feelings and the pain. The man who unjustly accused me came to visit and regretted his action. I asked no revenge and in the hands of the Lord I put my troubles. I did nothing for Hank, the wonderful, fantastic and simple old man, but he opened my heart.

In God's providence, Henrique Silva was later proved innocent and transferred to work at the military base at Tabatinga,

Amazonas, where he helped the ABWE pilots in various ways.

Two months later, Clif went to Peru to help Glenn Budd, who had damaged his aircraft on a newly built airstrip on a 5,000-foot-high mountain plateau. Phil Bowers, an ABWE MK and mechanic with Continental Airline, volunteered to help them. Clif also conducted Glenn's accident debriefing and flight safety review. Six days later, Glenn flew the repaired PA-12 from the isolated airstrip where the incident had occurred, to its home base in Chiclayo. As they prepared to return to Chiclayo by land, Clif and Phil were detained and interrogated by the Federal Police and released only at the insistence of the US Embassy in Lima. Clif told Hank, "Sounds scary, but it was a God-given opportunity to tell those police officers of the life-changing gospel of Jesus Christ. Amen!"

Clif arrived home with pneumonia and pleurisy, but after his recovery, he spent hours working on flight skills with ABWE pilots Randy Alderman and Steve Aholt, repainting the Cessna 206 for Togo, and then hauling it to Jacksonville, Florida, for shipping to Africa. Meanwhile, the turbocharged Cessna T206A (the former drug-runner), had had several major rebuild modifications for flying the mountain heights of Papua New Guinea, and it now needed to be tested and flown to work out any "bugs."

Short-term aircraft mechanics Herman Teachout, Bryan Wilson, Scott Resnick, and David Holmes also gave days and weeks to get these aircraft rebuilt and airborne. Melvin and Beverly Crowell, experts in auto refinishing, came from St. Johns, Michigan, to repaint the aircraft. These were busy days at "Hank's hangout and Ruth's restaurant" as God supplied extra hands to accomplish His tasks.

During the summer of 1996, after much prayer, Clif and Hannah determined to make a major change in ministry focus—from aviation to camp ministry at Doe River Gorge, Elizabethton, Tennessee. Looking back, the Jensens realized the importance of that contact with the director of the camp in 1992 when he had brought his youth group to minister in Benjamin Constant. Clif explained:

Our years in Brazil were very valuable as resource mate-rial for the camp ministry with which we are involved. One of its goals is to help mature young Christians get a vision of service in a missionary capacity. This was one of the rea-sons the director of Doe River Gorge Camp (the director who took the short-term group to Benjamin Constant in June of 1992) desired our contributions on the Doe River staff team. We have grown in directions never imagined in our Christian lives in this ministry. It's a different dynamic than an aviation ministry in a foreign setting, but much of what we learned and experienced in Brazil has been trans-ferred here.

TWENTY-TWO

ABWE AIR GOES TO PERU WITH NEW RECRUITS

Summer assistant missionary programs (AMP) for college students may be beneficial in more ways than one. Kevin and Bobbi Donaldson discovered this on their AMP trip to Peru in the early 1980s. Kevin wrote about his decision to go on an AMP trip:

> In high school my desires for an exciting career narrowed down to one in aviation, and what better place to start than flying exciting Air Force jets? Then I talked to Dr. Kempton at a winter camp retreat, and I saw I could serve the Lord and not have to give up my desires to be a pilot. After my junior year at Piedmont Bible College, I returned to Peru (where I had grown up as an ABWE MK) on AMP.

During this AMP trip, Kevin met his future bride, Bobbi Bingman. She had been intent on an engineering career, but when she heard the idea of using her technical abilities to gain entry into closed countries, she wanted to learn about missions firsthand. When an ABWE missionary described AMP at her church, Bobbi applied to go to Peru. She not only saw that technical training and an interest in missions could be combined in full-time ministry, she also found her life's partner.

After their appointment by ABWE in 1983 to Iquitos, Peru, the Donaldsons' sending church delegated them to revisit the field and learn all that might be required of a missionary pilot, both by the Peruvian government and by the missionary field council. This trip opened their eyes to the official requirements

of the Peru Department of Transportation and the Civil Aeronautics Administration. The aircraft (which they trusted the Lord
to provide) needed to be registered in Peru, and the paperwork
might take three years. All aviation tests would be in Spanish;
extensive physicals would be required; all mechanical work
would be inspected by a licensed Peruvian. Bobbi was pleased to
learn that her education and experience in engineering could
open the door to reach university students, a basis for church
planting among the middle class people. Before they returned
home, the Donaldsons took steps to begin registering ABWE as
a "flying entity" in Peru. Their trip confirmed the Lord's leading
to Iquitos, but, at the same time, they realized that missionary
work was not all glamour; it would entail hard work.

By September 1985, with financial needs supplied, Kevin was
ready to take his prefield flight training and evaluation with
Missionary Aviation Fellowship. However, this was not in preparation for Peru, but for a short stint in the Philippine Islands.
After clearing this "detour" with their supporting churches, the
Donaldsons had decided to go ahead with plans to fill in for a
year on the island of Leyte during David Nelson's furlough.

That same year, Scott DeWitt* and Hank began corresponding. Scott was a young family man with ten years of experience
as a youth pastor and two years of experience with Baptist Mid-
Missions in the Chad, and he was seeking to meet the requirements to become a missionary pilot. He and his wife, Robin,
graduated from Grand Rapids Baptist College before their short-
term service with Baptist Mid-Missions, and were now attending Miramar College and the School of Missionary Aviation at
San Diego Christian College to complete Scott's technical training for an A & P license. Scott had his private flying license, so
Hank encouraged him to build his flight time and get experience

---

*Another Scott DeWitt, along with his wife, Danielle, presently works with ABWE in
Paraguay. He is no relation to the Scott DeWitt mentioned above.

working on small aircraft. Scott and Robin applied themselves to the task, and they stood for appointment to Iquitos, Peru, in ABWE's 1987 Candidate Class. The Lord provided their financial partners and, by spring of 1989, the DeWitts completed Spanish language study. Scott earned his seaplane rating in a Super Cub floatplane on the Colorado River and, in July, completed his prefield flight evaluation and specialized maintenance training with MAF in California. Scott's excitement was contagious!

I am excited about stepping into a work where we are wanted and needed! I am excited about becoming part of a work that has been established for over 30 years! I am excited about working with the 24 plus students in our Peruvian Bible Institute—taking them out on campaigns, giving them firsthand experience in evangelism and discipleship, and then placing them in those newly established works as pastors and leaders. I am excited about flying an amphibious aircraft where a safe landing is always in sight! I am excited about joining with another pilot, Kevin Donaldson, someone with whom to share the load in piloting, maintenance, expense, etc. I am excited that there is an MK school and teacher on the field to teach our four children.

Meanwhile, the Donaldsons arrived back from their fill-the-gap assignment in the Philippines and traveled to Iquitos in ample time for Bobbi to birth their second son, Gregory, on November 24, 1988. Although Hank had located a Cessna 185, which would be registered in Peru as OB-1408, for Iquitos by this time, he, Scott DeWitt, and other assistants didn't complete the engine overhaul until the following summer. While they were at it, they mounted the floats and installed a Robertson STOL kit, wingtip fuel tanks, and a radio. But they faced a major setback when they discovered a cracked crankshaft. Again God blessed, and by the time the Cessna was ready to make the trip down to Iquitos, He provided the money to cover all expenses through the Donaldsons' and DeWitts' churches and individuals, as well as the volunteer mechanics to do the work.

While Scott worked with Hank in Georgia on the Cessna, Kevin collected building materials for the hangar project he had initiated. It would be built at the Iquitos city airport, to protect the mission plane that was tied down outside, exposed to the elements, vandalism, and theft. A team of thirteen dedicated people from the First Baptist Church of Ogden, Pennsylvania, spent two weeks building this hangar. Because the Cessna had amphibious floats, it could not only land and take off from the water, but also from regular airstrips, which was why it could be hangared at the airport.

The latter 1980s saw the culmination of what Hank had envisioned for Iquitos and coastal Peru. After a second survey made in the mission's Cessna turbo 210 in January 1979, Hank had presented his recommendations to the Board of ABWE to approve not only Iquitos, but also coastal Peru, for aviation ministry. He had also visited Don and Vivian Bond and Andy and Diane Large, who worked in Nasca and Ica in southwest Peru, two towns where most roads were unimproved and hazardous to travel, and towns above 10,000 feet in the Andes Mountains that were very difficult to get to.

Hank recommended that a small, fabric-covered aircraft be used to reach these places, one with short takeoff and landing capabilities, high-altitude performance, and simple and less-costly maintenance and repair requirements. This was when the 1976, tornado-wrecked 1948 Piper Super Cruiser (the PA-12) was taken out of the basket for repair and modification to fly the Andes Mountains.

Slowly over the years, the parts and pieces came together, rebuilt with the help of dozens of volunteers. While Hank supervised the preparation of the Cessna amphibian floatplane for Iquitos, he also engineered work on the PA-12. After covering the wings and fuselage with fabric, they installed a new larger engine, as well as larger wheels and tires so that the plane could be flown off rough surfaces. They modified the wings to have flaps, which gave the plane even slower takeoff and landing speed, and also altered the inside of the fuselage to include an interior compartment to accommodate a stretcher for medevac patients.

PREPARING THE WORKERS

During the late 1970s, God had been preparing Glenn and Dorothy Budd to fly this unique "rag-wing" aircraft. (A fabric-covered airplane has a fuselage made of steel tubing, and is also called a "pipe and rag" airplane.) First, the Lord moved Glenn from New York, after high school and Word of Life Bible Institute, to Christian Heritage College in San Diego, where he met Californian Dorothy Gilmore, who was also a student. With Glenn's Bachelor of Science in Aviation and Missions and Dorothy's degree in Elementary Education in hand, they married and applied to ABWE. They were appointed to pioneer an aviation ministry for the ABWE Coastal-Peru field, spending their first term in Ica and their second in Chiclayo.

In July 1987, the Budds and their two little daughters arrived in Lima to begin immigration, orientation to a new culture, and the complicated process of paperwork for the importation of the PA-12.

After Glenn visited one difficult-to-reach mountain town, eight-and-a-half hours by car as compared to twenty-five minutes by plane, he grew even more eager to get the PA-12 into action. Glenn spent the next year working full time with aviation officials and lawyers to obtain an operating license for ABWE in Peru and to import the plane.

While they waited for the plane, the Budds moved to the

coastal town of Ica, four hours south of Lima. They started working with ABWE missionaries Dave and Evelyn Stone in church-strengthening ministries such as the seminary, camp, and local Baptist congregations.

THE PA-12 FLIGHT TO PERU

On December 14, 1988, a flight of two aircraft departed from Concord, Georgia. Why two planes? The PA-12 would be flying over hostile territories, and long distances over water, without long-range navigational equipment, so it needed to be accompanied. At first, Hank had planned to fly the Iquitos Cessna 185 OB-1408 amphibious floatplane in formation with the PA-12. He thought the 185 was ready to fly, but when he discovered it had a cracked crankshaft, he opted to fly the Bonanza A-36 instead. Kay and I went along to serve as stewardesses, serving snacks and cold drinks. Delta Airline captain, Phillip LaBerge, our neighbor and long-standing partner with ABWE Air, took the controls of the yellow Piper PA-12 and flew alone.

One problem facing the two pilots was the tremendous disparity in the performance of these two aircraft. The Piper PA-12's capability was 100 miles per hour under the best conditions; the A-36 could barely fly that slowly. To maintain formation speed in flight next to the slower Piper PA-12, Hank would have to handle the A-36 much as if he were balancing on a barely moving bicycle. After trials to test compatibility, the pilots repitched the Piper's propeller for a bit more airspeed and installed large wheel pants taken from Phillip's Stinson Voyager aircraft. This added another five knots to the PA-12. Hank engineered a fuel system using two thirty-gallon plastic barrels that fit on the seat behind Phillip. He plumbed the barrels to drain from the upper to the lower tank and through a pump run by the aircraft battery that would push the fuel up into the right wing tank. He and Phillip also installed oxygen in a small bottle on the floor next to the pilot, because the planes would be flying at altitudes above 10,000 feet. Phillip described all the equipment he stored inside the Piper for his safety:

My weight of 140 was added to about 530 pounds of fuel, the spare parts for the airplane, and the survival equipment for the flight. It consisted of a two-man life raft, two life vests, a ten-day supply of canned food, three gallons of water, two hundred feet of rope for use in the jungle to lower myself from the top of the jungle canopy (if needed), a machete (but no firearms), signal mirrors, smoke and pyrotechnic flares for use at sea, a hand-held 720 channel VHF radio, two Emergency Locator Transmitters and spare batteries, a medicine kit, insect repellent, mosquito net and gloves, and warm clothing for the high mountains. Also in the plane was the propeller that was going to be used for the last part of the journey across the mountains in Peru that separate the coast from the jungle.

With all this weight on board, the Piper was tail-heavy, so Hank installed a small fixed trim-tab on the rear of the elevator to supplement the horizontal stabilizer trim system. The Piper passed muster, and the long flight began. The A-36 took the lead while Phillip prepared to tuck up and under in close formation when weather demanded—as he had been well trained to do when he was a Navy fighter pilot.

Forty minutes short of Fort Lauderdale, over the Everglades and already in the dark, Hank heard Phillip shout, "Keep me in sight. I've lost power!" When Phillip switched tanks and the engine burst back to life, he learned that the gas gauge indicated a little gas even when the tank was dry.

The next morning, although the FAA export license inspector didn't actually okay the thirty-gallon tanks in the back seat, he told the pilots that no one would stop them from taking off, and since the PA-12 wasn't likely to return to the US, the FAA couldn't care less. Off we went! Phillip took off ahead of Hank and circled, waiting for us to get airborne. He joined us on Hank's left wing, and we began one of the longest legs of the trip, 575 miles and six hours to Grand Turk Island.

Phillip later wrote in his journal:

> Hank's Loran C (Long Range Navigation) computer tells us that we are heading right for Aruba and we have a slight headwind. The Loran C is not supposed to work this far from the US, but Hank has rigged his ham radio with an antenna that can be switched over to the Loran C when he is not talking on the radio to the States or to other missionaries in South America. The antenna does wonders for the Loran C reception. . . . its best feature is the ability to mark one's present position. But I'm keeping my finger on the map and using my last groundspeed as a back-up. One diode in Hank's alternator is all that separates us from having the little black box go dead!

TENDER LOVING CARE FROM 'HAMS'

After a night's layover in Aruba, the two mission planes were detained by customs officials searching the airplanes and checking documents. The delay was long enough to cancel that day's flight to Bogotá, where ABWE missionaries were expecting us. After learning there were no phone connections to Bogotá, Hank remembered his ham radio and asked us to wait while he ran to the restricted zone on the other side of the airport where the Bonanza had been tied down. It was time for the Baptist Radio Amateur Group (BRAG) net. The ham operators who had been flight-following every hour on the half hour would be concerned because Hank hadn't reported in.

At the plane, Hank turned on the Kenwood 430S and transmitted, "Anyone on for the BRAG net? Here is WA4VSP aeronautical mobile."

"WA4VSP aeronautical mobile, here is WB2AUU. Where are you?" It was Ed Yoder, who worked in ABWE headquarters.

Ed's son, and our son-in-law, Al Yoder, in Bahia, Brazil, broke in, "PY6ZAJ checking in."

A few minutes later, Bob Trout in Bogotá reported in. Shortly, all flight-followers had been informed of the delay in Aruba and the new arrival time for Bogotá.

Afterward, Hank said to Phillip and me, "What a blessing to have this TLC (tender loving care) from hams!"

NO CLEARANCE FOR BOGOTÁ

At 9 a.m. the next morning, Phillip took off first. We strained to keep him in sight because the tower had delayed our departure. Soon we were over Venezuela and, about noon, we made contact with the first Colombian aeronautical radio in the town of Cucutá. "Can you verify the flight plan clearance to Bogotá for Bonanza N555JH and Piper 3967M?" Hank asked the control tower operator.

Twenty minutes later, Cucutá radio called us. "Be advised. You are *not* cleared to Bogotá. You must return to Venezuela."

After some time, we did receive clearance to land at Cucutá, but we were instructed to remain in the aircraft on the tarmac. Hank hurriedly advised Phillip by his en route frequency, "Don't be alarmed when you see policemen with automatic weapons surrounding us when we land. It's customary."

Waiting for the Colonel's office in Bogotá to clear us for entry stretched our patience. What had caused this delay?

It turned out that someone had transposed the PA-12's registration numbers—not an easy error to correct. By the time our aircraft registration had been verified and we received permission to fly into Bogotá, we would be flying over the Andes Mountains after dark. All of us agreed to spend the night in the picturesque town of Cucutá, in a hotel which proved to have rooms with no hot water, no towels, no windows, and communal toilets with no toilet seats.

Phillip was heard to mutter, "Remind me never again to complain about the accommodations on any Delta Airline layover!"

FLYING IN FORMATION

The following morning, December 21, around 11 a.m., our flight threaded its way through the Andes' beautiful green valleys and rugged peaks, each pilot keeping alert on oxygen at our 13,000-foot elevation. Kay and I also had oxygen as needed, but I remembered earlier trips in other aircraft when only Hank had regular access to oxygen. On those flights, he had reminded me to check my fingernails. Blue fingernails signaled oxygen deprivation, and if mine turned blue, I would breathe from his oxygen mask off and on until we returned to a lower elevation.

We had a three-hour flight to Bogotá, an hour to land and park at a fixed-base operator's facility, followed by official clearance of the planes and having our passports stamped by Colombian immigration. After lunch at the airport McDonald's restaurant, we caught a cab and arrived at the Trouts' residence, where ABWE missionaries Bob and Lynne treated us royally. The next morning the security checks, flight routines, and customary delays started up again as we continued the sixth leg of our journey, a six-hour flight to Iquitos, Peru.

"It's past 10 a.m.," Hank complained, as he went over his pre-flight procedures. "Well, at least the runway is over 12,000-feet long. Even with the high temperature and the 8,300-foot elevation, we should take off without a problem."

"What we won't have is very good performance after we get airborne," Phillip said, his thoughts working through the possible difficulties facing them. There were five minutes between his departure and ours in the Bonanza. The lightweight fabric PA-12 climbed at 1,000 feet per minute straight up, while the Bonanza, climbing at 250 feet per minute, had to circle to climb out of the valley surrounding Bogotá. Hank lost sight of the PA-12 and didn't find it until an hour later over the only VOR (radio station) en route. What a relief, especially for Phillip, who didn't speak Spanish! Some fifty miles south of Bogotá, at 10,500 feet, the planes were once again flying in a loose formation. At this altitude, the speed difference between the two planes became more critical. The Piper flew wide open, while the Bonanza maintained stall speed and, at times, began to settle. Hank had to speed up and do some 360 degree turns to keep his altitude. Phillip lost sight of him. At last, after finding one another, they descended and both broke out over the great expanse of the Amazon jungle. The Putamayo River, which delineates the border between Colombia and Peru was under us.

Phillip, knowing that his part of the trip would be finished soon, checked his groundspeed and looked over his survival equipment next to his seat in the cockpit. Food, water, and equipment were within easy reach in case the plane should end up in the canopy of trees. The air was muggy and humid, and he was thirsty, hungry, and stiff from sitting. He told us later, "I loved every minute of it!"

His aeronautical map was now pure white, indicating that relief data was incomplete for this area. When Phillip described flying over uncharted jungle to his family, he grinned and said, "I knew that the jungle floor teemed with all kinds of life, and perhaps, near the rivers, some human life, but I was content to let the jungle beneath remain unexplored."

MESSAGE TO IQUITOS VIA CHERRY HILL

One hour out of Iquitos, it was time for the BRAG net, but none of our missionaries from Iquitos were on the radio. Hank asked, "Anyone on frequency have an idea how we can advise

Kevin Donaldson or someone in Iquitos of our ETA?"

Ed Yoder from ABWE headquarters replied, "I'll be right back." Next we heard Kevin's voice. Ed had phoned him from Cherry Hill, New Jersey, on the land line to Iquitos, and Kevin was talking to Hank via phone patch. We were at Kevin's back door, yet Hank's message, "Hey, Kevin, we're arriving in forty minutes" had to be routed all the way through the US phone system!

After seeing Phillip off in an airliner to the US, and flying Kay and me in the Bonanza A-36 downriver to Benjamin Constant, where I was scheduled to run VBS, Hank left that plane in a hangar at the Iquitos Airport and finished the last leg of his trip in the PA-12. He flew solo for eight-and-a-half hours over the Peruvian jungle, Andes Mountains, and desert coastline to Lima, where he delivered the PA-12 to its new and excited pilot, Glenn Budd.

There, he spent several days helping Glenn with importation papers before his commercial flight back to Iquitos, from where he flew the Bonanza back to Benjamin Constant to get Kay and me, and to celebrate his sixtieth birthday on January 8.

On the return trip to Georgia, Al Yoder flew co-pilot with Hank so Al could get his floatplane rating in Florida. Including all the stops, typical delays, and minor problems with the Bonanza's fuel system, we arrived at the ABWE Airbase in Georgia on January 26, forty-two hours after leaving Brazil. God's loving hand had protected us and the planes and brought us safely through the entire trip without physical harm.

What happened next might have caused some to doubt God's love, but who can say that the painful experience which followed wasn't His loving hand upon our lives?

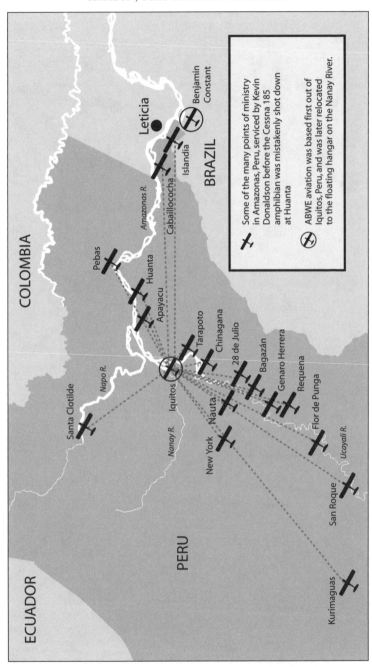

Some of the many points of ministry in Amazonas, Peru, serviced by Kevin Donaldson before the Cessna 185 amphibian was mistakenly shot down at Huanta

ABWE aviation was based first out of Iquitos, Peru, and was later relocated to the floating hangar on the Nanay River.

TWENTY-THREE

ACCIDENT!

On February 14, 1989, Hank was struck and badly injured by a falling tree.

One of his goals had been to clear the swamp on our property in Georgia in order to make a lake for floatplane operation. On this Valentine's Day, he had cut and felled one tree, about thirty inches in diameter, then turned away to work on another. What he didn't know then was that, when the first tree fell, it had balanced against two smaller trees. They bent under its impact, then catapulted it back up into the air and directly at Hank.

When he looked up and saw the first tree hurtling toward him, he threw the chain saw aside and dove for the ground to get out of the way. The tree hit his right foot first, and the impact jammed his leg up into his pelvis, which cracked in five places, but God saved Hank's life, protecting him from internal bleeding or injury to vital organs. Hank refused a complicated surgery suggested by the doctor, and opted for traction instead. He was fitted to a pelvic sling under sixty pounds traction and a right-leg boot under fifteen pounds traction. God supplied grace to allow "patience to have her perfect work" while Hank endured the pain and monotony of twelve weeks of confinement—though not inactivity.

From his hospital bed in our living room, he carried on many responsibilities by phone and ham radio, and through volunteers who came to his aid. Once again, Herman Teachout, who had volunteered with ABWE before, traveled from Michigan to assist Hank in various tasks. Although we should not have been surprised, we were amazed to see what God accomplished during Hank's convalescence. The following excerpt, taken from one of our prayer letters, relates how God worked:

> Phillip LaBerge gave check flights to Randy Alderman before he left for Togo, and to Tom Peace on his return to the Amazon. Two retirees from Alabama spent a few days clearing more trees out of the lake site. Bert Warren, a high school graduate, spent six weeks assisting with various jobs at the hangar, lake site, and airstrip. Five Delta mechanics continued repairs on two mission aircraft. Among these were Jim Rinehart and Tom Holmes, who traveled to several of ABWE Air ministries to assist our pilots in aircraft repair. Their wives and families sacrificed to enable them to "moonlight" for God's work.

By July, Hank was thirteen pounds lighter, but was back on his feet without a walker. One leg was slightly shorter than the other, while his pelvis, still slightly out of alignment, would continue to give Hank pain, especially when sitting, for the rest of his life.

BACK TO WORK

By November of that year, he and Scott DeWitt made the grueling flight of fifty-four hours and 6,727 air miles from the Concord air base to Iquitos in the Cessna 185 amphibian OB-1408, then Hank traveled on alone by commercial airlines to visit the other five aviation ministries in South America.

Most of the ABWE missionary family in Iquitos ran out onto the tarmac to greet Hank and Scott that memorable day. "What a day for us!" Kevin Donaldson said when he saw the Cessna, then quoted Proverbs 13:19: ". . . a longing fulfilled is sweet to the soul."

His next words were, "How soon can I take her up? I've been

out of the cockpit for over two years!"

The next few days, while the Cessna 185 OB-1408 was still under US registration, Scott and Kevin took each of the Iquitos riverboat missionaries up in the air to give them a bird's-eye view of the region where they served. On one survey flight, they discovered a village unknown to river missionaries after more than thirty years of ministry in that area.

As they traveled to the far extreme of one missionary's territory, he asked Scott, "How long a flight was it to get to this junction in the Itaya River?"

Scott, after a glance at his watch, answered, "Fifty minutes. Why?"

With a look of amazement, the missionary exclaimed, "It takes me twelve days in my launch. Incredible!"

Two days after the arrival of the Cessna, Scott's wife, Robin, arrived with their four children, who were affectionately known as A, B, C, and D (Aimee, Ben, Carissa, and Dallas). They endured the usual plagues of bites, boils, scabies, and lice typical of jungle living, but settled into their home. Meanwhile, Scott and Kevin made the sixteen-hour-round-trip, high-altitude flight over the Andes Mountains into the capital city of Lima to take care of official business.

Scott soon learned that the pendulum of departmental bureaucracy swings s-l-o-w-l-y. "There were enough forms, requests, copies, notarized documents, and printed material submitted to the Aeronautical Minister of Transportation to bulge a file folder two inches thick," Scott said. "Not to mention the months that followed of unnecessary shifting of paperwork to and from buildings, floors, offices, desks, and personnel for the express purpose of stamping, signing, legalizing, and confusing my North American mind."

Finally, after nine months, while the Donaldsons were in the US on a short furlough for their son Theodore's birth, the Peruvian authorities granted release from the customs agent and gave permission to operate the plane within Peruvian airspace as Cessna OB-1408.

SMOKE SIGNALS IN PERU

Meanwhile, Scott began holding evangelistic services, and, by August 1990, he had seen fifty-three Peruvians in previously unreached villages born into the family of God. Fellow missionaries were able to make discipleship visits to other villages more often and more easily because of the plane. As is always the case with missionary aviation, there were exciting moments, including a successful search and rescue, and a safe landing during an emergency caused by a failed airplane part.

But one of Scott's greatest thrills came in April 1991, delivered by a messenger via a thirty-two-foot, thatch-roofed wooden motorboat. It was a request from believers located in Paichehuahua and Bellavista on the Napo River, two villages where Scott had never ministered.

"Please come and preach the gospel here," they asked.

But how was he to find them in the heart of the jungle where every hut looked the same from the air? The villagers, Scott discovered, had a well-thought-out plan. They would keep fires burning throughout the day so the smoke would reveal their location, and when they heard the airplane approaching, the whole village would run into a clearing and wave towels, T-shirts, and rags. Someone would climb the highest palm tree and hold up their red and white Peruvian flag. They further promised to clear the river of all floating trees, logs, and debris so Scott could land the plane.

Within the week, Scott flew an evangelistic team, composed of five Bible Institute students and a Peruvian pastor and his wife, to hold a four-day campaign at these two villages. Paichehuahua was a forty-two minute flight away, but Scott couldn't miss it when he spotted the villagers' antics. After dropping off five of the team members on the riverbank, Scott flew the other team members upriver thirty-seven minutes to Bellavista. There, they easily sighted the flag-raiser, who lifted the fluttering Peruvian flag almost ten feet above the treetop. Approaching the steep twelve-foot bank, Scott held full left rudder and sufficient power to counter the whirlpools, wind, and water's flow while he maneuvered the plane toward a cove to tie up. He was so thrilled to reach another village in which to proclaim salvation in Christ that in his exuberance he locked the cabin door with his keys still in the ignition.

"How many keys do you suppose there are in a small jungle village?" he asked when he retold this story. "Well, believe it or not, I actually found a key that worked!"

When the Donaldsons arrived back in Iquitos from their furlough, they brought Theodore, their healthy month-old infant, with them. But a few weeks later, due to sudden infant death syndrome, baby Ted, just six-and-a-half weeks old, went to sleep in Jesus. God provided sufficient grace to Kevin and Bobbi to write the following:

> Ted's death had nothing to do with us being missionaries or with us being in Peru (perhaps it would be easier if it had), but his little body lies here waiting for the second coming of our Lord Jesus Christ. In that glad day of resurrection, we hope Ted will be but one of many going up from the Amazon jungle as a direct result of our presence here. Our experience with losing a child may help us minister to Peruvians. As God comforts us, we become more convinced than ever of His power and love, more confident in our work. We have a precious treasure laid up in heaven!

THE TERRORIST THREAT GROWS

In 1989, after the Donaldsons first arrived in Iquitos, Kevin had mentioned that the terrorists had arrived but, although the missionaries were careful to take precautions, they were not troubled. Now, after the annual inspection on the amphibian plane in March 1992, Kevin was warned that religious workers were more of a target for terrorism than ever.

"None of our churches or missionaries has had a problem yet, but rumors fly. We no longer announce dates or destinations of missionary trips over public radio as we did before," Kevin informed Hank.

By June, Peru's political situation deteriorated. However, Americans who lived in Peru and Peruvians, themselves, were applauding the new president's courage and democratic stand. The missionaries in Iquitos were praying that US support would be reinstated because, with its support, Peru had been gaining against drug trafficking and terrorism. But Peruvian government cutbacks had combined several departments and, in the shuffle, the paperwork for two aviation situations—validation of insurance and exoneration from airport taxes and fees amounting to over $4,000—had been stalled. A conference upriver had been scheduled, and the missionaries were praying that the amphibian could be used to make the two-hour round-trip flight. Otherwise, they faced a week's travel by riverboat.

About this time, the DeWitts left Peru for regular furlough. In the meantime, Kevin was discouraged because the government had raised taxes at the airport to an exorbitant level, and he had to make the following decision:

> If you can believe it, we have had to give up on being able to use the hangar that a US work team put up three-and-a-half years ago. It's being dismantled bit by bit and carted away. The good news is that the pieces are being built into churches and missionary housing. Cessna OB-1408 is still baked by the sun and drenched by the rain where it sits at the Iquitos International Airport.

Where Kevin had expected to receive official exemption from airport fees, this did not happen for several reasons. One was that ABWE, along with many other agencies, lost its general tax exemption status. Without it, the pilots faced a charge of $6,000 to start flying again, plus extra monthly fees; their aviation account couldn't cover it. The future for the aviation program in Iquitos seemed bleak, but Kevin and Scott chose to claim God's promise in I Corinthians 10:13. God promised to provide a way out of this trial.

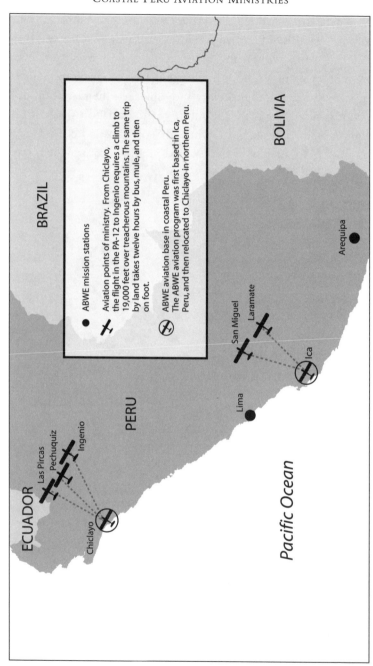

ABWE mission stations

Aviation points of ministry. From Chiclayo, the flight in the PA-12 to Ingenio requires a climb to 19,000 feet over treacherous mountains. The same trip by land takes twelve hours by bus, mule, and then on foot.

ABWE aviation base in coastal Peru. The ABWE aviation program was first based in Ica, Peru, and then relocated to Chiclayo in northern Peru.

TWENTY-FOUR

AVIATION CHANGES IN PERU

Have you ever tried to follow God's guidance, only to have a roadblock obstruct your plans? Did you conclude that God's plan was not what you thought—that the way He works is mysterious, beyond human comprehension?

Some of these questions went through Hank's mind as he watched the ebb and flow of the aviation ministry in Iquitos and coastal Peru over the next several years. Kevin Donaldson, Scott DeWitt, and Glenn Budd faced the same questions.

Kevin did not fly the Cessna OB-1408 amphibian the entire year the DeWitts were on furlough because of governmental problems with aircraft insurance and airport taxes and fees in Iquitos. As 1992 drew to a close, since they couldn't fly, the Donaldsons opted to be more involved in planting a church in Iquitos for the wealthy and educated, the nominally-Catholic middle class. Kevin and Bobbi helped facilitate other missionaries by keeping daily radio contact with those ministering on the rivers, fixing their appliances and equipment, assisting in bookkeeping and handling missionaries' accounts, acting as field council chairman, providing a guest room to those traveling through Iquitos, and even trekking up the mountains of Peru to help Glenn Budd repair some damage on the PA-12.

Glenn Budd and his family were busy starting up a new aviation ministry in northern Peru after having to leave the Ica area due to terrorism. Glenn also made evangelism visits to mountain towns, such as San Miguel, which was known to be a favorite haunt of the terrorists. The missionaries learned to live with that threat but trusted God for protection.

All too soon, the time came for the Budds' furlough, and Glenn flew the PA-12 to an airport north of Lima to "pickle" the engine and store the plane in a hangar for the year. But while the Budds were in the States, Peruvian pastors sent word that terrorism was on the rise in Peru, especially in the mountains.

In September 1991, the field council advised Hank and Glenn that "Laramate, one of Glenn's target towns, was attacked by an army of 100 terrorists, wiping out the entire police force and killing eleven policemen. Since there has been a buildup of subversive action in that area, and it is considered in a state of emergency, we therefore consider the door closed, at least temporarily, for flights into that area."

PRAYING FOR WISDOM AND DIRECTION

Glenn's return to Peru was delayed by surgery on his elbow. The tendons had to be cut off the bone and shortened, some damaged bone material was removed, and then the tendons were stitched back in place. The doctor advised him to give the elbow a full six months to heal, doing no lifting during that time. Glenn spent hours pouring out his heart to God and looking for answers. Should he forget his burden for the unreached people in the Andes? He remembered when he gave out tracts and Bibles, or dropped bundles of gospel literature from the plane. The people would grab them eagerly. How could he keep his promise to return to them? He knew it to be God's will that the mountain people hear the gospel, but if terrorism closed the door to the southern Andes, surely there was another location where he could work. Glenn wanted to be wise in discerning God's time and direction.

In December 1991, an invitation from a senior Peruvian pastor in northern Peru, Angel Colmenares, was passed on to Glenn via an ABWE colleague: "This pastor has started over 150 churches throughout the plains and mountains of northern Peru, most of which depend on lay pastors. These men and their congregations are zealous to spread the gospel further into the unreached mountain areas where there are few roads. Days of travel by mule could be saved with the use of the airplane, and the people there are willing to build airstrips."

A CHANGE OF LOCATION

With this information, Glenn traveled to Peru to survey areas of the country and see what God had prepared. The door opened to live and to base the PA-12 in Chiclayo, a location central to the northern Andes Mountains and closer to the Peruvian jungle. The mountains vary from the high, dry sierras to the *montaña*, which are humid, very green and lush, but not tropical. The area was uncharted, so Glenn's survey and later ministry flights were dependent on weather for visual reference. In Chiclayo, the Budds would minister alongside Peruvian pastors of the Association of Churches through teaching, camps, conferences, special projects, and much pastoral care.

Shortly after moving to Chiclayo in May 1992, Glenn met Pastor Hugo, a Peruvian missionary to the mountains. Together, Glenn and Pastor Hugo surveyed the mountain area using the plane. The pastor was able to pinpoint Ingenio, the town where he lived and pastored a growing church, and a few choices of location for an airstrip. From Ingenio, five other towns were being reached, so Ingenio was a logical choice for a ministry center.

Pastor Hugo's family had sacrificed a great deal in leaving their coastal culture of Lima to live in the poverty-stricken mountain villages. He was burdened to train lay pastors, but traveling conditions made it very difficult. Here, once again, missionary aviation was to prove a great help to evangelism and discipleship in the mountains.

Once they were back on the ground, Glenn and the pastor traveled overland to reach the town and determine whether or not an airstrip could be built at that location. It took thirty hours by bus and pickup truck, and then required a hike over terrain where even a motorcycle could not have gone. They completed the last hours of their hike to Ingenio first by moonlight and then by flashlight, until the batteries died.

After a day's recuperation, they surveyed the area and found a sloping plateau, twenty minutes walking distance from town, which appeared to be the best place to put an airstrip. Each evening of their stay, following a meal shared with a different church family, Glenn preached a series on Philippians, then met with the youth leaders late into the night.

Pastor Hugo, who had been a road engineer before he began to serve as a pastor in the mountains, offered, "If you'll lay out the airstrip, I'll make sure the brothers make it the way you want." Together, they measured, staked the airstrip with poles, and marked a center line through the brush. Then Pastor Hugo and the believers in Igenio built the strip—clearing, leveling, and even marking the center line with white crushed limestone—all by hand.

Early in January 1993 Glenn went to a pastors' conference in Las Pircas that Pastor Colemares sponsored, where he met and strategized with fifty lay pastors and leaders from the most northern mountains near the border with Equador. As a result, believers in a number of towns were ready to start construction on their own airstrips. They were eager to receive biblical training; two of the pastors pleaded with Glenn to return with them right then and survey their mountain plateau. So Glenn, Pastor Wilmer from the church the Budds attended in Chiclayo, and Pastors Umberto and Gumercindo made the trip by land in Glenn's Jeep to Las Pircas and Pechuquiz. The Jeep only made it through otherwise impassable stretches of road, with mud and water up to its floorboards, because of the shovels, picks, and pushing of the four men. The rugged terrain extended up past 11,000 feet and surrounded a large plateau where a number of towns are located. Glenn and the others had to leave the Jeep at Las Pircas and hike the last three hours to Pechuquiz and Overjeria, where Pastors

Umberto and Gumercindo came from.

The people who lived in these towns had to be tough to farm the hillsides and tend their herds of sheep and goats at this high elevation. Glenn and Pastor Wilmer were welcomed around the peoples' dark, smoky, crowded indoor cooking fires, to eat and to warm themselves. That night, after one of the pastors preached, the people insisted that Glenn also preach. He did so, wearing thermals, a shirt, a sweater, a heavy coat, and a wool poncho, but still found himself shivering. Although he ate plenty of tiny potatoes and goat cheese, he lost four pounds on that trip.

The next morning, they picked the best location for the airstrip, asked permission of the "town fathers" to build it, measured and marked out the boundaries, then hiked back to the Jeep.

ACCIDENT IN INGENIO

Glenn made his first landings at Las Pircas and Pechuquiz to participate in a successful weeklong Bible conference where he taught and showed Christian films at night with the generator and projector he carried in the plane. Back in Chiclayo, Glenn attempted to install his ham radio in the plane and another at home, then attended to some maintenance before he kept his promise to check out the new airstrip that had been built in Ingenio. A believer had arrived with pictures of the completed airstrip, and since Glenn was to be one of the featured speakers for their church anniversary Bible conference, he decided to look over the airstrip and land if all looked good. He loaded Bibles, a generator, projector, and Christian films into the cabin.

After one hour and forty-five minutes of flight over majestic, rugged mountains, canyons, and rivers, he was looking down on Ingenio from 200 feet above ground. The airstrip appeared to be finished. Glenn flew down the length of the field, checked its slope, and then noticed that trees, which had been marked to be cut down, were still standing. He thought, *I'll fly down, land at the beginning, right at the edge of the cliff, hold partial power, and then take off halfway down the strip to see how much altitude and speed I'll need to clear the trees. I think this'll give me an idea whether I can land and take off with the trees there.*

The airstrip proved to be narrow, about fifteen feet wide, but sufficient. Distracted by checking the airstrip's surface, Glenn allowed too little margin for takeoff, and when he looked up, the trees were very close—too close. Instantly, he hit the power and pulled back on the stick to climb, but he flooded the engine; it coughed and sputtered. Would the engine recover in time to clear the trees, or should he abort and set it back down? He chose to chop the power, set it back down on the surface, and braked hard. Then the thing pilots fear when landing a tail-dragger in that situation happened—the tail started to come up more and more. The PA-12's nose thrust forward and down, and the prop hit the ground, while the tail kept going up, up, up, and over. The plane flipped on its back, twenty feet from six-inch tree trunks hidden in taller grass at the end of the strip.

People from all directions ran to rescue him from the cabin. Glenn yelled, "No, no, no—let me do it!" He was concerned that more damage to the fabric wing might result from people step-ping on it. Glenn popped his seat belt, released his harness, and fell to the roof, gouging his helmet (thankfully, not his head), and crawled out. Glenn sent onlookers to gather tin cups and con-tainers to drain as much gas as possible, while others cut long poles. Within twenty minutes, they had the plane flipped back over on its main gear and had the broken left wing struts propped up with a stake.

Unharmed but dazed, Glenn assessed the damage: a bent prop, cracked windshield, broken left wing strut, and a mutilated inlet scoop for the air cleaner. Charo, the pastor's wife, looked on and lamented, "To me this feels like an expectant mother waiting nine months to see her child and then having that child die at birth."

Glenn excused himself from the crowd. "I need to get alone

with the Lord right now." Walking through the woods, he talked with God. "What am I to think? Am I in the wrong place? Is this the devil working to keep the gospel from going forward?" One thing he settled—not to give up. Glenn knew that God had led him to be a missionary pilot. In His strength, he would find a way to press on.

Leaving the plane guarded by the believers in the village, he ran almost the whole eight hours down the mountain, took a truck into town, and a bus back to Chiclayo. Having received his Peruvian ham license one week before, Glenn reported the incident on the BRAG net to Hank. Networking began immediately. Hank arranged for the needed equipment and, within three months, Glenn received the replacement parts. Phil Bowers and Clif Jensen from the US, along with Kevin Donaldson from Iquitos, all volunteered to travel with Glenn to the mountaintop airstrip to help get the PA-12 back up in the air. A crew of believers from Ingenio cleared trees and lengthened the airstrip another 130 feet. Missionaries and Peruvians encouraged him: "Twenty years from now this will seem a minor setback in light of the dozens of new churches established as a result of this thrust."

NEW BELIEVERS IN INGENIO

It wasn't easy to admit, but Glenn said, "I broke a cardinal rule by landing on a handmade airstrip without walking it first. I was foolish, but I've asked the Lord to bring something good out of it."

Later, Glenn heard that those who opposed his coming to Ingenio with a "new" religion had said, "That's the end of that missionary pilot. He'll never be back. He's wrecked the plane and we've seen the last of him." But when repairs were finished, and Glenn flew it back down the mountain, they were proved wrong. Glenn has now been ministering there for thirteen years, and many have turned to Christ for salvation and been discipled.

One of the ways God answered Glenn's request to bring good out of the plane crash was to allow him to witness to four Catholic lay priests who performed priestly functions in Ingenio. Two of these men received Christ—one became a deacon and the other a leader in the church there. Another man named Eloy, however, was an ardent antagonist, who encouraged his people to throw rocks on the roof of the Baptist church. He despised Glenn and took his hostility out on the believers every time he had the chance.

Other ABWE missionaries traveled to Ingenio to conduct a medical clinic as a ministry of compassion to believers and unbelievers alike. Eloy had fallen from his mule, hurt his shoulder, and showed up at the clinic for care. From then on, he changed his attitude towards the Peruvian lay pastor and the missionaries. He and his wife began attending gospel meetings and asked questions about the Bible. Finally, Eloy turned from his relationship with the traditional church, but he did not turn to Christ just yet.

In February 2003, Glenn, Dorothy, their son, David, their daughter Audra, and their new coworkers, the Farley family, all went by land to Ingenio for ladies' camp and to minister to the people there. The following morning before breakfast, several Peruvians came seeking help. "*Hermano* (Brother) Glenn, come quickly! Eloy is dying. He's been calling for you these past three weeks."

Glenn hurried to Eloy's house, where he found him cold and unresponsive, but still breathing. Knowing that Eloy had never trusted Christ as Savior and that time was running out, Glenn took things into his own hands. He began by calling for a deep bucket of warm water, then proceeded to get Eloy out of the dark, cold bedroom to the living room and into the sunshine. There, he sat his friend in a chair and put his legs in the warm water up to his knees. Eloy rallied and began munching the crackers handed to him, and Glenn confronted him earnestly: "Eloy, you've never made a decision to accept Christ as Savior.

Now is the time to make your decision. If that is what you want to do, you need to do it today."

Eloy shook his head, "No, not yet. I know what you've told me is true, but I can't let go of some things I've been taught."

Glenn reminded his friend that it was time to say goodbye to his wife. "Tell her you love her, because you will soon leave this world." As he left the room while husband and wife expressed their love, Glenn heard the initial wails and cries of the bereaved gathered in the next room.

Then Eloy called Glenn back to his side and said, "I'm ready to make a decision now." Glenn had shared the truth with him so many times that Eloy knew what he needed to do. He confessed his sin, trusted that Jesus' blood cleansed him from all sin, and asked Jesus to save him.

Glenn quizzed him carefully. "Where's your confidence? Is it in the church?"

"No, it's in Jesus Christ alone."

"Is your confidence in good works you can do?"

"No, it's in Jesus Christ alone."

In tears, Glenn hugged him good night and hoped Eloy would survive the night. The next morning, Eloy was weak, hardly able to be heard.

Glenn lifted him up closer and asked once again, "Are you trusting in Jesus?"

Eloy nodded.

Glenn told him that he would be with Jesus in heaven very soon, and Eloy died in his arms. God used Eloy's death and funeral as a mighty witness of His saving grace to the entire town.

None of Eloy's relatives were believers, so at their request, the fourth lay priest in Ingenio presided at the gravesite burial. Glenn, who had asked God for a way to present the gospel to the multitudes attending, helped carry the casket to the burial plot. While the lay priest went through his funeral ceremony and prayers, the people milled about, some of them wailing. At the same time, a large group of believers sang hymns. Glenn prayed, *It would be rude to take the liberty of speaking here without being invited. Lord, please open a way.*

Right then, the lay priest turned and said, "I'm done. We'd like to hear from our friend from Chiclayo."

Glenn didn't hesitate! Out came his Bible, and he presented Christ's love and sacrifice to save sinners, the same gospel message Eloy had received before his entrance into heaven. The Holy Spirit worked in hearts that day, and many later came to Christ.

"The fourth priest still follows the traditional church, but we continue to pray for his salvation," Glenn said.

Over the years of flying to the mountains or traveling by land, Glenn took along his three children whenever possible. Home schooling allowed them a flexible schedule and gave Amy, Audra, and David a vision for the ministry in those areas. Glenn's wife, Dorothy, continues her flight-following when her husband is in the air, as well as traveling often to hold ladies' camps and assisting with teams from the US that come to minister in these remote areas.

CHANGES IN THE PERU AVIATION MINISTRY

Just two months before the Donaldsons left for furlough in 1993, Kevin Donaldson finally received permission from the Ministry of Transportation to fly again. In less than two hours after receiving this news, the Cessna 185 OB-1408, which had been unable to fly for two years, was airborne.

"All our time of waiting and wondering vanished when the plane lifted off. As the nose pointed upwards, our hearts rose in grateful praise to God," Kevin wrote.

When the Donaldsons returned to the field in November 1994, they found the Cessna 185 OB-1408 sitting proudly in its new floating hangar, which had been built in their absence by volunteers. The hangar was located on the Nanay River, north of the city of Iquitos; it proved to be a huge help and blessing.

Not long after, when the DeWitts left the field, the Donaldsons leaned upon Romans 8:28–29a, believing that God's purpose in all things is to conform His children to the image of Christ. Kevin described how he felt about carrying on alone: "Missionary aviation on our own is overwhelming. Have you ever seen a person stagger under too heavy a load? That's us right now. Pray for wisdom as we prioritize our responsibilities at this time." Pondering God's mysterious ways that proved to be beyond human comprehension, he added, "We are learning to stick to an assignment until God changes the instructions no matter how discouraged or impatient we may feel." And that's exactly what they did.

The first flight of their term resulted in the salvation of a girl whose parents were the only believers in their town. In addition to regular two-to-four-day trips for TEE, Kevin flew special flights to settle church problems, to encourage new missionaries at their remote posts, and to answer emergency calls. Word of one emergency came at the one o'clock missionary radio rendezvous, and by 3 p.m., the sick man was at the city hospital. "That was fast—twenty-four hours faster than by other means," he explained. Kevin relished his flights to river villages for preaching, music, distributing literature, and showing a video. Many flights were to small, untaught groups that had no more than a few portions of Scripture and snatches of songs to aid them.

Keeping up with aviation regulations continued to be a challenge. All of the paperwork on the Cessna 185 OB-1408 would have to be done in Lima, where a faithful Peruvian pastor was responsible to keep the plane's documents current. This pastor suffered with a mysterious blood disease, and if he was unable to frequent the aviation offices on schedule, the plane program stood in danger of being shut down. In January 1997, Kevin learned that he would no longer be allowed to do his own annual inspection, and the Peruvian inspectors required more and charged more for their services.

The missionaries appreciated and benefited from Kevin's ministry; he was up in the air twenty hours per month. When they returned in August 1998 after another furlough, the Donaldsons saw that ministry in the city of Iquitos was transitioning: the maturing churches were taking more leadership in evangelism and training believers. The Association of Baptist Churches of the Jungle announced its desire to have foreign help in the form of money, not manpower.

Kevin knew that the future use of the airplane by missionaries would decrease due to retirements, but he intended to encourage Peruvian pastors to use it more; God had provided US dollars to fund their flights. The Lord had also provided a new engine for OB-1408, and Kevin made the engine swap and repainted the plane. He hoped to expand outreach through TEE to remote river villages outside of Iquitos.

Then, in April 2001, Kevin was forced to face one of the most difficult situations any missionary pilot could ever experience.

TWENTY-FIVE

A TRAGIC MISTAKE

Early on April 19, 2001, Kevin prepared the Cessna 185 OB-1408 for a routine flight to transport ABWE coworkers Jim and Roni Bowers. Jim was the son of Terry and Wilma Bowers, who had served with Hank and me in Amazonas, Brazil, during the 1960s and 1970s. On that April morning, Jim and Roni, their six-year-old son, Cory, and their adopted infant daughter, Charity, needed to get to Colombia, where the family could secure baby Charity's permanent residence visa at the Peruvian consulate.

Once Kevin confirmed his flight plan and got clearance from air traffic control at the Iquitos airport, he flew Jim and Roni and their children to the frontier tri-country area of Peru, Colombia, and Brazil. Since the ABWE floating hangar at Benjamin Constant was a secure place to ramp the OB-1408 and was located on an international waterway, Kevin landed at Islandia on the Javarí River in Peru, closed his flight plan, and taxied up the Javarizinho River to ramp the plane at the floating hangar. The Bowers family continued their trip to Leticia, Colombia, by speedboat to see the Peruvian consulate and settle Charity's visa paperwork.

Early the next morning, April 20, the missionaries met back at the ABWE hangar in Benjamin Constant and boarded OB-1408 once again to return to Iquitos. Kevin had followed standard pre-flight procedures, contacting the Iquitos airport controllers to make a verbal report of the flight plan, which he had faxed the day before to Lima, Peru. What happened next is best explained in Kevin's own words, taken from the Donaldsons' prayer letter written four months later:

> The Peruvian Air Force, aided by the CIA of the United States, mistook our mission plane for a drug runner and shot it down. Our ABWE colleagues, Roni Bowers, and her seven-month-old daughter, Charity, were killed. Kevin, with his right leg shattered and his left leg shot open to the bone, maintained control of the damaged aircraft while it dove 4,000 feet to the Amazon River. God's hand alone set the plane upright on the water. Villagers rescued Kevin and fellow survivors, Jim Bowers and his son, Cory (age 6), after OB-1408 burned and turned over.

Headlines from major US newspapers reported the incident this way:

"A gruesome shoot-down on the Amazon hints at a large and growing US narcowar in Latin America," wrote Joshua Cooper Ramo in the May 7, 2001, issue of *Time*.

"Peru downs plane bearing missionaries, not drugs," *The Atlanta Journal-Constitution* (April 21, 2001) read.

The Grand Rapids Press (April 21, 2001) reported: "Peru shoot-down shatters missionary family—father and son escape but the mother and new baby die when a Peruvian fighter mistakes their plane for a smuggler's."

The Donaldsons went on to describe the aftermath of this incident for their own family:

> Five trips to the operating room during a sixteen-day hospital stay, plus another surgery a month later, put Kevin's legs back together. Infection was not a problem, thanks to the Peruvian doctors who treated Kevin first. Grafts of bone, muscle, and skin took well. We graduated from a hos-

pital bed to a wheelchair to crutches. A cane came next. Nerve damage is beginning to correct itself. It may be a year before Kevin can walk normally on level surfaces and much longer before he can safely climb river banks or airplanes, but his recovery is progressing well.

What good has come out of this terrible accident? People all over the world are thinking about the gospel of our Lord Jesus Christ. In fact, a nurse was saved at the Peruvian clinic where Kevin spent the first night. . . . Christians awakening to the Great Commission has resulted in fervent prayer, increased financial support, and higher numbers of people moving into career missions.

One couple who had never heard of ABWE before April joined in June. May we all continue to watch expectantly to see what God will do.*

Hank was involved from the first day of the shoot-down: contacting the Peruvian and American embassy; meeting the Donaldsons upon their arrival in Texas aboard a Continental Airliner; debriefing Kevin to obtain accurate information; and assuring ABWE that its pilot had followed all required procedures before and during that memorable flight. Kevin was exonerated and retained his reputation and aircraft licenses. Hank worked throughout many months, alongside ABWE's corporate lawyer, Donald Davis, to locate an aircraft to replace OB-1408, and then to negotiate its payment by the Peruvian government, as promised; ABWE received this reimbursement in November 2004.

By the fall of 2001, the Donaldsons returned to Iquitos to resume their work in the church they had helped start, and to wait for God's direction for the future.

*Kristen Stagg's book, *If God Should Choose,* tells the complete story of this shoot-down. The book is available through ABWE Publications.

GOD CALLS NEW WORKERS TO THE PERU MINISTRY

During this time of transition and change, Ken and Ellen Fuss had been following all that was happening in Iquitos, for they hoped to become a part of the aviation program there and had worked for six years toward this goal. To fulfill the missionary apprentice program required at Piedmont Baptist College, in Winston-Salem, North Carolina, Ken had started corresponding with Hank in 1993. He took Hank's advice and, with Ellen, visited the three aviation ministries in South America. After graduation with his degrees in Theology and Aviation, Ken and Ellen attended the 1995 ABWE Candidate Class. They were appointed in November to partner in the aviation ministry with the Donaldsons in Iquitos.

Busy in prefield ministry, Ken also gained hands-on experience with a damaged Cessna 140, which had been donated as a "rebuild and fly" project. Over a six-year period of prefield ministry and Spanish language study, God tested Ken and Ellen's commitment to serve Him—through thick and thin—which included the loss of their little son, Christian. Christian went to be with Jesus just five days shy of his first birthday after a prolonged, exhausting, year-long battle with illness.

In spite of the shoot-down, Hank and Kevin encouraged the Fusses to continue on towards Iquitos. Having reached full support clearance, Ken, Ellen, and their other son, six-year-old Martin, flew to Costa Rica for language school. While there, they communicated with the Donaldsons, who had since returned to Iquitos. Kevin Donaldson reported to the Fusses that the US and Peru were dealing with the issue of flight safety with the Drug Interdiction Procedure. Also, Peru would be replacing the plane which had been mistakenly shot down. Kevin had met with Peru's Civil Aviation people and returned encouraged.

However, in the Donaldsons' next letter, the Fusses saw that they were considering making a change. When two years passed without a replacement aircraft, Kevin and Bobbi, now due for furlough, wrote the following to their stateside support team:

> We planned to extend our time on the field for six
> months to a year to orient a new plane and Ken Fuss. But
> since there is still no sign of a replacement plane, we will go
> back to the original schedule. . . . Our home of fifteen years
> will go to one of the two large ABWE families arriving
> mid-year. When or whether we return to Peru is unknown,
> depending on the developments for a Middle East project
> and the future of missionary aviation in Iquitos.

During their furlough in 2003, the Donaldsons did change
fields and received appointment with ABWE to work in the
Middle East.

After language school, Ken and Ellen returned to the US to
prepare for their anticipated release to the field and departure for
Iquitos. While in the States, Ken, along with Hank and Herman
Teachout, hoped to locate and purchase a replacement plane and
get it ready to fly down to Iquitos. However, the Peruvian
Embassy had assumed responsibility for replacing the Cessna 185
OB-1408, and two years passed before repayment was finalized.

By December 2003, the Fusses corresponded with Kevin and
sensed that the Iquitos Field Council now leaned toward not
reopening Iquitos to aviation. They determined that the door to
Iquitos had closed for them. Meanwhile, another door opened.
In 2004, Ken and Ellen were invited to join the ABWE Air support team at the air base to help with a backlog of aircraft projects. In March, Ken and a team of missionary pilot-mechanics
traveled to Papua New Guinea to perform a major overhaul on
the aircraft there.

As of this writing, the Fusses are corresponding with pilots on
various ABWE fields to determine where God would have them
serve long term. They agree, "God works in mysterious ways.
Some day, somehow, we'll be back up in the air for Him."

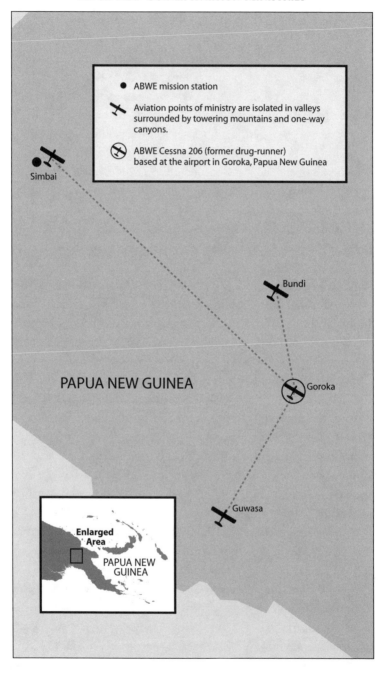

TWENTY-SIX

A CONVERTED DRUG-RUNNER FOR PAPUA NEW GUINEA

Sweaty and scrunched inside the extreme tail section of the damaged Cessna, I complained to my husband, "You didn't tell me when you asked me to help that there are *thousands* of these screws to take out."

Hank laughed as he worked to disassemble another part of the airplane. "I'm sorry, Ruth, but you fit up there in that cramped space much easier than I do."

In May of 1991, Hank had received notice that a county sheriff's department in New Mexico was open for bids on a damaged turbo-charged Cessna 206. It was highly modified with a STOL (short takeoff-landing) kit and wingtip tanks—an ideal aircraft to use in ABWE Air's new aviation program in Papua New Guinea (PNG).

On January 1, this plane had carried a big haul of marijuana from Central Mexico to New Mexico. But the inexperienced pilot caught the left wing while landing on a lonely road. The plane darted across a ditch and lost its nose wheel, and both payload and pilot disappeared before the sheriff arrived. Hank's bid bought the Cessna, and our work began.

Hank and I drove to Carlsbad, New Mexico, in Phillip LaBerge's king-sized pickup, pulling a trailer. There, under the hot, bright New Mexico sunshine, we disassembled and loaded the plane for the long haul back to the air base in Georgia. This former "drug-runner" was a good buy. Production of this particular plane had stopped in 1986; new models were no longer available. A late model in A-1 condition sold for $150,000 or more, and Hank and his many mechanic volunteers would be able to inspect it, repair it inside and out, and equip it for an estimated $45,000.

We asked God to provide partners to purchase the conversion parts and volunteer mechanics for the "hands-on" jobs, and then we mailed the information to our praying partners. Delta mechanics Tom Holmes and Jim Rinehart, along with other helpers too numerous to name, worked with Hank. Pastor Ledford, a former ABWE missionary from PNG, and his church members from Newman, Georgia, did the difficult work of stripping paint and etching the aluminum. Mel and Beverly Crowell, from St. Johns, Michigan, arrived to repaint the plane.

Meanwhile, pilot-mechanic Steve Aholt, who would eventually pilot the plane, along with his wife, Sandy, and their two children, completed their prefield ministry and headed for PNG with ABWE Air.

God's grace had brought Steve, once a devout Catholic, to accept Christ through the testimony of Sandy and the ministry of a Baptist church. In the late 1970s, God used two mission conference speakers at Evergreen Baptist Church in Michigan City, Indiana, to direct Steve and Sandy toward missionary aviation. One speaker presented his work in PNG; the other speaker was Hank. Steve had acquired his A & P license to work on aircraft after high school and he could see how God could use his aviation mechanics training to spread the gospel of Christ in Papua New Guinea, even before ABWE Air entered that country. The Aholts sold their house, Steve resigned his job, and they traveled to Piedmont Baptist College, in Winston-Salem, North Carolina, where he got his degree in Theology and Aviation.

Well-intentioned people told Steve he was crazy to step away from a secure career with Bethlehem Steel Corporation, but his response was, "I am crazy about following Christ and serving Him." Following graduation from college and aviation training in 1990, Salem Baptist Church ordained Steve before the Aholts left to attend ABWE Candidate Classes.

Past and present pilot-mechanics, multi-talented and diverse, have made and continue to make contributions to ABWE church-planting ministries worldwide, especially in remote, isolated regions where travel over land is difficult.

The Teachouts on duty in Papua New Guinea. (Back, left to right) Tami, Herman (the director of ABWE Air), and Caleb; (front) Brian and Andrea.

Ken and Ellen Fuss (with Martin in the background) prepare to serve in Togo, West Africa, where the Cessna 206 has been reassembled and awaits their arrival at the Carolyn Kempton Memorial Hospital.

Bob and Karen Hamilton fly one of ABWE's two Cessna 185 floatplanes in Brazil. They serve at the Baptist Hospital located in Santo Antonio do Iça, partnering with the doctors in medical evangelism and outreach to budding congregations in outlying areas.

Below:
In 2002, Mike and Sharon Thompson arrived in Asunción, Paraguay, to assume the aviation ministry begun by Dale and Beverly Fogg.

Above:
Sandy Aholt helps her husband, Steve, who flies the converted "drug-runner" (a Cessna 206 land plane) in Papua New Guinea.

Below:
After flying many years in Amazonas, Brazil, Clif Jensen (left) was reassigned to the ABWE Airbase in Concord, Georgia. He is shown here with Hank.

Above:
Enos (Butch) Jarvis uses the Cessna 185 floatplane to reach almost inaccessible Indian villages in the Colombian jungle.

Left:
Dale Fogg heads back to the Cessna 185 land plane after his service at Maranatha Baptist Church in Rosário, Paraguay.

Above:
Glenn Budd flies the PA-12 in tandem with Bryan Wilson (ABWE short-term pilot-mechanic) after the plane had been repaired on the 11,000-foot-high hand-made airstrip at Ingenio, Andes Mountains, Peru.

Below:
David and Becky Nelson with their young family in the Philippines.

Above:
As a part of the medical-evangelistic team working with the Baptist Hospital in Roxas, Palawan, Harry Rogers not only flew to outreach clinics, but also carried on supportive ministries to isolated churches.

Above:
Just prior to the shoot-down of the ABWE Cessna 185 amphibian, Kevin Donaldson had installed a new engine and repainted the plane. He had hoped to expand outreach through TEE to remote river villages outside of Iquitos, Peru.

Above:
Scott DeWitt reunites with his wife, Robin, and children (left to right, Ben, Dallas, Carissa, and Amy) after the grueling flight from the ABWE Airbase in Georgia to Iquitos.

Left:
Larry Holman stands beside a Cessna 180 land plane used for medical-evangelism ministry in Palawan, Philippines.

MORE HELP FOR PNG

At the same time the Aholts were preparing for missionary service and the drug-runner they would fly was being rebuilt, God was also orchestrating the events which directed Herman and Tami Teachout to become part of ABWE Air.

Herman had come to Christ for salvation at an early age, but it was during his studies at Cornerstone University, and through his reading about missionary aviation, that he came to feel strongly about his responsibility to help fulfill the Great Commission. He wondered if missionary aviation was something he had the ability to do. And if so, was it right not to do it? His path crossed that of a flight instructor, from the Missionary Aviation School at Grand Rapids School of the Bible and Music (GRSBM), who convinced him to enroll in this program and begin the journey that eventually led him to ABWE Air.

While still unmarried and a student at GRSBM, Herman went on an AMP trip to Liberia to help rebuild an airplane engine for Baptist Mid-Missions. After he graduated in 1983, he worked as a flight instructor for a Piper Aircraft dealership in Dallas, Texas. Fulfilling a longtime yearning to see Alaska, Herman found a flying job in Skagway, and it was during his time there that he began corresponding with Hank, who enlisted him to help out in the Amazon floatplane operation for three months.

That fall, he went to Louisiana to fly for a floatplane charter company that was doing oil-support work. Plunging oil prices and a floundering local economy prodded him to return to Michigan to "investigate" possibilities with Tami, who worked at Radio Bible Class in Grand Rapids, and they were married in 1988.

Tami also desired to serve God in missions. After she and Herman were married, they believed that their first step should be for Tami to also get some experience in third-world living, so they went on a five-week trip to Amazonas, Brazil, to help Clif and Hannah Jensen. Herman assisted Clif with airplane repairs and the construction of an apartment for missionary use. Tami helped Hannah prepare materials for home-schooling her children and helped Herman on the floating hangar.

The following year and into 1990, they volunteered for a seven-month stint with Evangelical Baptist Mission in Mali, West Africa, living in Timbuktu. Herman flew the plane, worked on construction projects, and repaired everything he could for the various missionaries. Tami took care of Herman, followed his flights on the radio, and helped the missionary wives whenever possible. Over the next five years, their children—Andrea, Brian, and Caleb—came along, but though their interest in missions and missionaries never waned, God had not yet led them to a full-time ministry.

Then in January 1995, God prompted Herman to contact Hank once again. "Do you have any work at the air base or overseas where we can serve?"

Hank had several possibilities, but believed that Papua New Guinea needed their assistance most. The converted drug-runner, now registered as P2-NOX, had been disassembled, packed into a forty-foot steel container along with the Aholts' household furnishings and equipment, and was on its way to PNG. Five months later, the Teachouts, supported by Grandville Baptist Church in Grandville, Michigan, arrived in PNG and remained for the next two years to help the Aholts begin their new aviation ministry.

Steve and Sandy and their children, Stephanie and Tyler, arrived in PNG on February 3, 1995, ahead of the container, which had been delayed in shipping. The container's delay was according to God's timing and plan; during that delay, the PNG government passed a law that allowed all aircraft being imported to be customs- and duty- free. This saved the Aholts a large amount of money that would otherwise have been charged. And by the time the container arrived, the Teachouts were on hand to help unpack the parts of the plane, reassemble them, and complete all the paperwork required by the PNG government.

THE WORLD'S MOST DIFFICULT FLYING CONDITIONS

Hank, our daughter Kay, and I arrived in September to help, also. That first week, the three pilots—Steve in the back seat with his video camera, Hank in the front right seat, and Herman at the controls—took the reassembled TP206 up for its trial flight within the Goroka valley area. They practiced canyon turns, takeoffs, and landings. Two days later, the pilots took Sandy and the children up for a spin. Looking down, they could see the only major highway in PNG that runs through the highland above 8,000 feet.

Granite clouds, Sandy thought, noticing the surrounding mountain peaks nearly engulfed by clouds. She remembered stories told of this danger. She also reminded herself that Steve would need God's protection in unpredictable weather and what are considered the most difficult flying conditions in the world.

In thirty-five minutes, they flew to Missionary Aviation Fellowship's base, then returned to Goroka, a four-and-a-half hour round-trip by PNG's best road. The next morning, they visited Kol, a beautiful village in the mountains that could only be reached in a four-wheel-drive vehicle by way of a hazardous trail and a four-and-a-half hour drive. It took them ten minutes by airplane.

On another day, Tami went along. The pilots planned a forty-minute flight to the Simbai region, which was usually three days away—that is, one day by truck and two days on foot. Tami wore a headset so that she could hear what the pilots were saying to one another. Flying conditions were not ideal, and Tami wondered if she was up to this flight.

She heard Herman, who was piloting, say, "I don't like the looks of the weather in that pass."

"Okay," Hank said, "let's try another way."

"I don't like this one either."

"All right, but let's go on a little farther. As long as we're already up and in no particular hurry to get back, we can get some experience flying in weather that's not ideal."

Yippee! Tami thought ironically, as she recalled Herman's explanation describing "granite cumulus." With bad weather closing in, she wanted to yell, "Watch out! Stay away from that cloud, a mountain may be hidden there." Instead, she listened silently to their remarks, one after the other:

"We can't get through that hole; it's too small."

"We can't fly over those clouds; they're building up too fast."

"Don't fly up into that valley; it's a dead end."

She braced herself to hear what they would say as they approached the airstrip at Bank. "You'll need quite a bit of power on this approach. Be sure to land right at the beginning of the strip to allow plenty of time to stop."

Once they were safely down, Hank got out to look around. When he returned to his seat, Tami heard him comment through the headset, "If you run out of runway, Herman, there's no place to go but over the end and on down the mountain."

Though she never actually felt as though she was in danger, Tami decided not to turn on the headset to listen to their comments on the way back to Goroka. It was too unnerving.

A MEMORABLE FLIGHT

September 24, 1995, was a memorable flight for Steve Aholt. Hank had studied the area navigation charts and pinpointed Bundi and Moki airstrips, located to the north of Goroka on the Ramu valley side of the Bismarck Range in Madang Province. While Herman and Hank practiced takeoffs and landings at Bundi, Steve got out of the plane to chat with the people gathered at the airstrip to watch. He wanted to practice his Neo-Melanesian Pidgin.

As he circulated among the people, he encountered Francisca Gendi, a Baptist. She had returned to the Bundi village after being run over by a vehicle in Madang town. Due to her disability, which left her on crutches and with speech impairment,

Francisca could no longer stay in Madang because her family deserted her. Returning to Bundi, Francisca began praying that God would send someone to start a Baptist church. That day, after praying fourteen years, she rejoiced to hear that Steve hoped to start his first ABWE aviation church plant there.

Steve sensed the villagers' desperate need of salvation in Christ, and this burden and hard work bore fruit. By 2004, the ministry in Bundi averaged 100 in attendance and had thirty baptized, active members who were responsible for starting and maintaining five other fellowships that met weekly. Many of those area fellowships, located in remote mountain villages, took four to eight hours to reach on foot.

At the end of September, Hank, satisfied that he could turn to responsibilities elsewhere, had Herman continue working on Steve's flight proficiency in flying the mountains, charting alternate routes in and out of canyons, and practicing takeoffs and landings on one-way strips. Flying in PNG was a challenge. Approaching Bundi one day, Steve piloted; Herman observed and encouraged. To clear the mountains and clouds obstructing their flight, the TP206 climbed to 10,000 feet. The weather was marginal, with rain and clouds surrounding the entire area. Steve had planned to show the Jesus video and preach the gospel of Christ in Bundi, but the village was completely socked in. Circling the area, Steve prayed, asking God to clear the way according to His plan. After circling again, Steve and Herman watched the clouds move as though God's hand had swept them out of the way to enable a safe landing.

The villagers crowded around as the pilots climbed from the cabin. "It's been raining all day, and when you flew around, it cleared for you to land!" God's control over the wind and rain, and His answer to prayer demonstrated His mighty power to all who witnessed it that day.

Those who knew the condition of the many steep mountain airstrips where Steve landed and took off were grateful for God's protection. Some of the airstrips were at a 12.5 percent slope, and once the plane started rolling for takeoff, it couldn't be stopped because the brakes wouldn't hold it on grass. But over the succeeding years of the Aholts' ministry in New Guinea, the Lord protected both pilot and aircraft from mishap.

TWENTY-SEVEN ✈

A NEW DIRECTOR FOR ABWE AIR

After seventeen months of working with Steve on PNG's challenging aviation program—testing alternate routes in case of severe weather, locating airstrips for emergency landings, and practicing various procedures—Herman and Tami talked and prayed about their next step in mission service. They knew that Hank was nearing retirement age and discussed the possibility of moving to Georgia to help at the air base part time while Herman got a flying job. They considered becoming full-time short-termers, to help out wherever God showed them a need.

Then, in 1996, as they prepared to return to the US, they received a fax from Hank with the following invitation:

> Let me present some thought-provoking ideas to you and Tami. Would there be any chance that you could go back out to PNG in the future to work with Tim Gainey for six months, and give Steve a refresher if he is there at that time? Also, we could use your help down in Brazil for a year. As you know Clif (Jensen) is gone for at least a few years. I need someone with your expertise, gifts, and experience. Would you and Tami pray about coming full time with ABWE Air?
>
> In less than three years, I'll be seventy years old. The Lord has led Ruth and me to pray for someone to pick up this mantle, and He has laid you on our hearts. Pray about it. We have talked to Dr. Kempton about it. It will be his job to make it known beyond this circle if God leads you to help us full time.

Herman and Tami had a *zillion* questions as they considered Hank's proposal. Though they knew it would mean a major change, including Candidate Class and more training, they were both excited. They were open to God's leading wherever and whatever it might entail.

After their return to the US and introduction to Dr. Kempton and the ABWE Board, Herman and Tami attended the July 1997 Candidate Class and received appointment to become ABWE Air's administrator upon Hank's retirement. In June 1998 they moved from Michigan to live near the air base in Concord, Georgia, and Herman became the new administrator in 2002.

ANOTHER PILOT FOR PNG

Meanwhile, having flown in all kinds of PNG weather, in and out of canyons and challenging airstrips throughout the highland while he instructed Steve, Herman was able to recommend criteria that Hank could use to better prepare Tim Gainey, another new pilot, for flying in PNG.

Tim and Rebekah Gainey had completed their Bible training, and Tim his aviation training, at Piedmont Baptist College. They attended ABWE Candidate Classes and were appointed in June 1994 to partner with the Aholts in PNG. The Gaineys' prefield ministry had to be partially postponed while both Tim and Rebekah held down full-time jobs in order to pay off college debts. Finally, in 1997, Tim quit his job and concentrated on full-time prefield ministry.

Between the time of their ABWE appointment and the fall of 1997, Tim didn't have extra funds to rent a plane to get in the flight hours needed to stay current. Nearly three years passed before he could climb into a cockpit again, when he received an unexpected gift from the ABWE VIPs, a group of retired missionaries who give an offering once a year to help out prefield missionaries with special needs. Their gift made it possible to rent a plane as needed, enabling Tim to get recurrent in flying, as well as save travel time by getting to meetings in a plane, when practical.

Before 1998 came to a close, Tim and Rebekah had paid off their $40,000 school debt, and God had supplied funds to enable Tim to get the 150 hours of flight time he needed. Hank and Herman suggested that banner flying would give him good experience for PNG, so Tim began flying for a company out of Conway, South Carolina, towing banners on the beach. Flying this way added up to a savings of $15,000, which he otherwise would have spent to rent an airplane, and he was building flight hours in a tail-dragger, a plane with a wheel on its tail. The banner-towing experience also saved Tim the time and expense of having to take a certification flight with the Civil Aeronautical Association in PNG in order to get his pilot's license, and it allowed him to get some airplane maintenance experience on the job.

GROWTH IN PNG

In PNG, Steve and Sandy Aholt, who were praying for the Gaineys to join them soon, began their fifth year of ministry. Steve and Sandy were rejoicing because in the midst of political turmoil and civil unrest in the Goroka area, God had protected them. They flew to Bundi three times each week. On Sundays, they conducted Sunday school and worship; on Tuesdays, Sandy taught a literacy class to women in the church, while Steve held evangelistic open-air meetings or visitation; and on Wednesdays, Sandy conducted evangelism and literacy review, while Steve counseled and encouraged believers and helped the men make improvements to the church property. A house on stilts had been built for a permanent pastor to live in; clean, fresh drinking water had been piped down from the mountain, supplying hundreds with water; and Steve had assisted many in emergency medical situations.

"I thought that my son Ben would have to have his leg amputated and that he would probably die," one father reported. "Ben snapped his right femur into two parts when he jumped from a fruit tree. We carried him for hours to reach the aid post near Bundi, only to learn that they could do nothing. On Sunday, the next morning, we heard the sound of the missionary's plane."

Steve transported Tobias, the father, and Ben to the hospital in Goroka. The fractured femur healed without complications. Through Steve's witness, Tobias trusted Christ as his personal Savior, and this Roman Catholic family began attending services.

When the Aholts couldn't get into Bundi because of rainy weather and thick cloud cover or aircraft repairs, the believers themselves met throughout the week to sing, pray, and listen to God's Word explained to them by one of the men Steve had mentored.

After trees were donated to the church, Steve and the believers cut them down to be sawed into lumber for the permanent church building. Before it was time for furlough, Steve, following blueprints and the advice of other missionaries, had the main posts up for this fifty- by twenty-two-foot structure.

THE GAINEYS ARRIVE IN PNG

Before the Aholts left on furlough, the Gaineys arrived in PNG, where Steve would orient Tim in flight operations. In their absence, Tim would continue the oversight of the building project and the church services. The Gaineys also spent their first months in PNG learning Neo-Melanesian Pidgin, until Hank arrived from the Amazon in May 2000 to give Tim his check flight and clearance to fly into the more difficult landing strips in the region. For Tim, the flight with Hank into Yomneki on May 20 was the culmination of a seven-year dream. Ever since Tim had spent a week there with ABWE missionary Rich Ernst while on their AMP trip in 1992, he had dreamed of piloting a plane to this village.

THE 'BIRD OF PARADISE' FLIES TO GUWASA

The Lord blessed the Gaineys' ministry at Bundi, but when the Aholts returned to PNG in October 2001, Tim and Rebekah expected to start mission work in another village. They asked God to supply as they looked for His choice of a PNG couple to partner with them. They especially prayed about two villages—Aiome and Guwasa. In answer to this prayer, the Lord allowed Tim to meet Peter Karo, from Guwasa, located in a remote area in the Eastern Highlands Province. Although Peter had been saved while in another town, he had a concern for his people and influenced the Gaineys to reach Guwasa with the gospel. The Church Planting Committee of the PNG Field Council approved.

Due to the ongoing responsibilities at Bundi, at first the Gaineys could make only infrequent flights to Guwasa to get acquainted with its villagers, hold special services, and assure those who attended that they intended to start a Baptist church there. From the beginning, Pastor Woemo and the members of Goroka Baptist Church in Goroka, where the ABWE air base was located, worked alongside the missionaries in this new endeavor.

On July 3, 2001, the Gaineys, along with Pastor Woemo and a Bible college student named Taitus, held a special day of meetings in Guwasa. Tim and Pastor Woemo had agreed to give Taitus the experience of preaching that day. After his message, twenty-three villagers made professions of faith. Though it became evident that not all of that number understood, and that they would need to be dealt with again later, the people were attentive and eager to listen to the Word of God. Rebekah met separately with the women, in a house packed with ladies who wanted to know how to be saved. After she presented the plan of salvation, nine ladies came to tell her that they had accepted Christ.

At the close of this special meeting, Peter Karo had a surprise

for the missionary family. Along with a large offering of fresh
fruits, vegetables, and assorted gifts of arrows, stone axes, *bilums*
(hand-woven string bags), he presented them with a beautifully
mounted red bird of paradise and told them the following story:

> This bird of paradise lives in the area surrounding
> Guwasa, but will fly from valley to valley in search of food.
> When it finds good food in a particular valley, it will fly to
> the top of a tall tree, perch, and call a message to tell all of
> the other birds of paradise, "Good news! Food is here. Come
> and eat with me."

Peter then turned to Tim and said, "You are our bird of paradise. We want you to fly into Guwasa to tell all of the people
here the good news that Jesus came to save us from our sins. We
want you to call out and tell everyone around us that they can
come and get spiritual food at the Baptist Church. You are our
bird of paradise."

Tears sprang to Tim's eyes as he received this special gift from
Peter's hand. He and Rebekah hung it in a prominent place on
the wall over their dining room table as a reminder of why they
are in PNG.

In August 2002, the Guwasa villagers finished building a bush
house for the Gaineys. PNG custom dictated that they open this
house, sectioned into three parts with walls about six feet high
separating each section, to others in the village. In the front section or community room, the Gainey family sat to talk with the
many people that came to visit. When everyone finished talking,
they lay down on the dirt floor and went to sleep. The first night
in their bush house, twenty-seven people slept in this section.
Cooking and eating took place in the second section, and the
third section was reserved for the Gaineys' sleeping quarters.

In September, the congregation moved their temporary meeting quarters from beside the airport to the church's new prop-

erty, on a hill overlooking the airstrip. For the New Believer's Class, there were thirty-nine inside the church and some twenty sitting under trees outside. From one week to the next, in Tim's absence, 200 villagers erected all the side posts and half of the roof posts for a permanent church structure. Other than helping them mark where they should put the building and bringing nails from Goroka, Tim had little responsibility in its construction, which was completed with grass roof and bamboo sides.

In 2003, Rebekah was expecting the birth of their fourth child, so the Gaineys had to be away from Guwasa for a couple of months. In June, the family flew to Cairns, Australia, for the baby's due date, which was late in that month, and in their absence, the ministry continued to grow.

The Gaineys described one event when a church member decided to follow the Lord instead of the PNG culture:

> Wan, a believer who was faithful to the services and did a lot of work to build both the house and the church, was going to take a second wife. Tim counseled with him and prayed with him on several occasions. Before the marriage was final, Wan decided to send the second lady home and not marry her. In the PNG culture, it is very acceptable for him to get a second wife; however, we praise the Lord that Wan obeyed Scripture instead of PNG culture.

The Gainey family arrived back in the US for their first furlough in June 2004, leaving the Guwasa ministry in the hands of Loya and Kanigi, missionaries of Goroka Baptist Church, until their return.

Back in Bundi, the ministry was also moving forward. On March 13, 2005, Bundi voted to call Timothy Barey to be their first national pastor. After furlough in 2005, Steve and Sandy Aholt hope to see Timothy ordained and hold the official church opening at Bundi. They look forward to joining a team of Simbai pastors, assisting them with transportation and ministry to un-reached people groups in the Simbai region.

By God's grace, the converted drug-runner TP206 that Hank and I rescued in Carlsbad, New Mexico, continues to play an effective part in spreading the gospel in PNG. Both the Aholts and Gaineys are raising funds to build a hangar for TP-206 at the Goroka airport.

Other workers are joining the PNG team, as well. In late 2005, John and Kisti Huffman left the US to join the aviation team in PNG, where they will complete language study and begin their ministry in Goroka. Joel and Rachel Prigge, now in prefield ministry, also plan to serve there, and future plans for ABWE Air in PNG include getting an additional Cessna 206 "up in the air for Him."

The air route that Al Yoder and Matt Cropsey flew from Benjamin Constant, Brazil, to the ABWE Airbase in Concord, Georgia

★ Marks the emergency landing on the Cuyuni River when a cylinder head blew

ABWE air bases

USA

Miami

Puerto Rico

Trinidad

Georgetown
Guyana

Boa Vista

Benjamin
Constant

BRAZIL

TWENTY-EIGHT ✈

NEVER A DULL MOMENT

Hank described a missionary pilot's life as one with "never a dull moment." After years of listening to the adventures of ABWE pilots, I'd have to say that's an understatement! One common factor in each unique tale is the truth of God's sovereignty. His sovereign purpose in allowing such events is to conform His children to the image of Jesus Christ.

The Brazil floatplane CJG had served 33 years of hard labor. There had been engine overhauls, float repairs after damages, repaint jobs, and constant preventive maintenance, but it was time for a complete overhaul. The amphibian floats were bad leakers. To ship and import a new set of floats to Brazil for $25,000 was out of the question, so it was decided to fly the plane to the US air base for repairs.

Al Yoder prepared CJG to make the flight. Matt Cropsey, who was preparing to serve in Togo, needed more flight hours. In an effort to help, Hank sent him to the Amazon to accompany Al. This flight became a memorable adventure, and a course in God's classroom of life.

Tuesday, March 11, 1997, dawned over the Javarizinho River, painting streaks of fluorescent yellow and magenta, mixed with deeper blues that glimmered on the water. Al and Matt had packed CJG with their flying gear before they shoved the aircraft off the ramp and into the Javarizinho current, ready to begin the long trip back to the US for the plane's overhaul. Kim and the children had shared breakfast and prayer with them earlier, then followed them down to the floating hangar. They waved goodbye, watching the plane taxi out to the Amazon for takeoff, headed to Boa Vista on Brazil's northern boundary. Kim silently entrusted their protection to the heavenly Father's care, little realizing how much they would need it before their trip ended.

Hank had contacted the Directors of Civil Aeronautics and the various embassies to advise them of our aircraft flying in their airspace, and secured permission for their flight plan: Benjamin Constant to Boa Vista, over Venezuela and the Guiana Highlands to Trinidad, a stop in Puerto Rico, and then to Georgia. He would be recording time and locations via GPS and giving the pilots flight-following by amateur radio every hour on the half hour, including weather information acquired through Jepp-Fax worldwide service. Also participating in the flight-following was Bill Sill, in Pennsylvania.

All went well the first day of the flight. On Wednesday, the second day, that changed. Dan Scheltema, our son, wrote a full account of this incident for the ABWE book *Jungle Myths.* Dan's chapter is titled, "Baptists Don't Believe in the Miraculous; Or Do They?" The following excerpts are taken from that account:

> At 7:30 a.m. EST, Al and Matt buckled themselves into the cockpit, lifted off, and flew north toward the mountains separating the Amazon Basin from the Caribbean and the coast of Guyana. . . .
>
> Coaxing the plane up to 12,400 feet to cross the mountains was difficult. Scanning the dials for overheating, Al found nothing to worry about. Uneasy because of the plane's resistance at climbing to less than ideal altitude, Al turned and headed for a lower pass through the mountains, where he could safely cross to an alternate landing location already listed on his flight plan. This was a logical response since maps aren't precise for this area of the world in spite of modern satellite mapping methods. Most elevations are listed as "estimated. . . ."
>
> At 8:30 a.m., Al made contact, reporting the change in

destination. The weather worsened; clouds closed in so that the world below was a grayish-white soup. Only the mountain peaks poked through, looking like spikes nailed through a sheet of plywood. But visibility was good and turbulence minimal at 9,500 feet. Matt was napping.

About 9:15 a.m., it happened: a loud explosion in the engine! Cockpit peace was instantly shattered; urgency drove the eyes and brains of both men as they sought the reason.

Al remembers being angry that his wife, Kim, was going to become a widow. Feeling silly that his mind had raced ahead to that extreme conclusion, he refocused his energies on the crisis at hand. The engine continued running, but with less power, and it vibrated badly.

"Mayday! Mayday!"

Bill responded immediately from his home, Hank minutes later from Atlanta. The invisible 1,800-mile umbilical cord would soon be carrying death-defying information to the pilots.

Fighting to stretch out the plane's glide path, Al estimated the plane was losing altitude at the rate of 400 feet per minute. Al and Matt did their best to plot a course between the mountain peaks as they descended into the soup; "estimated" mountain elevations didn't help. The whole situation had turned grim. Up north in the States, Hank and Bill frantically gathered charts and maps, looking for landmarks Al and Matt might be able to use.

The little plane sank into dense clouds and was lashed by rain. Waiting somewhere below was the hard ground, cushioned by trees 300-feet tall. From the air, the jungle looks like unending miles of giant broccoli: soft, nourishing, even inviting. But once below that deceptive vegetation, few come back—the last seven planes to take that plunge hadn't. The mountain peaks on either side waited silently to envelop the tiny plane.

From Atlanta, using information provided by the global positioning system (GPS), Hank was able to steer Al toward a local river. Since the plane could land on both runways and water, a river normally meant a safe landing spot.

The Amazon River at many places is miles wide and drops only 400 feet in 3,000 miles (Hank called it the longest runway in the world). The Cuyuni River—where Hank was directing Al and Matt—drops 450 feet in only 100 miles and boasts 75 whitewater rapids. Yet it held their best hope for a safe landing.

At this point, Al and Matt had been flying blind for 35 minutes. How close were they to a mountain? Were the 300-foot trees about to snare them? Minute by minute, the drama continued. That radio voice—a whole continent away—proved comforting.

Assured by Hank that the GPS coordinates showed a place to land, Al and Matt flew on. Breaking through the clouds at 1,500 feet, they were encouraged to see they were well above the trees, but no river was in sight. Nearby, they saw threatening mountain peaks thrusting up into the clouds. Al steered toward Georgetown, Guyana's capital, hoping to get as close to the city as possible.

Flying over a ridge, they suddenly saw the river! The plane was doing better in the heavier atmosphere and lower altitude, and holding steadier in the rich air. Al turned to follow the river, hoping to reach the coast and Georgetown.

It wasn't to be. The plane stopped holding altitude. Knowing they must land, Al looked for the best stretch of river and plotted his approach. Circling, they passed over a barge—civilization! People!

Most landings are made against the wind to slow the aircraft, but the situation here was the opposite. Not good, but at least the water was smooth, not whitewater rapids. The length and narrowness of the river would be tough—too short and too little room to maneuver.

"Loosen your seat belt, Matt. We may have to get out fast," Al told his co-pilot.

Once committed to the landing, Al had cut off the airplane's power, so they came down hard. Hard enough to force one float completely under the water. Before they could move to get out, the float popped above the surf. The tailwind turned the powerless airplane toward the riverbank, and directly ahead loomed a large tree. Planes normally slow quickly against the drag of the water on the floats. But that wasn't happening this time.

"Brace for impact!" yelled the captain.

In the providence of God, the tree was rotten and disintegrated like a feather pillow. The cushioning tree absorbed the crash energy and barely scratched the plane. They were down, safe and unhurt. Even the airplane, engine troubles aside, was in good shape.

Leaping out onto the floats, Matt and Al grabbed shoreline vegetation to anchor the plane against the strong current. They tied up the plane.

Back on the radio, Al shared the good news of their safe landing with Hank and Bill. Conserving battery power was now a major factor. They agreed to less frequent and shorter transmissions.

The current still had the potential to damage the airplane. As Al and Matt worked to ensure the plane's safety, they heard an engine in the distance. Around the bend came a motorized canoe from the barge they had flown over. These men were gold miners operating a suction barge.

The area was known to be on the drug traffic route north, and small planes are the transportation of choice in that trade. The miners were suspicious, but they were eager to help and won over by the deportment and composure of the two missionary pilots. They contributed food, water, and communications assistance. Al and Matt advised the Guyanese authorities that they had landed safely, but needed assistance. They waited with their aircraft.

Assured that the two men were down safely, Hank switched hats and called the office of the president of Guyana, then fired off the following fax to that office:

URGENT URGENT URGENT URGENT
AIRCRAFT CESSNA PT-CJG (AMPHIBIAN) FORCED DOWN BY ENGINE FAILURE ON CUYUNI RIVER WEDNESDAY, MARCH 12 AT 9:45 A.M. ATLANTA, GEORGIA TIME. COORDINATES: 6 DEGREES, 47 MINUTES, 87 NORTH, 59 DEGREES, 58 MINUTES, 86 WEST. PILOT ALLEN YODER, CO-CAPTAIN MATT CROPSEY ARE USA CITIZENS. I HAVE BEEN IN CONTACT BY AMATEUR RADIO. PLEASE SEND HELP AT ONCE AS THEY ARE IN DANGER. THANK YOU FOR YOUR KIND HELP.

HANK SCHELTEMA, DIRECTOR OF INTERNATIONAL AVIATION FOR THE ASSOCIATION OF BAPTISTS FOR WORLD EVANGELISM.

But Guyana was not indebted to Hank. So even this veteran experienced difficulty reaching the authorities in Guyana. Calling their embassy in Washington, D.C., he learned the reason. President Cheddi Jagan had died, and the nation's attention and resources were focused on his funeral.

Hank contacted Air Search & Rescue in Miami and Puerto Rico for any assistance they could give. The Miami office aided their communication with the Guyanese officials. But four hours passed before Hank heard from a Guyanese deputy. Provided with more information, the deputy promised to send a helicopter out, but not until the next morning. That discouraging news came first, then Al's radio battery went dead. Now, on-site, face-to-face communication was the only way to help. Hank had to get there!

At the river, Al and Matt opened the cowling to inspect the engine. Before the radio died, they had been able to tell Hank that a cylinder had blown, and the explosion had knocked off the exhaust system on the right side of the engine. The piston head had blown apart from the barrel, making visible a one-inch gap.

From years of servicing airplanes, Hank created a list of possibly needed parts and hunted for them. Hank was pleased to discover that a recent parts shipment from the supplier included a few more things than he had noticed when he inspected the shipment previously—including the essential cylinder.

The next morning, a Guyanese Army Air Force helicopter flew over the downed Cessna. It brought the federal police and the leader of the Civil Air Patrol to inspect the plane. They were touchy about paperwork and leery of drug traffic. Small airplanes arouse suspicion. Even though Hank had quickly arranged visas for Al and Matt by phone, officials started hassling the downed fliers.

The officials inspected the damaged airplane engine themselves. Colonel Michael Charles, the helicopter pilot, feeling an espirit de corps toward fellow pilots and knowing they had been through a grueling situation, stepped in to shield the two men from further examination. Colonel Charles was amazed that they had landed safely.

Al and Matt were airlifted to a nearby airstrip and then boarded a flight to Georgetown.

Another pilot, Colonel Miles Williams, was also a protector. "We know what you are going through—forced down in a strange country." Williams stayed with Al and Matt through six hours of interrogation and debriefing by the civil police, federal police, and Customs and Immigration officers. Finally, at 8 p.m. on Thursday, the paperwork was in order, and the two weary travelers were officially welcomed to Guyana.

Meanwhile, back in the States, Hank scrambled to arrange a flight south, get the parts he had ordered sent directly to Miami, make arrangements to meet Bob Cropsey, Matt's dad, and get on to Georgetown. With everything he could think of and find on short notice, he was en route to Miami by 11 a.m. The rendezvous in Miami was smooth, but the flight to Georgetown was canceled. The only other flight was overbooked, due to the earlier cancellation.

By explaining the emergency situation, Hank and Bob were able to get seats. Arriving at Timehri International Airport at 1 a.m. Friday, they were warmly welcomed by Al and Matt. By 2:30 a.m. they were in bed.

Time was an enemy. The clouds and rain, through which Al and Matt had descended, were having their normal effect: rising water. The miners reported that the river was rising fast. More water meant stronger currents, which would endanger the aircraft.

Up at 7:30 a.m., Al and Hank scavenged for parts Hank hadn't known he needed to bring with him. The US Ambassador, Ms. Heibern, was helpful in making contacts which produced a needed exhaust system from Guyana Sugar Corporation.

With everything in hand, Al called the Army Air Force to see about getting a chopper lift back to the river. Colonel Charles was busy and could not take them until the next day, unless they could be ready to leave in one hour. They were.

Arriving at a sandbar one mile from the plane, the pilots asked the miners to help them ferry the plane to the sandbar, where it would be easier to work on the engine.

The miners had been pumping out the floats, protecting

the plane against the current, and doing everything they could to keep the plane safe.

It was 6 p.m. on Friday before work on the engine could begin. Exhausted from accumulated stress, the men worked until 10 p.m. and then decided to get some sleep.

But the water was still rising. At the rate it was rising, their makeshift sandbar repair outpost would be underwater in fourteen hours. So by 2:30 a.m. they were back at work, using flashlights in calf-deep water, with little fish nibbling at their legs. A can of oil tipped over on the tools, making them slippery and hard to grip. Occasional thunder was answered by howler monkeys from trees on both sides of the river.

By 11 a.m., they had reassembled the engine and done the test runs. Al did a solo test flight, not wanting to risk any additional weight until the engine was proven and he'd had a chance to navigate a tricky takeoff from the winding river.

The chopper, due back to take the men out, was delayed. With the river rising, and their sandbar all but gone, the men decided to fly out in the repaired Cessna. Takeoff required the plane to gain speed around a bend in the river and leap into the sky before the trees claimed them. With full power on the newly repaired cylinder, Al coaxed the plane up to airspeed, and lifted her over the trees. Although not as difficult as the landing, takeoff proved a tense moment. They landed PT-CJG at Timehri International at 1 p.m. to a hero's welcome.

When Al and Matt landed in Miami on Thursday, they were only four days behind schedule. God keeps His promises. *And call upon Me in the day of trouble; I will deliver thee.* . . . Both missionary pilots survived without injury.

Psalm 50:15 also reads, . . . *and thou shalt glorify Me.* Through every phase of this perilous incident the Lord was glorified.

Though our aircraft developed engine failure in flight, through amateur radio, contact was made and maintained throughout the ensuing hours. This enabled Al and Matt to sustain a calm and confident spirit, knowing that physical help was on its way. The helicopter pilot who flew them from the Cuyuni River to Georgetown acknowledged God. Al and Matt overheard this conversation between the pilot and someone at the chopper base.

"Do you know where the American pilot is?"

The helicopter pilot answered, "In the chopper with me."

"He sure was lucky."

"No, it wasn't luck. He's a 'God man.' He talks to God and reads his Bible every day."

Over time, Al came to understand how God used this experience, even when his faith failed and questions assailed him. "Why did God allow me to spend twenty minutes thinking I would die? I lost my edge, my nerve, my confidence as a pilot. Why did I have to fly the plane from Guyana to the US? Why did God think I needed to be tested further when all I wanted was to be out of aviation?"

Peter Marshall, US Senate Chaplain in the 1940s, said, "God will not permit any troubles to come upon us, unless He has a specific plan by which great blessing can come out of the difficulty." Romans 8:28 and 29 says it even better!

The following year, Al wrote:

Much has happened this year to change me, to mold me to His image. I have learned that my disappointments are His appointments. I have learned that I should have no agenda; that is, no plan set in stone. No reserve—no holding back. No retreat; that is, no quitting and no regrets. God is faithful.

TWENTY-NINE

GOD'S HIGHER WAYS

Hank was all set to fly the refurbished amphibian floatplane back to Brazil in January 1999 when God changed the plan. God's thoughts are not our thoughts, neither are our ways His ways. Yet to those who walk with God and look to Him for guidance, He makes His thoughts and ways known.

The newly installed wing extensions on CJG legally allowed two extra passengers, but on a test flight with a full load of fuel and passengers, the old floats could not safely sustain the higher allowable gross weight. Larger floats were needed to get full utilization of the aircraft, so Hank searched for a good buy.

Then the FAA issued an AD (Advisory Directive) on CJG's new Continental 10-520 engine, and the Lord showed that His way was better than ours. A defective tool had been used when counterweight bushings on this engine were installed at the factory. Engines manufactured in 1998 had a potential crankshaft problem and had to be inspected by authorized factory personnel before further flight. For the inspection, Hank had to disassemble the new engine installed in the floatplane. Had Hank flown as scheduled, there might have been an engine failure en route to the Amazon or a complicated situation to get the engine inspected overseas.

Instead, Hank obtained larger, damaged, Wipline amphibian floats, less struts and all accessories, at a real bargain, and God sent experienced sheet-metal volunteer mechanics Mark Garris, Ralph Wethli, and assistant-in-training Bobby Burdette to help Hank repair the floats. As the work neared completion, funds ran out, but "Hurrah for God!" one friend said. "His servants, entrusted with His treasure and prompted by Him, supplied the need."

ANOTHER RETURN TO THE AMAZON

Our plan did not include a year of ministry in the Amazon; however, by August 1999, in order to keep the Amazon floatplane DNY up in the air, it became clear that God was directing Hank and me to fill in for the Yoders, who were returning stateside. (The thought of climbing up and down the slippery, fifty-foot-high embankments along the Amazon at seventy years of age is not what convinced us!)

We applied for permanent visas and they were granted within a month; Hank's Brazilian flying and mechanic licenses were still current. Our absence from the air base in Georgia, of necessity, thrust Herman and Tami Teachout into assignments besides pre-field ministry, providing them with valuable experience before they took full responsibility for ABWE Air.

Meanwhile, Colombia had become a center of terrorist activity during the latter 1990s. The ABWE Amazon aviation programs, both in Peru and Brazil, operated on its frontiers. ABWE aircraft and pilots were in danger, not only from civil-war guerrillas and drug-runners, but also of getting caught in the crossfire. The town of El Tigre had been attacked and reported twenty slaughtered. The ABWE mission hospital in Santo Antonio do Içá was located about one hundred miles downriver from this Colombian town, on the Putumayo River (known in Brazil as the Içá River). Al Yoder operated a strategic plane ministry with Indians halfway between the hospital and El Tigre. And when the Peruvian interdiction (shoot-down program) was activated, drug-runners deviated from Peruvian airspace to Brazilian airspace, flying over ABWE ministry areas.

Hank knew that, with this increased threat to the safety of ABWE personnel and families, it was time to follow through on his contingency plan, and our return to stand in the gap from

August 1999 to October 2000 facilitated this. The plan involved building a huge floating house-hangar to move at least one, and possibly both, floatplanes off the frontier if the situation demanded it. Hank and our daughter Kanda Way, an architectural designer, designed the floor plan.

Hank had several other obligations at that time: first, to visit the Zemmers in Bahia, Brazil, with a prospective missionary pilot; second, to attend graduation for his Master of Divinity and honorary doctorate from Immanuel Baptist Seminary, in Georgia; and last, a trip to Papua New Guinea to give Tim Gainey his check flight.

In the midst of all this, God brought Bob and Karen Hamilton and their family to Benjamin Constant. Hank had met the Hamiltons at a missions conference in Michigan and encouraged Bob, who had flown commercially for sixteen years, to consider a career as a missionary pilot with ABWE. The Hamiltons were appointed by ABWE, completed prefield, and were now ready to begin service in Benjamin Constant. I had been assigned to contract Portuguese language teachers for them and to oversee their language program. Hank, who had first introduced Bob to floatplane flying on the man-made lake back at the Georgia air base, now oriented him to missionary aviation in the right seat while flying to and from the island of Araria for a Sunday evangelical outreach, since Bob was unable to fly as pilot in command until he obtained his permanent visa.

In between Hank's trips and our efforts to help the Hamiltons get settled, Hank contracted workmen to cut and deliver lumber for the new floating house-hangar. The lumbermen used a winch, ropes, and up to eight men to haul each post from the boat up the embankment. The wood had to be washed free of sticky mud; separated according to width, length, and kind of wood; then stacked upright on sturdy beams to dry properly. Months in advance of building, supplies had been purchased and readied for the builders: three-foot handmade spikes, materials to make doors and cupboards, aluminum sheeting for the roof, and styrofoam for insulation.

BUILDING THE FLOATING HANGAR

On March 12, 2000, ten men and one woman, who was a nurse, from Grace Baptist Church of Kankakee, Illinois, arrived to build the floating house-hangar. Our daughter, Kim Yoder, and her friend, Gina Harlan, accompanied the travelers and came to help me cook and wash clothes for this energetic group of God's choice servants. Together, these volunteers raised $22,000 to fund most of the cost of construction. Only eternity will reveal the impact this ministry had on their lives, on those of Brazilians, and on the ABWE Air ministry in the Amazon. An e-mail message sent by one of the men told of one blessing:

> Sunday evening we all attended church in Benjamin Constant. There were over 120 in attendance. We sang a lot of choruses. The doctor and his fiancé that we witnessed to on Friday night were in attendance, and so were two other doctors studying here in the city. Ted got to preach, and Kim Yoder, Hank's daughter, was the interrupter. I mean interpreter! Five Brazilians accepted Christ as their Savior. We were so grateful.

It didn't take long to understand why God provided a nurse to travel with the builders. Working under the blazing Amazon sun, on tipsy logs bouncing on the river, took its toll. On the first day of work alone, a volunteer named Shane reported to Nurse Linnaea with a bruised wrist, banged-up knee, and injuries from straddling a log (Shane was often called "a walking band-aid"); Jesse came with a bruised ankle; Mark and Dave fell in the river and suffered heat exhaustion, and Dave lost his glasses; and Joe banged his shins. Linnaea daily treated one or more for sunburn, and e-mail messages to loved ones always included a medical report, which usually contained descriptions such as, "Everybody is peeling like an orange."

When asked what had been the hardest part of the trip up to that time, Linnaea said, "Dealing with the heat and the humidity. The steps to the house from the floating hangar are really steep and difficult when I'm helping with laundry." On average, Linnaea and I hung out seven to eight loads of laundry daily since most of the men changed clothing at midday and some again for supper.

She and I also helped Kim and Gina with the meals. With only one six-burner stove, we had to monitor our time carefully to boil five-gallon pans of drinking water for twenty minutes and still have time to prepare meals. We strained drinking water to remove critters, then filled five-gallon igloos with the purified water. Overnight hours provided time to freeze containers to cool the water in the igloos.

All the workers learned to keep a good grip on their tools. When the river dried up later in the year, along the muddy bank, Brazilians found hammers, pliers, screwdrivers, and other sundry equipment that had been dropped in the water. It was a happy day when the first-floor decking was finished; accidental falls into the river and the loss of tools almost ceased.

Twelve fifty-foot-long floating logs were locked together by two sixty-six-foot foundation timbers, weighing 1,000 pounds each and made of *masaranduba,* a heavy wood that doesn't float or rot in water. It took several men to lift, carry, and set them on top of the floating logs. The men wielded ten-pound sledgehammers, straining muscles to pound the three-foot spikes into the foundation timbers. The upright ironwood posts were twenty-three-feet high; the twenty-foot, hand-hewn floorboards had to be planed and sanded after nailing. There were no derricks to lift and place the roof trusses to support the twenty-three-foot-long aluminum sheets nailed to these high posts, thirty feet above water.

In two weeks, the volunteers finished the hard labor on the basic structure and the roof and built the stairs to the second floor. Despite long hours of backbreaking lifting, pounding nails into nail-resistant hardwood, balancing over the river, scorching under the equatorial sun, and enduring high humidity, these men exemplified self-control. There were no temper outbursts, no hurt feelings, no unwholesome talk—only a spirit of unity, cooperation, and love. What a testimony to the four Brazilian men who worked alongside them those eleven days!

A few weeks later, Hank's brother, Bill, arrived to build doors and cupboards and to nail walls in place. In August, two young people and two electricians from Griffin, Georgia, spent three days installing electrical wiring to run lights either by twelve-volt battery or through a gasoline generator. Three of them then had to return to their stateside jobs, but Tim Butler remained to help screen windows.

The Yoder family returned from the US in September 2000. Kim and I, with the help of two young Brazilian men, stuffed wads of cotton into cracks in the first- and second-level floors and shot liquid sealant into the wall cracks to protect from rain and invading bugs. With its final coat of paint, inside and outside, the floating house-hangar looked habitable and ready for occupancy.

The contingency plan could now be actualized. One of the ABWE floatplanes would be moved from the Peru–Colombia frontier and, if necessary, the house-hangar could accommodate both planes. It was mobile and could be towed and moored in a different location, as needed.

A NEW BASE FOR THE YODERS AND THE HAMILTONS

A few weeks after Hank and I returned to the US, the Yoders hired a tugboat to tow the house-hangar ninety miles downriver to its new location on the Camatiã River. Hank had negotiated the purchase of twenty-five acres at the threshold of the

Ticuna Indian Reservation near São Paulo de Olivença, a sizeable town in which the Yoders had previously started a church. This move would conserve flight time for outreach to the Ticuna settlements. Instead of a two-hour round trip from Benjamin Constant, ministry to several small Ticuna communities near the Camatiã could be done in less than 15 minutes, cutting the cost of flying to a fraction—from $200 to $25. The relocation put the Yoders closer to Santo Antonio do Içá, and Al would also be able to conserve fuel and time in serving ABWE missionaries at the Amazon Baptist Hospital.

While the Yoders were getting situated at their new station, where their acreage would eventually prove to be an ideal campsite for youth ministry, they assumed leadership of the international church plant—comprised of Brazilians, Ticunas, Peruvians, and now Americans—in São Paulo, a work they had started in a previous term.

The Yoders' schedule expanded to include activities nearly every day. On Mondays, they flew to Santo Antonio do Içá to train church leaders in biblical counseling. They worked with several men in drug rehabilitation and with couples that had marriage problems. They returned on Tuesday, stopping to minister in Betania to assist another ABWE missionary. On Thursdays, they taught Ticuna leaders at Decuampu Bible Institute, a ten-minute flight from home on the Camatiã River. By canoe, they paddled to São Paulo de Olivença on Wednesdays for evening Bible study, then again on Saturday, when they stayed overnight and through Sunday to teach ESL (English as a Second Language), conduct AWANA club, and teach training classes for church leadership, Sunday worship services, and youth group. Their youth camp ministries at the property on the Camatiã grew to include young people from other ABWE mission stations. Groups of AMPers spent weeks with them during summer months.

Meanwhile, the Hamiltons had also moved to a different location—from a mission house in town to the house on the Javarizinho River—so that Bob could better oversee the floating hangar and floatplane. Until Bob obtained permanent documents to fly the floatplane for ministry, he accepted various responsibilities in cooperation with the Brazilian pastor of the Benjamin Constant church and taught English in the church school. Both Bob and Karen continued taking four classes daily in Portuguese. There were many unchurched families in their immediate neighborhood. Through a weekly kids club, in which the four younger Hamilton children took part, ten neighborhood children prayed to receive Christ as Savior. On Tuesday, Thursday, and Saturday, Karen held a Bible memory program with seventeen children who wanted to earn a Bible. The Hamiltons began inviting neighbors over to share a meal, hoping to have more opportunity to witness to the parents of the children. They also ministered in two small communities, first at Araria, then at Star of Peace.

AMAZON DILEMMA

By the year 2003, the Amazon field again faced a dilemma. The Hamiltons would be leaving for their first furlough. Who could live in the Javarizinho River house in Benjamin Constant, care for their household things, fly for emergencies, and watch over the floating hangar and floatplane DNY? There was nothing to keep Hank and me from filling in for them. Hank had turned over the administration of ABWE Air to Herman Teachout in September 2002. We both passed physical exams and felt fit. Hank's Brazilian licenses were current, and we had our permanent visas. When the "Amazonian call" came, we left Georgia in July and moved into "the house that Hank built," 43 years earlier. We committed, by God's grace, to stay for eighteen months.

THIRTY

THE SHADOW OF THE CROSS

"Ruth, look out your window, down to the right," Hank told me.

It was early in our first term in the Amazon, and I had baby Linda on my lap. Our other three children sat in back of us on the wooden bench of the Aeronca Sedan, the first floatplane Hank flew to Brazil in 1961. Reflected on the clouds beneath us I saw a colorful rainbow. "Wow! I didn't know that the rainbow made a complete circle."

"Did you notice what's in the center, inside the halo?"

"The shadow of the floatplane. It's beautiful."

"It's what some call the airman's cross," Hank said. "Watch. The rainbow travels right along with us. Every time I see it, I think of Jesus' promise—*Lo, I am with you alway, even unto the end of the world*" (Matt. 28:20b).

Each time we saw this phenomenon, I marveled. We were reminded of God's promise and presence with us as we served "up in the air for Him." God reminded me of this promise more than once, but in different ways. One was during a circumstance that transpired in 2003 after Hank and I were back flying in the Amazon to fill in during the Hamiltons' furlough.

AN ANNIVERSARY CELEBRATION

An anniversary celebration was in the making. The First Regular Baptist Church of Benjamin Constant planned to celebrate its forty-fifth anniversary with the ordination of its pastor. Pastor Cristiano Dias had come to Christ under the Peaces' ministry and had been discipled as a youth by the Yoders. In 1996, a

Brazilian missionary from an ABWE church in southern Brazil arrived to serve as pastor of the church, and with his encouragement, Cristiano came to believe God had directed him to full-time ministry.

Cristiano was married to Cristiane, a third-generation believer, whose mother Hank had baptized when she was still a teenager. Her grandfather had served as deacon for many years.

After Cristiano served a year's internship, the church voted to ordain and call this gifted young man to be their senior pastor. The Brazilian missionary pastor returned for this special occasion. The crowning day of the celebration, Cristiano's ordination, fell on Sunday, October 23. Two Brazilian missionaries from nearby congregations, a pastor from Tabatinga, Pastor Josué from southern Brazil, and Hank were also there to dedicate Cristiano to the ministry.

Cristiano was special—to church members and to American and Brazilian missionaries alike. Ten other young men from the church had been sent in previous years to far-off places to prepare for ministry and had not returned; they were serving the Lord elsewhere. But Cristiano had come to Christ, had been discipled, had been taught in the church Bible Institute, and had prepared for service in Benjamin Constant. He was "home-grown."

STAYING ON IN BENJAMIN CONSTANT

After the Brazilian missionaries and pastors returned to their places of ministry, Hank and I remained in Benjamin Constant to fulfill definite assignments and responsibilities. The floating hangar needed to be renovated and restocked to pass the official relicensing as an approved repair shop. Several volunteers offered to work on this project, scheduled for 2005. When Lois Wantoch retired and returned stateside, Hank was appointed to advertise and sell the mission property in Tabatinga, upriver thirty-five minutes by speedboat. Bob Hamilton asked him to continue personal discipleship Bible study with João, a recent believer. Pastor Cristiano desired Hank's help to substitute preach and teach in the Bible institute. Pastor asked me to teach keyboard and music reading and assist his wife in ladies' ministries. I also completed the compilation of a new Portuguese songbook.

Every morning at 6:30, after Hank did the marketing by motorbike, he headed down the fifty-foot muddy bank and across a twenty-five by eight-inch plank to work at the floating hangar until 9:30 a.m. He and his friend and helper, Chico, climbed back up to the house at mid-morning for pancakes and coffee, then returned to work on DNY's engine, airframe, or floats. In order to keep within the time limits on aircraft accessories and comply with mandatory overhauls, Al Yoder had sent DNY's parts away for official overhaul. The parts had worked fine when Al sent them away, but not so after the overhaul. Hank had to rebuild a magneto and the alternator, as well as reset the governor. After lunch, I joined them at the hangar to help clean, paint, or sort aircraft nuts, pins, and bolts, in order to give Hank a better idea of what needed to be restocked. Work kept our hands busy, while our minds were occupied with international events.

We received a notice that the US and Colombia had put back into action the "Air Bridge"; that is, the shoot-down policy for civilian aircraft suspected of carrying drugs. The trapezoid-shaped area of Colombia, across the border and upriver from Benjamin Constant, was the bottleneck for south-to-north drug traffic. Hank kept the alarm system on the house and floating hangar well maintained; theft was a constant threat. It was not unusual for the ultra-sensitive siren to awake us in the middle of the night—as it did again—all too soon.

"What's setting it off now?" Hank grumbled one morning at 2 a.m. The last time this happened, a bat, fluttering in the proximity of the alarm, had set off the siren. This time it was the house alarm blaring its siren. "You check the fuel shack out back," he said to me. "I'll check the porch out front."

"Can't see anybody out here," I yelled, after shining the spotlight over the area.

"Nor here." All was quiet for a moment, then Hank burst out laughing. "I found the invaders. Come see."

Ants by the *thousands* were crawling across the telephone line and over and under the alarm on the porch. This time, ants were the culprits, but we couldn't let down our guard, regardless of what or who set off the alarm.

One evening, Pastor Cristiano invited us over for fellowship. Following dinner, Cristiane handed their baby son to Hank. "We want to dedicate our baby to the Lord. Please pray and ask God to bless him," she said. Hank cuddled the sleeping baby in his arms and asked, "Have you decided on a name?"

"We're naming him after you, Brother Henrique," Pastor Cristiano added. "We want *our* Henrique to become a servant of God as you have been for so many years."

Hank was deeply moved. Riding home on the seat behind him on the motorbike, I whispered in his ear, "I wouldn't have missed tonight for anything." Not long after this, Pastor Cristiano endeared himself to me in another way.

All of the church's Christmas events took place on Christmas Eve. The Yoders were planning to fly up for our family get-together the day after Christmas, so Hank and I spent a quiet Christmas Day, reading and sharing excerpts from our books. After lunch, he left on the motorbike, returned ten minutes later, read a while longer, and rode off again on the motorbike.

"Where'd you go?" I asked when he returned.

"I'm measuring the distance of my morning walk. I've started training for the stress test for my pilot's physical in two weeks. I want to be sure I'm walking the right distance." (When they get older, commercial pilots are required to have a treadmill test.)

"Are you? Or do you need to add more?"

"It's okay now. I'll walk a bit farther in the morning."

Later that afternoon, Hank telephoned his 96-year-old mother to wish her a Merry Christmas, reminding her to pray for his trip to Manaus for his pilot's physical, and then talked with our children in the US.

Before we went to bed that night Hank reminded me to write my list of vegetables and fruits to get at the open market and leave it on the table for him. "I'm planning to leave earlier tomorrow morning," he said. "I want to be back and waiting to help when Al and Kim arrive."

On December 26, Hank left at 5:30 a.m. to take his daily rapid walk. His plan was interrupted by God. Within ten minutes, he returned home. I was surprised when I heard him on the porch, and I walked out to the living room, thinking, *He must have forgotten to take my shopping list.*

Through the window I saw him stagger, seeming to bend over to reach for something. *The cat must be in my flower box again,* I thought. But Hank stayed down, and I hurried to his side. I found him on his back in a dead faint, unnaturally cold, his shirt soaked to the skin.

I moved his head from side to side. I slapped his cheeks. I kissed him, then shook him, but I couldn't rouse him. *Oh, Lord, don't let him be dead!*

Frightened, I cried out, "Oh, God. Help. Who can help me? I need someone to pray." It was 5:40 a.m., too early for the neighbors to be out and about. I ran to the telephone to call Pastor Cristiano. No answer. Next, I dialed Flavio, who was like family, having lived with us in the US. *He'll be up this early, I know. Oh, Lord, please don't let Hank die.*

Within minutes, Flavio arrived with his wife, Eda, and their youngest daughter. Flavio's uncle, a longtime friend of ours, followed them in his taxi. Together, Flavio and his uncle lifted Hank, who roused and directed them to seat him at the dining room table. He sat with his head on his hands, looking white as a sheet, and frail, almost too weak to breathe.

While Flavio vigorously rubbed Hank's upper body to warm him and get blood circulating, I tried to persuade him to go to the hospital. "Senhor Venancio is here with his taxi, Hank. Let us take you to the hospital where they can check you and put you on oxygen."

It startled me when Hank answered, "No!"

"Please, Uncle Hank," Flavio pleaded. Hank shook his head. Instead he asked us to help him lie down in the air-conditioned office.

Bill, Hank's brother and also a pilot, later explained that a pilot knows if he faints or passes out for any reason, he can be grounded from flying. "I'm sure that Hank did not want one fainting spell to be an issue for grounding him, and that could have happened if he had gone to the hospital."

Flavio, who is not much taller than I am, lifted Hank in his arms and carried him to the office, where I had prepared a pallet on the floor. While Flavio got Hank settled, I hurried to get the blood pressure cuff. Hank brushed it from his arm when I tried to put it on. Then he sat up, struggling to get up from his pallet. "What do you want, Hank? Can I get something for you?" I asked. He collapsed in my arms.

Meanwhile, Eda had telephoned Pastor Cristiano, who appeared as we were getting Hank resettled on the pallet and gave me a loving hug.

"Please pray, Pastor." We knelt beside Hank to pray. My heart was broken as I beseeched the Lord for mercy and grace to trust. *Save Him, Lord; but if not, then do what is best.*

As we prayed and wept, Flavio's father entered the office, walked over, and put his fingers on Hank's carotid artery. I didn't notice when he shook his head in answer to Flavio's unvoiced question because, just then, I made a decision to disobey my husband's command. "I think we should take him to the hospital," I told the others. "Can you get an ambulance, Senhor João?"

Giving me a tender embrace, Flavio's father answered, "It's

waiting outside. I think you've made the right decision, Sister Ruth." I rode next to Hank's stretcher in the ambulance, asking for Hank's life to be spared, not realizing that he was already gone from me.

But Senhor João knew that Hank had passed into eternity. He encouraged me to take Hank to the hospital because he believed that a doctor at a hospital should validate Hank's death. After all, Hank was an American, a foreigner, and the American Embassy would require an official death certificate.

After the doctor pronounced Hank dead, he reprimanded me for waiting too long to get him to the hospital. The Lord gave me grace to witness to him of God's sovereignty. Life and death are in God's hand; He determines our time to be born and to die.

Flavio was at my side, asking, "*Tia* (Aunt), what shall we do . . . about his body?"

"Hank and I discussed what to do should one of us die here in the Amazon. He wanted to be buried here, but I have no notion how to go about it," I said, wringing my hands. The Brazilians were amazed and awed that an American would choose to be buried there. Even in death, Hank was a blessing to those he served. And in his death, many Brazilians served him, and in my distraught condition, they served me, as well.

"I'll take care of it," he answered. Flavio had asked me to give him Hank's documents and identification papers before I left for the hospital, and he had them with him now. He began the process of notifying the US representative in Manaus, requesting a grave site at the city cemetery and getting Hank's death certificate and the needed official copies made. He arranged for a believer to dig and cement the brick lining in the grave.

Flavio's brother, José, asked me, "Do you think any of the family would have time to get here before his burial? If you wish, I can arrange to have the hospital inject formaldehyde." (Embalming was not practiced in Benjamin Constant, but formaldehyde would help preserve his body beyond the normal time limits that a tropical climate permits.)

I agreed, and José and Flavio told me they would also order the casket and have it delivered from Leticia.

Pastor Cristiano left me to contact ladies in the church to get flowers and prepare the sanctuary for the viewing and funeral. My friends at church served coffee and soft drinks to those who came to view Hank's body and again following the funeral service.

Distressed as I was, I can't recall who took me or how I got back home to get Hank's razor, comb, bathing needs, and clean clothes, but I do remember being alone with Hank in a hospital room with the things I needed. In the strength of the Lord, I shaved and bathed him, and changed his clothes, all the while weeping and talking to the Lord. Isaiah 23:6 comforted me as I repeated its words over and over: *Thou wilt keep him in perfect peace whose mind is stayed on Thee because he trusteth in Thee.*

"I trust in You, Lord," I whispered. I completed this task, gazed at Hank's dear face, and kissed him one last time.

Then the ambulance delivered his body to the church for viewing. The Yoders were there waiting for us.

In retrospect, I'm glad I had the privilege of seeing him before strangers handled his body to inject the formaldehyde. Afterward, Al and Kim sealed the coffin with silicone because of the large gaps in the wood. We viewed only his face through a glass pane, and it looked grotesque. Brazilians in the Amazon were accustomed to seeing a cadaver with cotton wadded into his nostrils, his mouth closed with a white bandage tied under his chin and around his head. Unlike me, they had not seen how life like and pleasing an American mortician can make a dead face become.

THE RESURRECTION AND THE LIFE

I had an hour at home before the time set for the viewing. During that time, I asked to be alone in our office. My Bible seemed to open of itself to the passage that God knew I needed.

Jesus seemed to whisper to me, *I am the resurrection and the life, he that believeth in me though he were dead, yet shall he live. And whosoever liveth and believeth in me, shall never die. Believest thou this?* (John 11:25). The Holy Spirit quickened my sorrowing spirit to answer in faith, *I do believe. I trust You, Lord. I know Hank is alive with You right now, and I know that I'll see him again.*

The viewing at the church was set from 2 p.m. until midnight. Had we followed Amazon custom, Hank would have been buried by late afternoon or early the next day. Pastor Cristiano held Hank's funeral service on Saturday evening and did not have the casket brought into the sanctuary. Besides the injection of formaldehyde, Al and Kim suggested that the coffin be kept locked in the air-conditioned office of the church after Friday's viewing, until the graveside burial on Sunday at 3 p.m. We figured that Kanda, Linda, and David, who were to arrive on Sunday afternoon, might want to open the coffin before burial. Along with the formaldehyde, twenty-four hours in air conditioning would certainly help to preserve the body.

I dreaded the viewing, not realizing that God was preparing blessings for me. As I chatted with people, I discovered the answer to recurring questions: How far did Hank get that morning on his rapid walk? Had anyone seen him or noticed anything wrong with him?

Several people who routinely sold Hank vegetables and fruits reported that he had not been to the market that morning. Others recounted that they missed Hank's customary wave and smile as he passed their houses. It was evident that Hank had not gone far before he sensed something wrong and returned, his walk unfinished. A dear friend in the US sent me a sweet note when she heard about Hank. She wrote, "He went for his morning walk, and kept on walking—right on up to be with the Lord."

It was a blessing to hear stories about Hank's escapades as a young missionary who played soccer with the Brazilian boys; to

hear from many who came to Christ under his ministry; to meet
several from the headwaters—preaching points upriver where we
had gone in our earliest years; to talk with folks whose lives had
been rescued by Hank's medevac flights.

The funeral service on Saturday night comforted me and honored the Lord as testimonies of the impact Hank's life had on
others; music and message pointed to the hope a believer has in
Jesus Christ. Several unsaved businessmen who had known Hank
for many years heard the message—to be absent from the body
is to be present with the Lord.

ABWE President Dr. Michael Loftis sent an e-mail to be read
at the funeral; he followed his comforting words with a touch of
humor, writing:

> My heart is still struggling to accept the reality that your
> beloved Hank is with the Lord he loved and served so faith-
> fully. He must have been grinning from ear to ear as his final
> lift off from Benjamin Constant took place without a run-
> way or even a plane. In my mind's eye, I can see him step-
> ping up to the podium there in glory with his big easy grin
> to have his eternal wings pinned on his chest.

On Sunday afternoon the trip to the cemetery was delayed as
we waited for my children—Kanda, and Linda with her husband—to arrive from the States. I had no way of knowing that
their plane had been detained in Bogotá, but the mayor of
Benjamin Constant had his van waiting at the port for their
arrival by speedboat from Leticia and would rush them to the
church. A few minutes prior to transferring the casket into the
pickup that would transport it to the cemetery, the mayor's van
pulled up, bringing my children in time to accompany the Yoders
and me. Bob Trout, ABWE representative from Bogotá, and
Michael Guerink, our most recent missionary in the Amazon,
joined us in the mayor's van. The pickup carrying the coffin pre-

ceded us. Crowds of believers and acquaintances followed on foot and motorbike as we drove the mile to the cemetery.

Within a week following the burial, my family and I had packed or distributed Hank's belongings. Bob Hamilton arrived to take care of their household furnishings, which had been loaned to us, making arrangements for hired help to guard the house and hangar for the remaining months of their furlough. The Yoders accompanied me home to Georgia.

HANK SCHELTEMA
1929–2003

EPILOGUE

IN MEMORIAM

Before I left Benjamin Constant, concerned that Hank's tomb was unfinished and surrounded by mud, I hired a believer to build a decorative white fence to enclose it until I could arrange to have the tomb and tombstone completed. I wanted John 11:25 to be engraved in large letters for all to read God's message of hope for those who trust Him. Because the granite and engraving was unavailable locally, the Yoders ordered it, selected ceramic tile, and had the materials freighted by boat from Manaus; Flavio did the finishing work on the tomb. When I returned in May 2004 to look over the completed grave site, I found it just as I had hoped. Decorative granite and ceramic tile had transformed Hank's tomb and surrounding space from a muddy quagmire into a beautiful memorial site that honored the Lord.

Talking with Pastor Cristiano before I departed, I probed to determine how best to use funds that were given in Hank's memory. Having worked in the Baptist church school beginning in 1961, I saw how God used its teaching to direct many students to serve Him. Young men, taught to read and write and love the Lord in that school, left our jungle town to get Bible training to serve as pastors in other places. Many of the young ladies married Christians and now teach and serve in scattered churches. Long ago, the former school building fed the voracious jungle termites, and the present wooden structures were fast deteriorating. I believed God would have us provide a cement building to serve for the long haul. The Yoders, Pastor Cristiano, Flavio, and I discussed how best to do this. I returned to Georgia expecting to organize groups of volunteers who would be willing to help build it. Flavio, fluent in English, agreed to supervise the construction process.

While I waited and prayed for further guidance on the school project, I was interested to hear what was happening in ABWE Air. The air base adjoins our property, and I knew that the Cessna T210 was getting an overhaul before it was put up for sale. I could see the Taylorcraft tied down in front of the hangar. Herman and Dale must be repairing that damaged tail wheel, I thought, and I wondered if progress had been made on the Cessna 180 stored in the hangar.

"That's not your problem now, Mom," my daughter Kanda cautioned me. "It's in good hands."

"I know," I admitted. "But those planes are like family, and I can't help but be interested."

The several ABWE aircraft that God entrusted to Hank's care during his years as director were still up in the air on various fields. The seven pilots flying these aircraft had been appointed under Hank's leadership. I could still be a praying partner, aware of the specialized needs they face.

I knew that the Teachouts and Foggs were hard at work. In a letter dated in September 2004, Herman detailed answers to questions asked him:

> For quite some time we have fielded questions regarding the ABWE Airbase. Some of the questions were "Why are you guys in Georgia when the mission headquarters is in Pennsylvania?" and other queries to that effect. We have recently completed a lengthy and thorough study of the situation, and ABWE, "with the help of many counselors," has come to a decision for the future. I won't include all the data in this letter, but the consensus was that to best position us for the future, it would be best to stay here in Georgia and expand at our present location.

Expansion and construction involve needs: volunteer workers and dollars to accomplish them. New ABWE fields hope to begin aviation ministries. Additional aircraft will be needed. In leadership positions, the Teachouts and Foggs know, as Hank and I, that though the need be great, our God *"shall supply all your need, according to his riches in glory by Christ Jesus."* He is faithful. ABWE Air is as much in His hand as it ever was when Hank birthed it.

GOOD NEWS FOR THE AMAZON CHRISTIAN SCHOOL

Weeks passed; I had a tentative floor plan and possibilities for volunteers to build the Amazon Christian school in Benjamin Constant. Then I heard from Pastor Cristiano; he had exciting news to share. "Dona Ruth, across the street, directly in front of our church, a concrete building and property is to be sold. It has twelve large rooms with several bathrooms, ceiling fans, adjustable glass windows, and a good-sized yard. Flavio heard about it and inquired about the price. They are asking $50,000."

My first response was, "Whew! That's a lot of money. More than what's in Hank's memorial fund."

While Pastor Cristiano waited for my response, thoughts raced through my mind. Getting volunteers rounded up, organized, and sent or accompanied to the Amazon is going to be a Herculean job for me without Hank. There are no missionaries presently living in Benjamin Constant to offer hospitality and help work crews from the US. It will make it easier for the church if it doesn't have to build a school because then its classes can continue without interruption. And the property behind the church will still be open and unoccupied for future church expansion. Was this God's plan? Was I willing to trust God for that much money?

"Negotiate the price," I said. "If you can get the price down to $45,000, we'll believe this is what God intends. He is able to provide."

God blessed our faith, and through His choice stewards, He supplied first the $11,000 for the down payment and, by February 2005, the funds for the final payment. Elementary school classes met in the new building for first sessions on February 13. "The Bible institute, Sunday school classes, youth groups, and AWANA club will also use these classrooms," Pastor Cristiano told me.

A NEW STAGE IN MINISTRY

Officially retired from ABWE now, I am a prayer partner and interested follower of ABWE Air's progress into the twenty-first century. Our children, the Yoders, continue to fly the Amazon floatplanes, CJG and DNY, which were a vital part of Hank's early ministry. Like children, those planes required much of our time and energy. I look forward in the future to flying as a passenger once again in both planes when I return to help in the ministry of the First Baptist Church in Benjamin Constant. It may be nostalgia that I feel, but I am eager to see the airman's cross again from above the clouds over the Amazon River.

Remembering that day in 1961 when I first saw that cross encircled by a rainbow, I researched, hoping to learn more about it. What we saw that day, and many times since, is a natural phenomenon called a "glory," a sight only seen from above the clouds. It is caused under certain conditions by sunlight striking water droplets within a cloud. The sunlight is split into its constituent colors and then is reflected back toward the sun along the same path. As the floatplane penetrated the sunlight forming the rainbow, its shadow appeared in the form of a cross within the halo, and as we flew, God's "glory" accompanied us.

Wherever and whenever ABWE pilots fly "in the air for Him," His glorious promise is there in the rainbow: *I am with you alway, even unto the end of the world.*

No wonder Hank used to say, "Pilots are more heavenly minded!"

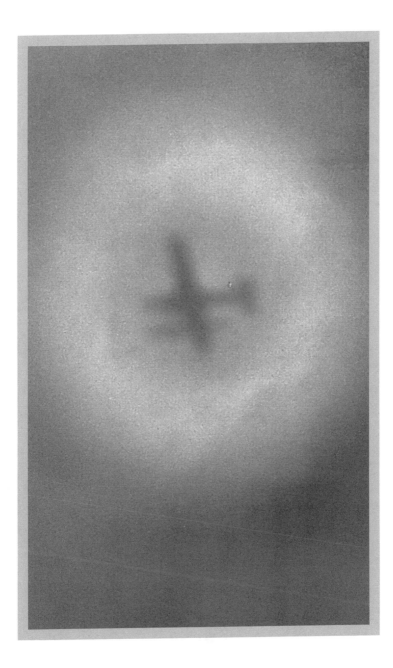

TIMELINE ✈

Note: Only ABWE pilots who completed at least one term on the field or are currently engaged in prefield ministry are included in the timeline and chapters of this book.

TENURE OF SERVICE	COUNTRY	NAME	ARRIVAL AFTER LANGUAGE STUDY	AIRCRAFT FLOWN
1958–2003	Amazon, Brazil	Scheltema	1961	3-place Aeronca Sedan floatplane & 1964 Cessna 185 floatplane
1962–1989*	Amazon, Brazil	Bowers	1964	1968 Cessna 185 floatplane
1968–1980	Amazon, Colombia	Fanning	1974	Cessna 185 floatplane
1970–1988*	Amazon, Colombia	Jarvis	1975	Piper PA-18 Super Cub wheelplane
1973–1986*	Palawan, Philippines	Holman	1976	Cessna 180 wheelplane
1974–1988*	Palawan, Philippines	Rogers	1976	Cessna 180 wheelplane
1974–1991*	Amazon, Brazil	Peace	1976	Cessna 185 floatplane
1975–1988*	Mindanao, Philippines	Nelson	1977	Cessna 180 wheelplane

*Continued with ABWE, but not in aviation

TENURE OF SERVICE	COUNTRY	NAME	ARRIVAL AFTER LANGUAGE STUDY	AIRCRAFT FLOWN
1976–1989	Togo, West Africa	Washer	1983	Cessna 182 wheelplane
1976– transferred to US in 1999	Asunción, Paraguay	Fogg	1980	Cessna 185 wheelplane
1977–1986 transferred to US in 1993	Amazon, Brazil	Jensen	1982	Cessna 185 floatplane
1993–1996	USA Airbase	Jensen	—	—
1978–1985	Bahia, Brazil	Jertberg	1982	—
1979–1988	Amazon, Brazil	Chiano	1985	Cessna 185 floatplane
1980–1989 transferred to Amazon in 1989	Bahia, Brazil	Yoder	1982	Embraer Piper Arrow wheelplane
1989–	Amazon, Brazil	Yoder	—	Cessna 185 floatplanes
1980–1988*	Bogotá, Colombia	Bolin	1983	—
1982–1998	Togo, West Africa	Alderman	1989	Cessna U-206 wheelplane

*Continued with ABWE, but not in aviation

TENURE OF SERVICE	COUNTRY	NAME	ARRIVAL AFTER LANGUAGE STUDY	AIRCRAFT FLOWN
1982–2001*	Iquitos, Peru	Donaldson	1988	Cessna 185 amphibian
1984–1999*	Bahia, Brazil	Zemmer	1987	Embraer Piper Arrow wheelplane
1984–	Ica/Chiclayo, Peru	Budd	1987	PA-12 wheelplane
1987–1995	Iquitos, Peru	DeWitt	1989	Cessna 185 amphibian
1990–	Papua New Guinea	Aholt	1995	Cessna T206
1994–2006	Papua New Guinea	Gainey	1999	Cessna T206
1995–	Togo, West Africa	Fuss	2006	Cessna U-206 wheelplane
1996–	Amazon, Brazil	Hamilton	1999	Cessna 185 floatplanes
1996–	Asunción, Paraguay	Thompson	2002	Cessna 185 wheelplane
1997–	USA Director	Teachout	1998	Taylorcraft
1999–	Togo, West Africa	Cropsey	2001	Cessna U-206 wheelplane

*Continued with ABWE, but not in aviation

ASSOCIATION OF BAPTISTS FOR WORLD EVANGELISM

The Association of Baptists for World Evangelism is an independent mission agency with headquarters in Harrisburg, Pennsylvania. ABWE exists to serve local churches in the task of sending missionaries around the world. Founded in 1927, ABWE now has 1,250 missionaries in over 75 countries, and serves over 5,000 churches.

ABWE's goal is to plant churches, and many means are used to reach this goal. These include Bible clubs, Sunday schools, camps, kindergartens, primary schools, centers for the blind and deaf, literature production, literacy programs, hospitals and clinics, radio, Bible schools, student centers, campus work, and aviation. In each of these ministries, ABWE missionaries faithfully share Christ with men, women, and children.

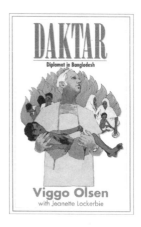

Daktar
by Viggo Olsen

The classic missionary story that continues to thrill readers with its exciting, inspiring account of Viggo Olsen, a young Christian doctor who helped establish the first modern medical facility in the new nation of Bangladesh.

Suggested Donation: $16.00
(includes shipping and handling)

NOW IN ITS THIRD PRINTING!

Interwoven
by Russ & Nancy Ebersole

Four years after the deaths of their mates, God led Russ and Nancy together and blended their families. *Interwoven* describes the many threads God wove together and recounts unusual situations they have experienced, such as a hijacking to communist China.

Suggested Donation: $15.00
(includes shipping and handling)

Singlehearted
by Mary Lou Brownell

Mary Lou Brownell served as a missionary in Bangladesh for thirty years, nursing in jungle clinics, directing nursing at the ABWE mission hospital, establishing a training center for destitute women widowed by the war, and sharing the gospel at every opportunity.

Suggested Donation: $15.00
(includes shipping and handling)

Port of Two Brothers
by Paul Schlener

The astonishing story of how God led and used brothers Paul & John Schlener to draw hundreds of indigenous people in an Amazon village to Himself.

Suggested Donation: $15.00
(includes shipping and handling)

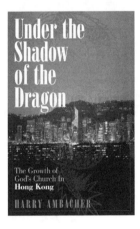

Under the Shadow of the Dragon
by Harry Ambacher

In the twentieth century, God used events in China and fear of the impending Chinese takeover to bring many Chinese people in Hong Kong to salvation. From 1965 to 1999, ABWE's ministry in Hong Kong grew from three small missionary churches to over 30 vibrant churches with Chinese pastors, transformed through the strategies of discipleship and partnering with nationals.

Suggested Donation: $18.00
(includes shipping and handling)

HOW TO ORDER

Write to:
ABWE Publishing
P.O. Box 8585
Harrisburg, PA 17105

Call toll-free:
1-877-959-ABWE (2293)

publish@abwe.org
www.abwe.org